Critical Essays on
Anton Chekhov

*Critical Essays on
World Literature*

Robert Lecker, General Editor
McGill University

Critical Essays on
Anton Chekhov

Thomas A. Eekman

G. K. Hall & Co. • Boston, Massachusetts

Library of Congress Cataloging in Publication Data

Critical essays on Anton Chekhov / [edited by] Thomas A. Eekman.
     p. cm. — (Critical essays on world literature)
   Bibliography: p.
   Includes index.
   ISBN 0-8161-8843-2
   1. Chekhov, Anton Pavlovich, 1860-1904 — Criticism and inter-
pretation. I. Eekman, Thomas. II. Series.
  PG3458.Z8C75 1989
  891.72'3 — dc19   89-31906
                                          CIP

CONTENTS

INTRODUCTION   1
    Thomas A. Eekman

On The Prose

    Anton Chekhov (Creation from the Void)   10
       Leo Shestov
    Anton Chekhov   21
       Conrad Aiken
    Chekhov's Prose   26
       Vladimir Nabokov
    Structural Features in Chekhov's Poetics   34
       Avram B. Derman
    Warm Heart, Cold Eye   45
       George P. Elliott
    On the Nature of the Comic in Chekhov   61
       Vladimir B. Kataev

On Specific Stories

    Chekhov's "An Attack of Nerves" as "Experimental"
       Narrative   70
       Phillip A. Duncan
    Vestiges of Romantic Gardens and Folklore Devils in
       Chekhov's "Verochka," "The Kiss," and
       "The Black Monk"   78
       Joseph L. Conrad
    Chekhov's "A Woman's Kingdom": A Drama
       of Character and Fate   92
       Robert Louis Jackson
    Narrative Technique and the Art of Story-telling
       in Anton Chekhov's "Little Trilogy"   103
       John Freedman
    "The Lady with the Dog"   118
       Virginia Llewellyn Smith

Contents

On The Plays

[An Introduction to Chekhov's Plays]   126
    Richard Peace

Anton Chekhov and His Play without a Title   139
    Thomas A. Eekman

A Russian Hamlet (*Ivanov* and His Age)   154
    Tatiana Shakh-Azizova

Microsubjects in *The Seagull*   160
    Zinovii S. Paperny

Craftsmanship in *Uncle Vanya*   169
    Eric Bentley

The Three Sisters   186
    Maurice Valency

The Cherry Orchard   192
    John L. Styan

SELECTED BIBLIOGRAPHY   201

INDEX   205

INTRODUCTION

Brought together in this volume are the views of eighteen essayists on Anton Chekhov — views of diverse personalities ranging from the Russian philosopher-essayist Leo Shestov and the American poet and critic Conrad Aiken, writing at the beginning of this century, to some present-day critics and literary scholars. This collection seeks to help satisfy a demand for information and illumination, for knowledge and understanding of Chekhov among a large general readership and a large number of literary and theater critics and students of Chekhov's works; and also to show how judgments, opinions, feelings, and knowledge about him have changed, expanded, and matured in the course of some eighty years.

Chekhov's double claim to his high reputation among world authors rests on his prose works — the abundant harvest of stories and novellas he created — and his theater pieces, the one-act and full-length plays that are a constant fixture on stages of the world. Attention is paid on the following pages to both aspects of Chekhov's creativity. A question often asked about Chekhov is "What is more significant and artistically valuable, his prose or his drama?" This question has never been satisfactorily answered, nor can it ever be, because the answer largely depends on personal taste. Chekhov's active interest both in writing and in the theater appeared at an early age (we know how he loved to visit the Taganrog theater and to act in performances he organized at home), and when he was twenty he started his career as both a short-story writer and a playwright. We can only speculate what might have happened had the grand actress Maria Ermolova accepted and staged his first play, or at least encouraged him to continue writing dramas. The rebuffs Chekhov endured as a serious dramatist contrast with his success and rapidly escalating popularity as a short-story writer (and also as an author of one-act comedies) in the 1880s and 1890s. The comedies were largely reworkings of his short stories. While there were many years in his career during which he did not write anything for the theater, there were no years, and few months, in which he did not write any prose at all. Later in his life a certain equilibrium between his work in prose and his work in drama was attained. Actually, because of the founding of the Moscow Art Theater and his close

1

association with it and because of his marriage to the actress Olga Knipper, the last few years of his life stood more in the sign of the stage than of prose. When he talked or wrote about future creative plans, they involved drama, not prose. For our times, a hundred years after the flourishing of his talent, the two aspects of his creativity are equally important.

Some of the typical features of Chekhov's talent are characteristic of his short stories and novellas, and only applicable to them: brevity, the "impressionistic" selection of secondary details that acquire significant meaning, the absence in many stories of an introduction, background information, or formal conclusion. Other features are typical of his dramatic works: the pauses in the dialogues, their contemplative character, the conversation at cross purposes, the often elegiac atmosphere, the feeling of frustration, uselessness, and loss. This situation certainly does not evidence a split between Chekhov the prose writer and Chekhov the dramatist: one has only to remember the ease with which he transformed some of his humorous stories into one-act plays (partly because they already consisted largely of dialogue). The mood and the atmosphere of some of his more mature and significant prose works is similar to that of his five main plays. And parallels in theme, content, and character have been established as well. There are elements in stories like "At Home" or "A Visit to Friends," for example, that remind us of *Uncle Vanya, The Three Sisters*, or *The Cherry Orchard.*

It should not surprise us that Chekhov was viewed and evaluated very differently in various periods and countries and by different critics. Among his earliest critics were traditional Russian utilitarian and populist publicists, men like Nikolai K. Mikhailovsky, who blamed Chekhov for his supposedly indifferent, irresponsible way of writing without social concern, and also for the negative, amoral picture he drew of the Russian peasantry (in his story "The Peasants"). Socialists considered him bourgeois and lacking in revolutionary spirit (a negative attitude toward Chekhov shared by some Marxist critics of the early Soviet period). Taking a different viewpoint, Leo Shestov in his 1905 essay regarded hopelessness as the overriding quality of his later (not, of course, of his earlier) work: "He is constantly, as it were, in ambush, to watch and waylay human hopes." This opinion was echoed in the same year by Dmitri S. Merezhkovsky: "Daily existence and death — those are the two fixed poles of Chekhov's world." And in a lecture, also published in 1905, S. N. Bulgakov expressed the view that, like Byron, Chekhov was a "poet of world grief." This opinion has influenced many readers of and writers about Chekhov. The title of Nina Toumanova's book *Anton Chekhov: The Voice of Twilight Russia* (1937) is typical of this view: Chekhov voiced the dark, pessimistic forebodings prevalent among educated Russians in the decades preceding the revolution. Thus it seems appropriate to open this volume with at least part — the most characteristic part — of Shestov's extended essay.

In the twenties several prominent English men (and women) of letters expressed praise and admiration for Chekhov: John Middleton Murry, William Gerhardi(e), Edward Garnett, Virginia Woolf, John Galsworthy, among others. Interest in him was more general and more intense in Great Britain than in other European countries or the United States; but it was slowly growing there too. In the Soviet Union, which diverged so sharply from the old Russia in which Chekhov had lived and created, many critics saw him as a typical representative of the spirit of that bygone period. Some Soviet critics attempted to interpret him from a Marxist, dialectical-materialist point of view, explaining his writings totally by his class origins.[1]

A completely different Chekhov emerged from various memoirs that were published after his death, notably those of his younger brother Mikhail (*Anton Chekhov and His Subjects*, 1923; *Anton Chekhov on Vacation*, 1929; *Around Chekhov*, 1933). They showed a cheerful, very hospitable, energetic young man with a strong will and sense of responsibility, who was involved in all sorts of social activity, and who even in his later years preserved a lively sense of humor. This image was also presented convincingly in Kornei Chukovski's book *Chekhov the Man* (English edition 1945), a study that has done much to correct the gloomy picture of the writer that was prevalent both in Russia and the West. More literary critics, scholars, and theater directors and experts started to emphasize the positive, cheerful, optimistic side of Chekhov's work.[2] However, the debate over Chekhov's pessimism or optimism had by no means ended. It is a question of interpretation that largely depends on the interpreter, an issue that can never be finally decided and should probably occupy our minds less than it has for so long. Much more fruitful are the in-depth studies and analyses of his works in which numerous scholars have been involved during the last three decades, both in the West (Robert L. Jackson, Simon Karlinsky, Thomas Winner, John L. Styan, Donald Rayfield, Richard Peace, Nils Åke Nilsson, Herta Schmid, to name just a few), and in the Soviet Union, where the authoritative voice of V. V. Ermilov (whose book of 1946 was translated into English in Moscow, with several reprints), representing a narrow Marxist-Leninist view of Chekhov and his work, has gradually faded and where younger, less biased literary scholars have come to the fore: Alexander P. Chudakov (*Chekhov's Poetics*, 1971; English 1983), Emma A. Polotskaia, M. P. Gromov, Vladimir B. Kataev, V. Ia. Linkov, and several others.

Whatever the image that Chekhov's stories and plays produced in European and American minds during the early decades of this century, his work and his fame penetrated everywhere. Thorough knowledge and understanding of his achievement was still hampered by insufficient data about his life and times and the background of his work, incomplete, nonchronological editions, and inadequate translations of his works. Yet when in 1921 the American poet, novelist, and essayist Conrad Aiken devoted one of his short critical essays to Chekhov — one of the first critical essays by an American man of letters — he evinced good insight into the character of Chekhov's stories. He is the second author included in this collection. Aiken calls Chekhov "possibly the greatest writer of the short story who has ever lived" — quite a commendation for the Russian writer from a compatriot of Edgar Allan Poe — and he makes valid, interesting comparisons with Maupassant, Turgenev, and Henry James, stressing the poetical quality of Chekhov's creations and his strong evocation of "mood."

There was another "American" who had a more intimate and profound knowledge of the Russian writer: the Russian-born but truly cosmopolitan novelist Vladimir Nabokov. In his 1940 lecture notes for a course on Russian literature he devoted a long chapter to Chekhov, in which he points to Chekhov's unobtrusive, artless style. "His dictionary is poor, his combination of words almost trivial," Nabokov remarks with typical overstatement, because Chekhov was "quite satisfied with the man-in-the-street among words," words that have "a tint between the color of an old fence and that of a low cloud." Nabokov sees Chekhov as the quintessence of Russian literature and Russian life, and even of universal literary art.[3]

By contrast, Avram B. Derman was one of the numerous literary scholars who, in the Soviet era, attempted new interpretations of Chekhov and his work within the framework of Marxist ideology. Yet he obviously tried to evade strict ideological guidelines, even though he could not completely ignore them. In a time when there was strong pressure to interpret Chekhov exclusively as a castigator of feudal bourgeois society, a harbinger of the coming revolution, Derman turned to the intrinsic literary values of Chekhov's work. He pays particular attention, in a chapter from one of his books translated and reprinted in this volume, to the beginnings and endings of Chekhov's stories, especially those of his mature years.

Before we give the floor to a whole series of contemporary Chekhov specialists, it is good to listen to the American writer George P. Elliott, who acknowledges his indebtedness to Chekhov. In his essay, one of the longest in this volume, originally written as a public lecture, he agrees with Nabokov (and with many people in many countries, not just the Americans he mentions) that Chekhov is one of those very few writers for whom the reader develops a particular feeling of closeness and friendship. Elliott does not regard Chekhov merely as a congenial author of supranational appeal, he goes much further: in Chekhov "we can see what educated, cultivated, enlightened Americans now are essentially like." It is true that he qualifies that opinion later as "at least a defensible exaggeration of the truth" and he goes on to stress the thoroughly Russian nature of Chekhov's characters. His next thesis is that of the "warm heart, cold eye," the title of his essay, with which Chekhov, in his view, relates to his heroes. And the third point he makes is that Chekhov's world was not yet psychoanalyzed, that is, that Freudian ideas had not yet started to influence and change European-American literature, mostly in a negative fashion.

The contribution of Vladimir B. Kataev, author of one of the best monographs on Chekhov that have appeared in the Soviet Union during the last two decades (*Chekhov's Prose*, 1979) deals with an important aspect of Chekhov's creativity: his humor, which not only pervades the early stories and sketches, but also crops up in the later prose works and plays. He views these works as an internal unity, from the beginning to the end of his career, no matter whether they have tragic or comic overtones.

After these more general studies, a second group of essays addresses more specifically one or a few of his short stories or novellas. This part begins with an essay by Phillip A. Duncan on the story "An Attack of Nerves." Duncan discusses this story in terms of Chekhov's "experimental writing," of which it is one of the best examples. These stories resemble, and seem to be indebted to, Émile Zola's ideas concerning the experimental novel.

In an essay specifically written for this volume, Joseph L. Conrad studies three Chekhov stories (two from 1887, one from 1894) in which he discloses certain romantic and diabolic elements. Such typical Chekhovian narratives evidently have more in common than just these elements, but by tracing and singling out the motifs of romantic flora and demoniacal apparitions, Conrad is able to shed new light on their character and significance.

Next is Robert Louis Jackson's study of "A Woman's Kingdom," which he views as "an artistic masterpiece in every respect." The story contains little action, but "a momentous drama is underway" within the main character, the factory owner Anna, for whom the episode described in the text is "a decisive point in time, a moment of self-discovery." With his usual perceptiveness Jackson discerns in "A Woman's Kingdom" an "essentially Greek drama of Character and Fate" that merges with biblical events and imagery, which "form an organic part of the semantic structure of the work."

John Freedman's essay sheds new light on the often-discussed "Little Trilogy": "The Man in a Shell," "Gooseberries," and "About Love." He argues that the hero of the first story, Belikov, is not the only "man in a shell" in the story and that the narrator, Burkin, gives a subjective, colored picture of the entire Belikov episode. In the second text we discover that the words of the narrator, Ivan Ivanych, should also be taken very cautiously. The credibility of the narrator and hero of the third story is likewise in doubt: Freedman shows convincingly that Chekhov "allows the reader to arrive at a very different interpretation of the affair" from the one Alekhin tries to impart to us.

Virginia L. Smith's essay is a chapter from her book *Anton Chekhov and the Lady with the Dog*, the first book entirely devoted to the question of women in Chekhov's writings. She sees many analogies between the behavior of the male hero of the story, Gurov, and Chekhov himself, and she concludes that "the history of Gurov's relationships with women is a transmutation of Chekhov's history." The essay contains valid remarks on the question of Chekhov and love.

The third group of essays focuses on Chekhov's plays. This part opens with the introductory chapter from Richard Peace's book, the most recent and doubtless one of the best of the numerous monographs devoted to Chekhov's drama. The essay shows how some of the distinctive features of Chekhov's theater are linked—in their symbolism and their atmosphere—to other, earlier Russian dramatic works. Some elements reach back even to eighteenth-century comedy. Peace's study is rich in references to other Russian works; the juxtaposition with Oblomov is especially revealing.

Ivanov was preceded by a strange, lengthy, un-Chekhovian play that, as I show in my own essay, "Anton Chekhov and His Play without a Title," contains innumerable elements that anticipate his later dramatic works and reappear in them. It is, therefore, a fascinating nursery and testing field for those works. At its base lies Chekhov's adolescent trauma caused by the loss of the parental home.

The next selection, devoted to *Ivanov*, Chekhov's first recognized play, is by prominent contemporary Soviet Chekhovist, Tatiana Shakh-Azizova. It is relatively brief, but deals with a central problem in *Ivanov*: the protagonist's relation to Hamlet (touched upon by Peace as well) and Chekhov's "complex attitude to Russian Hamletism and to the sort of people who are represented by Ivanov," whose tragedy she interprets as that "of a man with a capacity for life but who cannot adapt himself to it."[4]

Zinovii S. Paperny, the doyen of Russian Chekhov scholars, is represented by an essay on *The Seagull*, in which he discusses "microsubjects," the small themes and motifs connected with most of the main characters, which are not just accidental and subordinate, but active, sometimes disturbing, elements of the play and crucial for the general development of the action and the fortunes of the protagonists.

Uncle Vanya and Chekhov's craftmanship are discussed by Eric Bentley, the well-known writer on the theater. He juxtaposes, throughout his essay, the first version of the play, *The Wood Demon*, and the final version, pointing to its transition from "a farce spiced with melodrama" to a tragicomedy in which farce and melodrama are subordinated to a higher art.

Maurice Valency writes about *The Three Sisters*, contending that it, more clearly than any other of Chekhov's plays, "reflects his spiritual tension." It is laden with symbolism; Chekhov "developed a more complex counterpoint than anyone had so far attempted in the theatre." He opposes Chekhov, who seems to indicate that all the hopes and dreams of his Vershinins are ultimately futile and meaningless, to Henrik Ibsen, who takes the cosmic processes within his characters much more seriously.

The final essay is from John L. Styan's book *Chekhov in Performance* and deals with the last play. Styan does not reiterate the often-heard interpretation of *The Cherry Orchard* as an allegory, a metaphor for the passing of old Mother Russia, but he does indicate that the setting and action of the play stand for a wider world beyond "the microcosm of the cherry orchard family." He carefully traces the various groupings or patterns among the characters (by social status, age, sex, etc.) and their continuous interactions.

These eighteen essays could easily be augmented by another eighteen or many more than that: there seems to be no end to the books and articles on Chekhov and his works, in the Soviet Union, in Eastern and Western Europe, in America. Each generation and each culture has its own viewpoints and interpretations, and it is hard to decide which of them are more lastingly valid than others. The fact remains that Chekhov continues to fascinate a wide public as well as literary and theatrical scholars in all these generations, countries, and cultures. The present volume is meant as a collection of some of the more profound and provocative essays written by Russians and Americans over a period of some eighty years, but mostly during the last three decades — essays that show the high level of expertise in decoding and elucidating Chekhov's texts that has developed over this period and that demonstrate the special genius that gave rise to this wealth of interpretive effort.

THOMAS A. EEKMAN

University of California, Los Angeles

Notes

1. For the changing image of Chekhov in Russian literary criticism, see Victor Terras, "Chekhov at Home: Russian Criticism," in *The Chekhov Companion*, ed. Toby Clyman, 167 ff. (Westport, Conn.: Greenwood Press, 1985). See also Simon Karlinsky, "Russian Anti-Chekhovians," *Russian Literature* (Amsterdam) 15 (1984): 183 ff.

2. See K. A. Lantz's "Introduction: Images of Chekhov" in his *Anton Chekhov, A Reference Guide to Literature* (Boston: G. K. Hall, 1985), xxiii–xxiv.

3. For a comparison of the two, see Simon Karlinsky, "Nabokov and Chekhov: The Lesser Russian Tradition," *TriQuarterly* 17 (1965): 7 ff.

4. Shakespeare's *Hamlet* and Chekhov's *The Seagull* are the theme of an essay by Thomas G. Winner in *American Slavic and East European Review* 15 (1956): 101 ff.; reprinted in René and Nonna D. Wellek, eds., *Chekhov, New Perspectives* (Englewood Cliffs, N. J.: Prentice Hall, 1984), 107 ff.

On The Prose

Anton Chekhov
(Creation from the Void)

Leo Shestov*

Résigne-toi, mon coeur, dors ton sommeil de brute.
— Charles Baudelaire

I

Chekhov is dead; therefore we may now speak freely of him. For to speak of an artist means to disentangle and reveal the "tendency" hidden in his works, an operation not always permissible when the subject is still living. Certainly he had a reason for hiding himself, and of course the reason was serious and important. I believe many felt it, and that it was partly on this account that we have as yet had no proper appreciation of Chekhov. Hitherto in analyzing his works the critics have confined themselves to commonplace and cliché. Of course they knew they were wrong; but anything is better than to extort the truth from a living person. Mikhailovsky alone attempted to approach closer to the source of Chekhov's creation, and as everybody knows, turned away from it with aversion and even with disgust. Here, by the way, the deceased critic might have convinced himself once again of the extravagance of the so-called theory of "art for art's sake." Every artist has his definite task, his life's work, to which he devotes all his forces. A tendency is absurd when it endeavours to take the place of talent, and to cover impotence and lack of content, or when it is borrowed from the stock of ideas which happen to be in demand at the moment. "I defend ideals, therefore every one must give me his sympathies." Such pretences we often see made in literature, and the notorious controversy concerning "art for art's sake" was evidently maintained upon the double meaning given to the word "tendency" by its opponents. Some wished to believe that a writer can be saved by the nobility of his tendency; others feared that a tendency would bind them to the performance of alien tasks. Much ado about nothing: ready-made

*From *Chekhov and Other Essays*, by Leon Shestov (Ann Arbor: University of Michigan Press, 1966), 3–26. (First publication in 1916 by Maunsel & Co., Dublin-London.)

ideas will never endow mediocrity with talent; on the contrary, an original writer will at all costs set himself his own task. And Chekhov had his *own* business, though there were critics who said that he was the servant of art for its own sake, and even compared him to a bird, carelessly flying. To define his tendency in a word, I would say that Chekhov was the poet of hopelessness. Stubbornly, sadly, monotonously, during all the years of his literary activity, nearly a quarter of a century long, Chekhov was doing one thing alone: by one means or another he was killing human hopes. Herein, I hold, lies the essence of his creation. Hitherto it has been little spoken of. The reasons are quite intelligible. In ordinary language what Chekhov was doing is called crime, and is visited by condign punishment. But how can a man of talent be punished? Even Mikhailovsky, who more than once in his lifetime gave an example of merciless severity, did not raise his hand against Chekhov. He warned his readers and pointed out the "evil fire" which he had noticed in Chekhov's eyes. But he went no further. Chekhov's immense talent overcame the strict and rigorous critic. It may be, however, that Mikhailovsky's own position in literature had more than a little to do with the comparative mildness of his sentence. The younger generation had listened to him uninterruptedly for thirty years, and his word had been law. But afterwards every one was bored with eternally repeating: "Aristides is just, Aristides is right." The younger generation began to desire to live and to speak in its own way, and finally the old master was ostracized. There is the same custom in literature as in Terra del Fuego. The young, growing men kill and eat the old. Mikhailovsky struggled with all his might, but he no longer felt the strength of conviction that comes from the sense of right. Inwardly, he felt that the young were right, not because they knew the truth—what truth did the economic materialists know?—but because they were young and had their lives before them. The rising star shines always brighter than the setting, and the old must of their own will yield themselves up to be devoured by the young. Mikhailovsky felt this, and perhaps it was this which undermined his former assurance and the firmness of his opinion of old. True, he was still like Gretchen's mother in Goethe: he did not take rich gifts from chance without having previously consulted his confessor. Chekhov's talent too was taken to the priest, by whom it was evidently rejected as suspect; but Mikhailovsky no longer had the courage to set himself against public opinion. The younger generation prized Chekhov for his talent, his immense talent, and it was plain they would not disown him. What remained for Mikhailovsky? He attempted, as I say, to warn them. But no one listened to him, and Chekhov became one of the most beloved of Russian writers.

Yet the just Aristides was right this time too, as he was right when he gave his warning against Dostoevsky. Now that Chekhov is no more, we may speak openly. Take Chekhov's stories, each one separately, or better still, all together; look at him at work. He is constantly, as it were, in ambush, to watch and waylay human hopes. He will not miss a single one of them, not one of them will escape its fate. Art, science, love, inspiration, ideals — choose out all the words with which humanity is wont, or has been in the past, to be consoled or to be amused — Chekhov has only to touch them and they instantly wither and die. And Chekhov himself faded, withered and died before our eyes. Only his wonderful art did not die — his art to kill by a mere touch, a breath, a glance, everything whereby men live and wherein they take their pride. And in this art he was constantly perfecting himself, and he attained to a virtuosity beyond the reach of any of his rivals in European literature. Maupassant often had to strain every effort to overcome his victim. The victim often escaped from Maupassant, though crushed and broken, yet with his life. In Chekhov's hands, nothing escaped death.

II

I must remind my reader, though it is a matter of general knowledge, that in his earlier work Chekhov is most unlike the Chekhov to whom we became accustomed in late years. The young Chekhov is gay and careless, perhaps even like a flying bird. He published his work in the comic papers. But in 1888 and 1889, when he was only twenty-seven and twenty-eight years old, there appeared *The Tedious Story* and the drama *Ivanov*, two pieces of work which laid the foundations of a new creation. Obviously a sharp and sudden change had taken place in him, which was completely reflected in his works. There is no detailed biography of Chekhov, and probably will never be, because there is no such thing as a full biography — I, at all events, cannot name one. Generally biographies tell us everything except what it is important to know. Perhaps in the future it will be revealed to us with the fullest details who was Chekhov's tailor; but we shall never know what happened to Chekhov in the time which elapsed between the completion of his story *The Steppe* and the appearance of his first drama. If we would know, we must rely upon his works and our own insight.

Ivanov and *The Tedious Story* seem to me the most autobiographical of all his works. In them almost every line is a sob; and it is hard to suppose that a man could sob so, looking only at another's grief. And it is plain that his grief is a new one, unexpected as though it has fallen from the sky. Here it is, it will endure for ever, and he does not know how to fight against it.

In *Ivanov* the hero compares himself to an overstrained laborer. I do not believe we shall be mistaken if we apply this comparison to the author of the drama as well. There can be practically no doubt that Chekhov had overstrained himself. And the overstrain came not from hard and heavy labor; no mighty overpowering exploit broke him: he stumbled and fell, he slipped. There comes this nonsensical, stupid, all but invisible accident,

and the old Chekhov of gaiety and mirth is no more. No more stories for
The Alarm Clock. Instead, a morose and overshadowed man, a "criminal"
whose words frighten even the experienced and the omniscient.

If you desire it, you can easily be rid of Chekhov and his work as well.
Our language contains two magic words: "pathological," and its brother
"abnormal." Once Chekhov had overstrained himself, you have a perfectly
legal right, sanctified by science and every tradition, to leave him out of all
account, particularly seeing that he is already dead, and therefore cannot
be hurt by your neglect. That is if you desire to be rid of Chekhov. But if
the desire is for some reason absent, the words "pathological" and
"abnormal" will have no effect upon you. Perhaps you will go further and
attempt to find in Chekhov's experiences a criterion of the most irrefrag-
able truths and axioms of this consciousness of ours. There is no third way:
you must either renounce Chekhov, or become his accomplice.

The hero of *The Tedious Story* is an old professor; the hero of *Ivanov*
a young landlord. But the theme of both works is the same. The professor
had overstrained himself, and thereby cut himself off from his past life and
from the possibility of taking an active part in human affairs. Ivanov also
had overstrained himself and become a superfluous, useless person. Had
life been so arranged that death should supervene simultaneously with the
loss of health, strength and capacity, then the old professor and young
Ivanov could not have lived for one single hour. Even a blind man could
see that they are both broken and are unfit for life. But for reasons
unknown to us, wise nature has rejected coincidence of this kind. A man
very often goes on living after he has completely lost the capacity of taking
from life that wherein we are wont to see its essence and meaning. More
striking still, a broken man is generally deprived of everything except the
ability to acknowledge and feel his position. Nay, for the most part in such
cases the intellectual abilities are refined and sharpened and increased to
colossal proportions. It frequently happens that an average man, banal
and mediocre, is changed beyond all recognition when he falls into the
exceptional situation of Ivanov or the old professor. In him appear signs of
a gift, a talent, even of genius. Nietzsche once asked: "Can an ass be
tragical?" He left his question unanswered, but Tolstoy answered for him
in *The Death of Ivan Ilyich.* Ivan Ilyich, it is evident from Tolstoy's
description of his life, is a mediocre, average character, one of those men
who pass through life avoiding anything that is difficult or problematical,
caring exclusively for the calm and pleasantness of earthly existence.
Hardly had the cold wind of tragedy blown upon him, than he was utterly
transformed. The story of Ivan Ilyich in his last days is as deeply
interesting as the life-story of Socrates or Pascal.

In passing I would point out a fact which I consider of great
importance. In his work Chekhov was influenced by Tolstoy, and particularly by Tolstoy's later writings. It is important, because thus a part of
Chekhov's "guilt" falls upon the great writer of the Russian land. I think

that had there been no *Death of Ivan Ilyich*, there would have been no *Ivanov*, and no *Tedious Story*, nor many others of Chekhov's most remarkable works. But this by no means implies that Chekhov borrowed a single word from his great predecessor. Chekhov had enough material of his own: in that respect he needed no help. But a young writer would hardly dare to come forward at his own risk with the thoughts that make the content of *The Tedious Story*. When Tolstoy wrote *The Death of Ivan Ilyich*, he had behind him *War and Peace*, *Anna Karenina*, and the firmly established reputation of an artist of the highest rank. All things were permitted to him. But Chekhov was a young man, whose literary baggage amounted in all to a few dozen tiny stories, hidden in the pages of little known and uninfluential papers. Had Tolstoy not paved the way, had Tolstoy not shown by his example, that in literature it was permitted to tell the truth, to tell everything, then perhaps Chekhov would have had to struggle long with himself before finding the courage of a public confession, even though it took the form of stories. And even with Tolstoy before him, how terribly did Chekhov have to struggle with public opinion. "Why does he write his horrible stories and plays?" every one asked himself. "Why does the writer systematically choose for his heroes situations from which there is not, and cannot possibly be, any escape?" What can be said in answer to the endless complaints of the old professor and Katya, his pupil? This means that there is, essentially, something to be said. From times immemorial, literature has accumulated a large and varied store of all kinds of general ideas and conceptions, material and metaphysical, to which the masters have recourse the moment the over-exacting and over-restless human voice begins to be heard. This is exactly the point. Chekhov himself, a writer and an educated man, refused in advance every possible consolation, material or metaphysical. Not even in Tolstoy, who set no great store by philosophical systems, will you find such keenly expressed disgust for every kind of conceptions and ideas as in Chekhov. He is well aware that conceptions ought to be esteemed and respected, and he reckons his inability to bend the knee before that which educated people consider holy as a defect against which he must struggle with all his strength. And he does struggle with all his strength against this defect. But not only is the struggle unavailing; the longer Chekhov lives, the weaker grows the power of lofty words over him, in spite of his own reason and his conscious will. Finally, he frees himself entirely from ideas of every kind, and loses even the notion of connection between the happenings of life. Herein lies the most important and original characteristic of his creation. Anticipating a little, I would here point to his comedy, *The Seagull*, where, in defiance of all literary principles, the basis of action appears to be not the logical development of passions, or the inevitable connection between cause and effect, but naked accident, ostentatiously nude. As one reads the play, it seems at times that one has before one a copy of a newspaper with an endless series of news paragraphs, heaped upon one another, without order and without previous plan. Sovereign accident reigns everywhere and in everything, this time boldly throwing the gauntlet to all conceptions. In this, I repeat, is Chekhov's greatest originality, and this, strangely enough, is the source of his most bitter experiences. He did not want to be original; he made superhuman efforts to be like everybody else: but there is no escaping one's destiny. How many men, above all among writers, wear their fingers to the bone in the effort to be unlike others, and yet they cannot shake themselves free of cliché — yet Chekhov was original against his will! Evidently originality does not depend upon the readiness to proclaim revolutionary opinions at all costs. The newest and boldest idea may and often does appear tedious and vulgar. In order to become original, instead of inventing an idea, one must achieve a difficult and painful labour; and, since men avoid labour and suffering, the really new is for the most part born in man against his will.

III

"A man cannot reconcile himself to the accomplished fact; neither can he refuse so to reconcile himself: and there is no third course. Under such conditions 'action' is impossible. He can only fall down and weep and beat his head against the floor." So Chekhov speaks of one of his heroes; but he might say the same of them all, without exception. The author takes care to put them in such a situation that only one thing is left for them, — to fall down and beat their heads against the floor. With strange, mysterious obstinacy they refuse all the accepted means of salvation. Nikolai Stepanovich, the old professor in *The Tedious Story*, might have attempted to forget himself for a while or to console himself with memories of the past. But memories only irritate him. He was once an eminent scholar: now he cannot work. Once he was able to hold the attention of his audience for two hours on end; now he cannot do it even for a quarter of an hour. He used to have friends and comrades, he used to love his pupils and assistants, his wife and children; now he cannot concern himself with any one. If people do arouse any feelings at all within him, then they are only feelings of hatred, malice and envy. He has to confess it to himself with the truthfulness which came to him — he knows not why nor whence — in place of the old diplomatic skill, possessed by all clever and normal men, whereby he saw and said only that which makes for decent human relations and healthy states of mind. Now everything which he sees or thinks only serves to poison, in himself and others, the few joys which adorn human life. With a certainty which he never attained on the best days and hours of his old theoretical research, he feels that he has become a criminal, having committed no crime. All that he was engaged in before was good, necessary, and useful. He tells you of his past, and you can see that he was always right and ready at any moment of the day or the night to answer the severest judge who should examine not only his actions, but his thoughts as well. Now not only would an outsider condemn him, he condemns himself. He confesses openly that he is all compact of envy and hatred.

"The best and most sacred right of kings," he says,

> "is the right to pardon. And I have always felt myself a king so long as I used this right prodigally. I never judged, I was compassionate, I pardoned every one right and left. . . . But now I am king no more. There's something going on in me which belongs only to slaves. Day and night evil thoughts roam about in my head, and feelings which I never knew before have made their home in my soul. I hate and despise; I'm exasperated, disturbed, and afraid. I've become strict beyond measure, exacting, unkind and suspicious. . . . What does it all mean? If my new thoughts and feelings come from a change of my convictions, where could the change come from? Has the world grown worse and I better, or was I blind and indifferent before? But if the change is due to the general decline of my physical and mental powers—I am sick and losing weight every day—then I am in a pitiable position. It means that my new thoughts are abnormal and unhealthy, that I must be ashamed of them and consider them valueless. . . ."

The question is asked by the old professor on the point of death, and in his person by Chekhov himself. Which is better, to be a king, or an old, envious, malicious "toad," as he calls himself elsewhere? There is no denying the originality of the question. In the words above you feel the price which Chekhov had to pay for his originality, and with how great joy he would have exchanged all his original thoughts—at the moment when his "new" point of view had become clear to him—for the most ordinary, banal capacity for benevolence. He has no doubt felt that his way of thinking is pitiable, shameful and disgusting. His moods revolt him no less than his appearance, which he describes in the following lines: ". . . I am a man of sixty-two, with a bald head, false teeth and an incurable tic. My name is as brilliant and prepossessing, as I myself am dull and ugly. My head and hands tremble from weakness; my neck, like that of one of Turgenev's heroines, resembles the handle of a counter-bass; my chest is hollow and my back narrow. When I speak or read my mouth twists, and when I smile my whole face is covered with senile, deathly wrinkles." Unpleasant face, unpleasant moods! Let the most sweet natures and compassionate person but give a side-glance at such a monster, and despite himself a cruel thought would awaken in him: that he should lose no time in killing, in utterly destroying this pitiful and disgusting vermin, or if the laws forbid recourse to such strong measures, at least in hiding him as far as possible from human eyes, in some prison or hospital or asylum. These are measures of suppression sanctioned, I believe, not only by legislation, but by eternal morality as well. But here you encounter resistance of a particular kind. Physical strength to struggle with the warders, executioners, attendants, moralists — the old professor has none; a little child could knock him down. Persuasion and prayer, he knows well, will avail him nothing. So he strikes out in despair: he begins to cry over all the world in a terrible, wild, heartrending voice about some rights of his: ". . . I have a passionate and hysterical desire to stretch out my hands and moan aloud. I want to cry out that fate has doomed me, a famous man, to death; that in some six months here in the auditorium another will be master. I want to cry out that I am poisoned; that new ideas that I did not know before have poisoned the last days of my life, and sting my brain incessantly like mosquitoes. At that moment my position seems so terrible to me that I want all my students to be terrified, to jump from their seats and rush panic-stricken to the door, shrieking in despair." The professor's arguments will hardly move any one. Indeed I do not know if there is any argument in those words. But this awful, inhuman moan. . . . Imagine the picture: a bald, ugly old man, with trembling hands, and twisted mouth, and skinny neck, eyes mad with fear, wallowing like a beast on the ground and wailing, wailing, wailing. . . . What does he want? He had lived a long and interesting life; now he had only to round it off nicely, with all possible calm, quietly and solemnly to take leave of this earthly existence. Instead he rends himself, and flings himself about, calls almost the whole universe to judgment, and clutches convulsively at the few days left to him. And Chekhov — what did Chekhov do? Instead of passing by on the other side, he supports the prodigious monster, devotes pages and pages to the "experiences of his soul," and gradually brings the reader to a point at which, instead of a natural and lawful sense of indignation, unprofitable and dangerous sympathies for the decomposing, decaying creature are awakened in his heart. But every one knows that it is impossible to *help* the professor; and if it is impossible to help, then it follows we must forget. That is as plain as *a b c*. What use or what meaning could there be in the endless picturing — daubing, as Tolstoy would say — of the intolerable pains of the agony which inevitably leads to death?

If the professor's "new" thoughts and feelings shone bright with beauty, nobility or heroism, the case would be different. The reader could learn something from it. But Chekhov's story shows that these qualities belonged to his hero's old thoughts. Now that his illness has begun, there has sprung up within him a revulsion from everything which even remotely resembles a lofty feeling. When his pupil Katya turns to him for advice what she should do, the famous scholar, the friend of Pirogov, Kavelin and Nekrasov, who had taught so many generations of young men, does not know what to answer. Absurdly he chooses from his memory a whole series of pleasant-sounding words; but they have lost all meaning for him. What answer shall he give? he asks himself. "It is easy to say, Work, or divide your property among the poor, or know yourself, and because it is easy, I do not know what to answer." Katya, still young, healthy and beautiful, has by Chekhov's offices fallen like the professor into a trap from which no human power can deliver her. From the moment that she knew hopelessness, she had won all the author's sympathy. While a person is settled to some work, while he has a future of some kind before him, Chekhov is utterly indifferent to him. If he does describe him, then he usually does it hastily and in a tone of scornful irony. But when he is entangled, and so entangled that he cannot be disentangled by any means, then Chekhov begins to wake up. Color, energy, creative force, inspiration make their appearance. Therein perhaps lies the secret of his political indifferentism. Notwithstanding all his distrust of projects for a brighter future, Chekhov like Dostoevsky was evidently not wholly convinced that social reforms and social science were important. However difficult the social question may be, still it may be solved. Some day, perhaps people will so arrange themselves on the earth as to live and die without suffering: further than that ideal humanity cannot go. Perhaps the authors of stout volumes on Progress do guess and foresee something. But just for that reason their work is alien to Chekhov. At first by instinct, then consciously, he was attracted to problems which are by essence insoluble like that presented in *The Tedious Story:* there you have helplessness, sickness, the prospect of inevitable death, and no hope whatever to change the situation by a hair. This infatuation, whether conscious or instinctive, clearly runs counter to the demands of common sense and normal will. But there is nothing else to expect from Chekhov, an overstrained man. Every one knows, or has heard, of hopelessness. On every side, before our very eyes, are happening terrible and intolerable tragedies, and if every doomed man were to raise such an awful alarm about his destruction as Nikolai Stepanovich, life would become an inferno: Nikolai Stepanovich must not cry his sufferings aloud over the world, but be careful to trouble people as little as possible. And Chekhov should have assisted this reputable endeavour by every means in his power. As though there were not thousands of tedious stories in the world—they cannot be counted! And above all stories of the kind that Chekhov tells should be hidden with special care from human eyes. We have here to do with the decomposition of a living organism. What should we say to a man who would prevent corpses from being buried, and would dig decaying bodies from the grave, even though it were on the ground, or rather on the pretext, that they were the bodies of his intimate friends, even famous men of reputation and genius? Such an occupation would rouse in a normal and healthy mind nothing but disgust and terror. Once upon a time, according to popular superstition, sorcerers, necromancers and wizards kept company with the dead, and found a certain pleasure or even a real satisfaction in that ghastly occupation. But they generally hid themselves away from mankind in forests and caves, or betook themselves to deserts where they might in isolation surrender themselves to their unnatural inclinations; and if their deeds were eventually brought to light, healthy men requited them with the stake, the gallows, and the rack. The worst kind of that which is called evil, as a rule, had for its source and origin an interest and taste for carrion. Man forgave every crime — cruelty, violence, murder; but he never forgave the unmotived love of death and the seeking of its secret. In this matter modern times, being free from prejudices, have advanced little from the Middle Ages. Perhaps the only difference is that we, engaged in practical affairs, have lost the natural *flair* for good and evil. Theoretically we are even convinced that in our time there are not and cannot be wizards and necromancers. Our confidence and carelessness in this reached such a point, that almost everybody saw even in Dostoevsky only an artist and a publicist, and seriously discussed with him whether the Russian peasant needed to be flogged and whether we ought to lay hands on Constantinople.

Mikhailovsky alone vaguely conjectured what it all might be when he called the author of *The Brothers Karamazov* a "treasure-digger." I say he "dimly conjectured," because I think that the deceased critic made the remark partly in allegory, even in joke. But none of Dostoevsky's other critics made, even by accident, a truer slip of the pen. Chekhov, too, was a "treasure-digger," a sorcerer, a necromancer, an adept in the black art; and this explains his singular infatuation for death, decay and hopelessness.

Chekhov was not of course the only writer to make death the subject of his works. But not the theme is important but the manner of its treatment. Chekhov understands that. "In all the thoughts, feelings, and ideas," he says, "[which] I form about anything, there is wanting the something universal which could bind all these together in one whole. Each feeling and each thought lives detached in me, and in all my opinions about science, the theatre, literature, and my pupils, and in all the little pictures which my imagination paints, not even the most cunning analyst will discover what is called the general idea, or the god of the living man. And if this is not there, then nothing is there. In poverty such as this, a serious infirmity, fear of death, influence of circumstances and people would have been enough to overthrow and shatter all that I formerly considered as my conception of the world, and all wherein I saw the meaning and joy of my life. . . ." In these words one of the "newest" of Chekhov's ideas finds expression, one by which the whole of his subsequent creation is defined. It is expressed in a modest, apologetic form: a man confesses that he is unable to subordinate his thoughts to a higher idea, and in that inability he sees his weakness. This was enough to avert from him to some extent the thunders of criticism and the judgment of public opinion. We readily forgive the repentant sinner! But it is an unprofitable clemency: to expiate one's guilt, it is not enough to confess it. What was the good of Chekhov's putting on sackcloth and ashes and publicly confessing his guilt, if he was inwardly unchanged? If, while his words acknowledged the general idea as god (without a capital, indeed), he did nothing whatever for it? In words he burns incense to god, in deed he curses him. Before his disease a conception of the world brought him happiness, now it had shattered into fragments. Is it not natural to ask whether the conception actually did ever bring him happiness? Perhaps the happiness had its own independent origin, and the conception was invited only as a general to a wedding, for outward show, and never played any essential part. Chekhov tells us circumstantially what joys the professor found in his scientific work, his lectures to the students, his family, and in a good dinner. In all these were present together the conception of the world and the idea, and they did not take away from, but as it were embellished life; so that it seemed that he was working for the ideal, as well as creating a family and dining. But now, when for the same ideal's sake he has to remain inactive, to suffer, to remain awake of nights, to swallow with effort food that has become loathsome to him— the conception of the world is shattered into fragments! And it amounts to this, that a conception with a dinner is right, and a dinner without a conception equally right—this needs no argument—and a conception *an und für sich* is of no value whatever. Here is the essence of the words quoted from Chekhov. He confesses with horror the presence within him of that "new" idea. It seems to him that he alone of all men is so weak and insignificant, that the others . . . well, they need only ideals and concep-tions. And so it is, surely, if we may believe what people write in books. Chekhov plagues, tortures and worries himself in every possible way, but he can alter nothing; nay worse, conceptions and ideas, towards which a great many people behave quite carelessly—after all, these innocent things do not merit any other attitude—in Chekhov become the objects of bitter, inexorable, and merciless hatred. He cannot free himself at one single stroke from the power of ideas: therefore he begins a long, slow and stubborn war, I would call it a guerilla war, against the tyrant who had enslaved him. The whole history and the separate episodes of his struggle are of absorbing interest, because the most conspicuous representatives of literature have hitherto been convinced that ideas have a magical power. What are the majority of writers doing but constructing conceptions of the world—and believing that they are engaged in a work of extraordinary importance and sanctity? Chekhov offended very many literary men. If his punishment was comparatively slight, that was because he was very cautious, and waged war with the air of bringing tribute to the enemy, and secondly, because to talent much is forgiven.

Anton Chekhov

Conrad Aiken*

You are traveling from New York to Chicago, and the stranger with whom you have been talking leans with restrained excitement towards the car window, as the train passes a small town, and says: "I lived in that town for three years." It looks like any other town. But you stare at it as if it concealed something amazing, had some secret; and when, after a pause, he begins telling you the story of something odd that happened to him there, a story not very remarkable in itself nor involving very remarkable people, nevertheless the story, the people, the town all seem to you very extraordinary: you listen with an intensity of pleasure that is almost painful, you strive desperately to hold in mind the picture of that town with its small brick shops, dingy fences, white wooden church, to penetrate it, to live in it; and when the narrative is finished you have suddenly an overwhelming desire to tell the stranger a similar narrative, something real, convincing. You have, maybe, no such story at your disposal. You might tell him of something that happened to your friend S., but that, you feel, would not be so satisfactory: the effect of it would not be so powerful. What you desire to say is: "That reminds me of something that occurred when I was living in a small town in Vermont, two years ago. . . ." You are silent, and wonder why it is that the stranger's simple tale has so absorbed you.

Its charm, of course, is simply in the fact that it is actual, that it really happened. This charm is intensified by the fact that it is narrated by the protagonist himself, simply and artlessly, and by the fact that you have actually seen the town that served as a setting, two things that combine to make the reality overwhelming. You have been treated to a "slice of life," a "human document" . . . It is in this kind of actuality that we find, perhaps, a key to the work of Anton Chekhov, possibly the greatest writer of the short story who has ever lived. The stories of Chekhov have precisely this quality of natural, seemingly artless, actuality — casual and random in appearance, abrupt, discursive, alternately overcrowded and thin. Chekhov is the stranger who sits in the train beside us, who suddenly exclaims, "You see that town? I know a queer thing that happened there," and he tells us, in a normal, conversational tone, of the real things that happened there to real people. Observe his openings, taken in order from his volume, *The Schoolmistress, and Other Stories*.

At half-past eight they drove out of town.

A medical student named Mayer, and a pupil of the Moscow School of Painting, Sculpture and Architecture, called Rybnikov, went one

---

*From *Collected Criticism* (formerly *A Reviewer's ABC*) by Conrad Aiken (London, Oxford, New York: Oxford University Press, 1968), 148–53.

evening to see their friend Vasilyev, a law student, and suggested that he go with them to S Street.

The twilight of evening. Big flakes of wet snow are whirling lazily about the street lamps, which have just been lighted.

In the year in which my story begins I had a job at a little station on one of the south-western railways.

Nadia Zelenin had just come back with her mamma from the theatre, where she had seen a performance of *Yevgeni Onegin*.

In every instance the pitch is at once plausibly colloquial. "I am not," Chekhov seems to say, "up to any literary tricks, I have no artistic designs upon you — literature bores me, with its exaggerations and flowerinesses. No, I simply happen to know about this case, and this is how it was." This disarms us — we are now ready to believe literally anything. The primitive desire to listen to a story has been aroused in us, but that is not all: we have been convinced a priori by the speaker's very tone of voice, by his calm, and above all by the absence, on his part, of any *desire* to convince, that what he is about to tell us is true. His audience is already half hypnotized with the first sentence.

In this regard, Chekhov is obviously in the tradition of the Goncourts, with their "human documents," and of Gogol: he was a contemporary of Maupassant in more than mere moment. The theory of the "slice of life" was, at that moment, the thing, and Chekhov, with Maupassant, remains as the chief exemplar, in the short story, of that theory. Yet that theory as it worked through Chekhov is not what it was as it worked through Maupassant: a world of difference sunders the two men. Basically, the difference lies in the fact that Maupassant was a logician of the short story, and Chekhov a poet. Maupassant's mere "mechanics" are superb; far better than Chekhov's. There is no waste, his items are well chosen and "clear"; he arranges them with precision and economy and in a sequence logically overwhelming; he makes his case with a miracle of cold dexterity. Grant his hypothesis, his Q. E. D. will punctually flower.

There is little of this in Chekhov. His stories have not this flat, swift trajectory, are not logically "rounded," do not move, as narratives, to an overwhelming provided conclusion, through an unalterable certainty which one has been permitted, or rather compelled, now and again terrifyingly to feel. Many of his stories do not, in this sense, conclude at all — they merely stop. In fact, the conclusion in itself did not interest Chekhov. He did not desire to emphasize, as Maupassant emphasized, the "final" event, nor, indeed, any single event; his method was more copious, and his concern was not so much with the possibility that in this copiousness a narrative current should be felt, as with the certainty that through it should be perceived a living being or group of beings, beings through whose rich consciousness, intense or palpable, we are enabled to live, backward and forward, in time, lives as appallingly genuine as our own.

Here we reach naturally the question of psychology, and must observe that while Maupassant's characters obey a logic in this regard, obey it mechanically, like marionettes, and have no life apart from it, Chekhov's characters are complex, indeterminate, diffuse a consciousness wider than the bounds of the particular event in which we see them participating: they come to it from "somewhere" (we know only vaguely where), and depart from it for somewhere else. This is due not merely to the fact that Chekhov is more concerned with the effect of "actuality" than with "story," to the fact that, as was said above, he was a poet. His sensibilities were rich and of an immense range, had thrust their roots, one dares to think, almost as widely and deeply into life as Shakespeare's: his understanding was unsurpassed, and if he falls short of the greatest of artists it is not for a lack of that faculty. No artist has known, by introspection, more "states of mind," no artist has known better, by observation, what shapes they assume in talk or behavior. This, after all, is Chekhov's genius — he was a master of mood. His stories offer not only an extraordinary panorama of scenes, actions, situations but, more importantly, a range of states of consciousness which is perhaps unparalleled. It was this pluralism, this awareness of the many-sidedness of life, that sent him to the short story rather than to the novel, and made of his longer stories, as he himself says, mere accumulations. These accumulations — "A Dreary Story," "My Life," "The Steppe" — do not disintegrate, as the short stories do not, simply because, like the short stories, they depend for unity not on the formal working of a theme, but on verisimilitude, on the never-diminishing saturation of consciousness in the life to be "given": their unity is a unity of tone.

If we evade for the moment the question of the precise value, in fiction, of the "actual," and of the extent to which it may be permitted to supplant all other values, and evade, also for the moment, the question of the kind of actuality toward which Chekhov felt a compulsion, it is perhaps profitable to note how interesting are the aesthetic problems raised by the effort to capture, in fiction, that tone. We have already observed that Chekhov instinctively or consciously uses, at the outset of a story and throughout, a colloquial tone — he is never better than when he tells his story in the first person singular. He wishes, in other words, to keep the pitch of the story down, to diminish what is called "the psychic distance"; his picture is to be frameless and immediate, so close to us that we can touch it. He does not want us to be conscious of his style, nor of any arrangement. He wants us to see his people and scenes just as they are, neither larger nor smaller than life. Every trace of sympathy must therefore be excluded: "When you depict sad or unlucky people try to be colder — it gives their grief, as it were, a background. . . . Yes, you must be cold. . . . Every trace of stylization, of heightening, must be expunged. . . . Beauty and expressiveness in Nature are attained only by simplicity, by such simple phrases as 'The sun set,' 'It was dark,' 'It began to rain,' and so on. . . ." In everything we see the avoidance of the phrase, the detail, the attitude, the sense of "frame," of "scheme," which might mitigate the effect of immediacy. "But of the word 'art' I am terrified. . . ." No wonder — by art he meant conscious art, and Chekhov was only intermittently a conscious artist; he knew that he was at his best when, on a theme out of memory — a face, an incident — he gave himself up to rapid improvisation, an improvisation which took the form of a complete surrender to that face, that incident, a submersion of the senses.

This, of course, *was* his art — an art, of its sort, perfect. Yet we come back to question again the extent to which this effect of overwhelming actuality may be permitted to supplant other effects — the effects, for example, of an art more deliberate, more conscious. The two sorts of art ("two" if we take merely the extremes, say, Chekhov and Henry James) are not of course mutually exclusive, there will be room for both; the generation, like the individual, will make its natural choice and rationalize its choice ex post facto. Yet if we need not necessarily at the instant choose between them, it is none the less fruitful to observe their distinguishing characteristics, and we can do no better at the outset than to quote Henry James himself, speaking, in his essay on "The New Novel," of precisely this question of the degree in which mere immersion in the actual may be sufficient.

> Yes, yes — but is this all? These are the circumstances of the interest — we see, we see; but where is the interest itself, where and what is its center, and how are we to measure it in relation to that? . . . That appreciation is . . . a mistake and a priggishness, being reflective and thereby corrosive, is another of the fond dicta which we are here concerned but to brush aside . . . appreciation, attentive and reflective, inquisitive and conclusive, is in this connection absolutely the golden *key* to our pleasure.

This is a statement of a theory of art so antithetical to that of Chekhov (insofar as he consciously entertained one), that it is reasonable to suppose that he simply would not have understood it. Here we have an artist who not only selects one from among many themes because it is richest in possibilities of being "worked," but also positively invites his reader to observe at every moment the "working" of it, to look, as it were, at the back of the clock no less often than at its face, so that he may know not merely what it says but how it says it. This is a pleasure to which Chekhov does not invite us: to make that invitation is, in the same breath, to take a deliberate step away from the "actual."

Compare Chekhov's *In the Ravine* with Turgenev's *A Lear of the Steppes*. The themes have much in common. But whereas Chekhov has richly and beautifully improvised, always in the key of the actual, giving us an immense number of scenes, dialogues, persons, all of them palpitantly real and caught in an exquisite, quiet beauty of tone, Turgenev has gone more deliberately to work: he strikes sharply, even artificially, his "theme" in the opening, giving us thus in advance a glimpse of the whole, and then proceeds to the fine development of this theme through a series of delicate exaggerations—he aims not at the immediate but at the distant, slightly distorted by a trick of atmosphere; not at the actual, but at the larger than the actual. One feels the artificiality, certainly; but one enjoys it, and in retrospect it is the Turgenev story that one clearly remembers, not the Chekhov story. Kharlov we still see, but we do not even recall the name of Chekhov's Lear, any more than we see him as a person. He was living as long as we read of him—more so perhaps than Kharlov. That whole life, in which Chekhov drowned us, how beautiful, resonant, full of echoes it was, how aromatically it ended! But it is our joy in the tone of it that we recall, and not the things that created that tone.

We come back, therefore, to the point from which we started, to a clear realization that Chekhov was in essence a poet, a poet of the actual, an improviser in the vivid. His compulsions drove him to seek character, perhaps—more precisely, to seek mood, state of mind; he profoundly knew the quality, the light, the timbre, the fluctuations of mood, particularly those of a melancholy tinge; and if, in retrospect, we find that his characters have an odd way of evaporating, it is because so often our view of them was never permitted for a moment to be external—we saw them only as infinitely fine and truthful sequences of mood. Chekhov was great because his sensibilities were of sufficient range to enable him to apply this method almost universally. His sympathy, his pity, his tenderness, were inexhaustible. He lived, and thus permitted us to live, everywhere.

Chekhov's Prose   Vladimir Nabokov*

A difference exists between a real artist like Chekhov and a didactic one like Gorky, one of those naive and nervous Russian intellectuals who thought that a little patience and kindness with the miserable, half savage, unfathomable Russian peasant would do the trick. One may compare Chekhov's story "The New Villa."

A rich engineer has built a house for himself and his wife; there is a garden, a fountain, a glass ball, but no arable land — the purpose is fresh air and relaxation. A couple of his horses, splendid, sleek, healthy, snow-white beasts, fascinatingly alike, are led by the coachman to the black-smith.

"Swans, real swans," says the latter, contemplating them with sacred awe.

An old peasant comes up. "Well," he says with a cunning and ironic smile, "white they are, but what of it? If my two horses were stuffed with oats, they would be quite as sleek. I'd like to see those two put to plow and whipped up."

Now, in a didactic story, especially in one with good ideas and purposes, this sentence would be the voice of wisdom, and the old peasant who so simply and deeply expresses the idea of a modus of life regulating existence would be shown further on as a good fine old man, the symbol of the peasant class consciousness as a rising class, etc. What does Chekhov do? Very probably he did not notice himself that he had put into the old peasant's mind a truth sacred to the radicals of his day. What interested him was that it was true to life, true to the character of the man as a character and not as a symbol — a man who spoke so not because he was wise but because he was always trying to be unpleasant, to spoil other people's pleasures: he hated the white horses, the fat handsome coachman; he was himself a lonely man, a widower, his life was dull (he could not work because of an illness that he called either "gryz' " (hernia) or "glisty" (worms). He got his money from his son who worked in a candy-shop in a big town, and all day long he wandered about idly and if he met a peasant bringing home a log or fishing, he would say, "That log is rotten" or "In this weather fish don't bite."

In other words, instead of making a character the medium of a lesson and instead of following up what would seem to Gorky, or to any Soviet author, a socialistic truth by making the rest of the man beautifully good (just as in an ordinary bourgeois story if you love your mother or your dog you cannot be a bad man), instead of this, Chekhov gives us a living

*Excerpts from *Lectures on Russian Literature*, ed. Fredson Bowers (New York, London: Harcourt Brace Jovanovich, 1981), 249–56 and 262–63. © 1981 by the Estate of Vladimir Nabokov. Reprinted by permission of Harcourt Brace Jovanovich, Inc.

human being without bothering about political messages or traditions of writing. Incidentally, we might note that his wise men are usually bores, just as Polonius is.

The fundamental idea of Chekhov's best and worst characters seems to have been that until real moral and spiritual culture, physical fitness and wealth, come to the Russian masses, the efforts of the noblest and best-meaning intellectuals who build bridges and schools while the vodka pub is still there, will come to naught. His conclusion was that pure art, pure science, pure learning, being in no direct contact with the masses, will, in the long run, attain more than the clumsy and muddled attempts of benefactors. It is to be noted that Chekhov himself was a Russian intellectual of the Chekhovian type.

No author has created with less emphasis such pathetic characters as Chekhov has, characters who can often be summed up by the quotation from his story "In the Cart": "How strange, she reflected, why does God give sweetness of nature, sad, nice, kind eyes, to weak, unhappy, useless people — and why are they so attractive?" There is the old village messenger in the story "On Official Business" who tramps through the snow miles and miles on trifling and useless errands which he neither understands nor questions. There is that young man in "My Life" who left his comfortable home and became a miserable house-painter because he could not endure any longer the nauseating and cruel smugness of small-town life, symbolized for him by the dreadful straggling houses that his father the architect builds for the town. What author would have withstood the temptation of drawing the tragic parallel: father builds houses, son is doomed to paint them? But Chekhov does not so much as allude to this point, which if stressed would have put a pin through the story. There is in the story "The House with the Mezzanine" the frail young girl with a name unpronounceable in English, frail Misyus, shivering in her muslin frock in the autumn night and the "I" of the story putting his coat on her thin shoulders — and then her lighted window and then romance somehow fizzling out. There is the old peasant in "The New Villa" who misunderstands in the most atrocious way the futile and lukewarm kindness of an eccentric squire, but at the same time blesses him from all his heart; and when the master's doll-like pampered little girl bursts into tears as she feels the hostile attitude of the other villagers, he produces from his pocket a cucumber with crumbs sticking to it and thrusts it into her hand, saying to that pampered bourgeois child, "Now don't cry, lassy, or else Mummy will tell Daddy, and Daddy will give you a thrashing" — which suggests the exact habits of his own life without having them stressed or explained. There is in the story "In the Cart" that village school mistress whose pathetic daydreaming is broken by the accidents of a rough road and the vulgar though good-natured nickname by which the driver addresses her. And in his most astounding story "In the Ravine" there is the tender and simple young peasant mother Lipa whose naked red baby is murdered with one splash of boiling water by another woman. And how wonderful the preceding scene when the baby was still healthy and gay and the young mother played with it — would go to the door, return, respectfully bow to the child from afar, saying good-morning Mister Nikifor, and then would rush to it and hug it with a scream of love. And in the same wonderful tale there is the wretched peasant bum telling the girl of his wanderings over Russia. One day a gentleman, probably exiled from Moscow for his political views, meeting him somewhere on the Volga, and casting a glance at his rags and face, burst into tears and said aloud, so the peasant relates, "Alas," said the gentleman to me, "black is your bread, black is your life."

Chekhov was the first among writers to rely so much upon the undercurrents of suggestion to convey a definite meaning. In the same story of Lipa and the child there is her husband, a certain swindler, who is condemned to hard labor. Before that, in the days when he was still successfully engaged in his shady business, he used to write letters home in a beautiful hand, not his own. He casually remarks one day that it is his good friend Samorodov who pens those letters for him. We never meet that friend of his; but when the husband is condemned to hard labor, his letters come from Siberia in the same beautiful hand. That is all, but it is perfectly clear that the good Samorodov, whoever he was, had been his partner in crime and is now undergoing the same punishment.

A publisher once remarked to me that every writer had somewhere in him a certain numeral engraved, the exact number of pages which is the limit of any one book he would ever write. My number, I remember, was 385. Chekhov could never write a good long novel — he was a sprinter, not a stayer. He could not, it seems, hold long enough in focus the pattern of life that his genius perceived here and there: he could retain it in its patchy vividness just long enough to make a short story out of it, but it refused to keep bright and detailed as it should keep if it had to be turned into a long and sustained novel. His qualities as a playwright are merely his qualities as a writer of long short stories: the defects of his plays are the same that would have been obvious had he attempted to write full-bodied novels. Chekhov has been compared to the second-rate French writer Maupassant (called for some reason de Maupassant); and though this comparison is detrimental to Chekhov in the artistic sense, there is one feature common to both writers: they could not afford to be long-winded. When Maupassant forced his pen to run a distance that far outreached his natural inclination and wrote such novels as *Bel Ami* (*Sweet Friend*) or *Une Vie* (*A Woman's Life*), they proved to be at the best a series of rudimental short stories more or less artificially blended, producing a kind of uneven impression with none of that inner current driving the theme along that is so natural to the style of such born novelists as Flaubert or Tolstoy. Except for one faux-pas in his youth, Chekhov never attempted to write a fat book. His longest pieces, such as "The Duel" or "Three Years," are still short stories.

Chekhov's books are sad books for humorous people; that is, only a reader with a sense of humor can really appreciate their sadness. There exist writers that sound like something between a titter and a yawn — many of these are professional humorists, for instance. There are others that are something between a chuckle and a sob — Dickens was one of these. There is also that dreadful kind of humor that is consciously introduced by an author in order to give a purely technical relief after a good tragic scene — but this is a trick remote from true literature. Chekhov's humor belonged to none of these types; it was purely Chekhovian. Things for him were funny and sad at the same time, but you would not see their sadness if you did not see their fun, because both were linked up.

Russian critics have noted that Chekhov's style, his choice of words and so on, did not reveal any of those special artistic preoccupations that obsessed, for instance, Gogol or Flaubert or Henry James. His dictionary is poor, his combination of words almost trivial — the purple patch, the juicy verb, the hothouse adjective, the crème-de-menthe epithet, brought in on a silver tray, these were foreign to him. He was not a verbal inventor in the sense that Gogol was; his literary style goes to parties clad in its everyday suit. Thus Chekhov is a good example to give when one tries to explain that a writer may be a perfect artist without being exceptionally vivid in his verbal technique or exceptionally preoccupied with the way his sentences curve. When Turgenev sits down to discuss a landscape, you notice that he is concerned with the trouser-crease of his phrase; he crosses his legs with an eye upon the color of his socks. Chekhov does not mind, not because these matters are not important — for some writers they are naturally and very beautifully important when the right temperament is there — but Chekhov does not mind because his temperament is quite foreign to verbal inventiveness. Even a bit of bad grammar or a slack newspaperish sentence left him unconcerned. The magical part of it is that in spite of his tolerating flaws which a bright beginner would have avoided, in spite of his being quite satisfied with the man-in-the-street among words, the word-in-the-street, so to say, Chekhov managed to convey an impression of artistic beauty far surpassing that of many writers who thought they knew what rich beautiful prose was. He did it by keeping all his words in the same dim light and of the same exact tint of gray, a tint between the color of an old fence and that of a low cloud. The variety of his moods, the flicker of his charming wit, the deeply artistic economy of characterization, the vivid detail, and the fade-out of human life — all the peculiar Chekhovian features — are enhanced by being suffused and surrounded by a faintly iridescent verbal haziness.

His quiet and subtle humor pervades the grayness of the lives he creates. For the Russian philosophical or social-minded critic he was the unique exponent of a unique Russian type of character. It is rather difficult for me to explain what that type was or is, because it is all so linked up with the general psychological and social history of the Russian nineteenth century. It is not quite exact to say that Chekhov dealt in charming and ineffectual people. It is a little more true to say that his men and women are charming because they are ineffectual. But what really attracted the Russian reader was that in Chekhov's heroes he recognized the type of the Russian intellectual, the Russian idealist, a queer and pathetic creature that is little known abroad and cannot exist in the Russia of the Soviets. Chekhov's intellectual was a man who combined the deepest human decency of which man is capable with an almost ridiculous inability to put his ideals and principles into action; a man devoted to moral beauty, the welfare of his people, the welfare of the universe, but unable in his private life to do anything useful; frittering away his provincial existence in a haze of utopian dreams; knowing exactly what is good, what is worth while living for, but at the same time sinking lower and lower in the mud of a humdrum existence, unhappy in love, hopelessly inefficient in everything—a good man who cannot make good. This is the character that passes—in the guise of a doctor, a student, a village teacher, many other professional people—all through Chekhov's stories.

What rather irritated his politically minded critics was that nowhere does the author assign this type to any definite party or give him any definite political program. But that is the whole point. Chekhov's inefficient idealists were neither terrorists, nor Social Democrats, nor budding Bolsheviks, nor any of the numberless members of numberless revolutionary parties in Russia. What mattered was that this typical Chekhovian hero was the unfortunate bearer of a vague but beautiful human truth, a burden which he could neither get rid of nor carry. What we see is a continuous stumble through all Chekhov's stories, but it is the stumble of a man who stumbles because he is staring at the stars. He is unhappy, that man, and he makes others unhappy; he loves not his brethren, not those nearest to him, but the remotest. The plight of a negro in a distant land, of a Chinese coolie, of a workman in the remote Urals, affects him with a keener pang of moral pain than the misfortunes of his neighbor or the troubles of his wife. Chekhov took a special artistic pleasure in fixing all the delicate varieties of that pre-war, pre-revolution type of Russian intellectual. Those men could dream; they could not rule. They broke their own lives and the lives of others, they were silly, weak, futile, hysterical; but Chekhov suggests, blessed be the country that could produce that particular type of man. They missed opportunities, they shunned action, they spent sleepless nights in planning worlds they could not build; but the mere fact of such men, full of such fervor, fire of abnegation, pureness of spirit, moral elevation, this mere fact of such men having lived and probably still living somewhere somehow in the ruthless and sordid Russia of to-day is a promise of better things to come for the world at large—for perhaps the most admirable among the admirable laws of Nature is the survival of the weakest.

It is from this point of view that those who were equally interested in the misery of the Russian people and in the glory of Russian literature, it is from this point of view that they appreciated Chekhov. Though never concerned with providing a social or ethical message, Chekhov's genius almost involuntarily disclosed more of the blackest realities of hungry, puzzled, servile, angry peasant Russia than a multitude of other writers, such as Gorky for instance, who flaunted their social ideas in a procession of painted dummies. I shall go further and say that the person who prefers Dostoevsky or Gorky to Chekhov will never be able to grasp the essentials of Russian literature and Russian life, and, which is far more important, the essentials of universal literary art. It was quite a game among Russians to divide their acquaintances into those who liked Chekhov and those who did not. Those who did not were not the right sort.

I heartily recommend taking as often as possible Chekhov's books (even in the translations they have suffered) and dreaming through them as they are intended to be dreamed through. In an age of ruddy Goliaths it is very useful to read about delicate Davids. Those bleak landscapes, the withered sallows along dismally muddy roads, the gray crows flapping across gray skies, the sudden whiff of some amazing recollection at a most ordinary corner—all this pathetic dimness, all this lovely weakness, all this Chekhovian dove-gray world is worth treasuring in the glare of those strong, self-sufficient worlds that are promised us by the worshippers of totalitarian states.

"The Lady with the Little Dog" (1899)

Chekhov comes into the story "The Lady with the Little Dog" without knocking. There is no dilly-dallying. The very first paragraph reveals the main character, the young fair-haired lady followed by her white Spitz dog on the waterfront of a Crimean resort, Yalta, on the Black Sea. And immediately after, the male character Gurov appears. His wife, whom he has left with the children in Moscow, is vividly depicted: her solid frame, her thick black eyebrows, and the way she had of calling herself "a woman who thinks." One notes the magic of the trifles the author collects—the wife's manner of dropping a certain mute letter in spelling and her calling her husband by the longest and fullest form of his name, both traits in combination with the impressive dignity of her beetle-browed face and rigid poise forming exactly the necessary impression. A hard woman with the strong feminist and social ideas of her time, but one whom her husband finds in his heart of hearts to be narrow, dull-minded, and devoid of grace. The natural transition is to Gurov's constant unfaithfulness to her, to his general attitude toward women—"that inferior race" is what he calls them, but without that inferior race he could not exist. It is hinted that these Russian romances were not altogether as light-winged as in the Paris of Maupassant. Complications and problems are unavoidable with those decent hesitating people of Moscow who are slow heavy starters but plunge into tedious difficulties when once they start going.

Then with the same neat and direct method of attack, with the bridging formula "and so . . . ," we slide back to the lady with the dog. Everything about her, even the way her hair was done, told him that she was bored. The spirit of adventure—though he realized perfectly well that his attitude toward a lone woman in a fashionable sea town was based on vulgar stories, generally false—this spirit of adventure prompts him to call the little dog, which thus becomes a link between her and him. They are both in a public restaurant.

> He beckoned invitingly to the Spitz, and when the dog approached him, shook his finger at it. The Spitz growled; Gurov threatened it again.
> The lady glanced at him and at once dropped her eyes.
> "He doesn't bite," she said and blushed.
> "May I give him a bone?" he asked; and when she nodded he inquired affably, "Have you been in Yalta long?"
> "About five days."

They talk. The author has hinted already that Gurov was witty in the company of women; and instead of having the reader take it for granted (you know the old method of describing the talk as "brilliant" but giving no samples of the conversation), Chekhov makes him joke in a really attractive, winning way. "Bored, are you? An average citizen lives in . . . (here Chekhov lists the names of beautifully chosen, super-provincial towns) and is not bored, but when he arrives here on his vacation it is all boredom and dust. One could think he came from Grenada" (a name particularly appealing to the Russian imagination). The rest of their talk, for which this sidelight is richly sufficient, is conveyed indirectly. Now comes a first glimpse of Chekhov's own system of suggesting atmosphere by the most concise details of nature, "the sea was of a warm lilac hue with a golden path for the moon"; whoever has lived in Yalta knows how exactly this conveys the impression of a summer evening there. . . .

All the traditional rules of story telling have been broken in this wonderful short story of twenty pages or so. There is no problem, no regular climax, no point at the end. And it is one of the greatest stories ever written.

We will now repeat the different features that are typical for this and other Chekhov tales.

First: The story is told in the most natural way possible, not beside the after-dinner fireplace as with Turgenev or Maupassant but in the way one person relates to another the most important things in his life, slowly and yet without a break, in a slightly subdued voice.

Second: Exact and rich characterization is attained by a careful selection and careful distribution of minute but striking features, with perfect contempt for the sustained description, repetition, and strong emphasis of ordinary authors. In this or that description one detail is chosen to illume the whole setting.

Third: There is no special moral to be drawn and no special message to be received. Compare this to the special delivery stories of Gorky or Thomas Mann.

Fourth: The story is based on a system of waves, on the shades of this or that mood. If in Gorky's world the molecules forming it are matter, here, in Chekhov, we get a world of waves instead of particles of matter, which, incidentally, is a nearer approach to the modern scientific understanding of the universe.

Fifth: The contrast of poetry and prose stressed here and there with such insight and humor is, in the long run, a contrast only for the heroes; in reality we feel, and this is again typical of authentic genius, that for Chekhov the lofty and the base are *not* different, that the slice of watermelon and the violet sea, and the hands of the town-governor, are essential points of the "beauty plus pity" of the world.

Sixth: The story does not really end, for as long as people are alive, there is no possible and definite conclusion to their troubles or hopes or dreams.

Seventh: The storyteller seems to keep going out of his way to allude to trifles, every one of which in another type of story would mean a signpost denoting a turn in the action — for instance, the two boys at the theatre would be eavesdroppers, and rumors would spread, or the ink-stand would mean a letter changing the course of the story; but just because these trifles are meaningless, they are all-important in giving the real atmosphere of this particular story.

Structural Features in
Chekhov's Poetics

Avram B. Derman*

1

Chekhov occupies one of the highest places among those literary artists who in their work not only use the resources allowed by scholarship — they all use them, even those who deny that they resort to them and state that they rely exclusively on their own intuition — but also among those who repeatedly express the principle of creative cooperation between the artist and the scholar. . . .

There is something scholarly in his approach to the structure of a work; he divided it into distinct stages, and for each of them he had carefully reasoned methods for the creative embodiment of his ideas.

Regarding the first stage, one must say that if Chekhov's poetics is, as a whole, polemical, that is, if he presents new devices in contrast to old ones, then it is especially polemical with even a paradoxical emphasis as far as it pertains to the first stage of structure, which is the so-called "beginning of the plot,"[1] "preface," "introduction," "prologue," etc.

His poetics of the "story's beginning" amounted in effect to the demand that there be no overt "complication" or, in an extreme case, that it consist of no more than two or three lines. This, of course, was quite a revolutionary step in relation to the poetics of the time, which was dominated by Turgenev (who was its greatest representative). In Turgenev's main and longest works, that is, in his novels, he went through dozens of pages with retrospective biographies of his heroes before they appeared. Chekhov wrote no novels; the short story and short novel were the dominant genres in his works, and that, perhaps, is partly the reason why the nature of his formal requirements was adapted to the short story or the short novel.

There is no doubt, however, that the main reason for Chekhov's sharp hostility towards more or less extended "introductions" was based on something else: they seemed superfluous and in contradiction to his idea about the active reader. He believed that even without the help of specific introductions this sort of reader would reconstruct what was most important in the hero's past life; he would do this through a skillfully depicted present, and if something in the past remained unknown to such a reader,

*From *Anton Chekhov as a Master of Story Writing, Essays in Modern Soviet Literary Criticism*, ed. and trans. L. Hulanicki and D. Savignac (The Hague, Paris: Mouton, 1976), 107–18. Reprinted by permission of Mouton de Gruyter Publishers, Berlin. This essay originally appeared as chapter 4 (pp. 74–88) of Derman's *O Masterstve Chekhova* (Moscow: Sovetsky pisatel, 1959).

then to balance it, a more substantial danger would be avoided: that of the diffusion of an impression which a superabundance of particulars creates. Chekhov's most merciless demands concerned the brevity of the "beginning of the plot," "preface," "introduction," etc.

This is stated with great expressiveness in the valuable memoirs of S. Shchukin, a priest, who appeared before Chekhov as an author with a manuscript. Taking the notebook, Chekhov remarked:

> "A novice writer should do the following: bend it in two and tear out the first half."
>
> "I looked at him with disbelief", Shchukin writes.
>
> "I say this in all seriousness", Chekhov said. "Novice writers usually attempt, so to speak, to 'introduce a reader to the story' and half of what they write is superfluous. One should write in such a way that the reader understands what was going on not through any explanation on the part of the author, but rather through the movement of the story and through the conversations and actions of the characters. Try tearing out the first half of your story; you will only have to change the beginning of the second half a bit, and the story will be completely understandable. And in general, you shouldn't have anything that is superfluous. You have to discard mercilessly everything that is not directly related to the story. If, in the first chapter, you say that a rifle is hanging on the wall, then it absolutely must be fired in the second or third chapter. If it is not going to be fired, then it ought not to be hanging there."[2]

Instructions of this sort are rarely absent in letters to authors who had sent him their works. He was no less merciless in his own personal creative practice, and his severity steadily increased as time went by. If in Chekhov's earlier works one could still find "beginnings" in the spirit of traditional poetics, with some specific traces of an "introduction" — they later disappear without a trace, and Chekhov begins the story either with one (literally!) sentence introducing the very essence of the narration, or else he manages even without this. As an example of the first sort, we shall refer to "Ariadna": "On the deck of a steamer travelling from Odessa to Sevastopol a rather handsome gentleman with a little round beard came up to me to ask for a light, and he said. . . ." This is a bit more than the *whole* introduction: the note about the gentleman's appearance, strictly speaking, already belongs to the corpus of the narrative because this gentleman, being the narrator, is, at the same time, an important protagonist. Everything further is already the corpus of the work, the narrative itself. Too, it is impossible to remain silent about yet another fact. Evidently sensing some sort of unnaturalness in such a "beginning" where a man goes up to someone he does not know to ask for a light and without any apparent reason relates to him a long, complicated and intimate story, Chekhov took care to render this device harmless. Having allowed the narrator to speak a bit at first not on the main theme but on a closely related subject, the author observes: "It . . . was clear that he was somewhat upset and that he would rather talk about himself than about women, and that I would not escape without hearing some long story in the nature of a confession" (IX, 63)[3].

Such a story, of course, follows later. There is, however, a second shock-absorber against artificiality: once he has begun the story, the narrator, that is, the gentleman with the little round beard, soon turns to the listener-author: "I'm sorry, but I must ask you again: is this boring you?"

"I told him that it was not at all boring, and he continued," this time, we might add, uninterrupted by the author to the very end of the story.

As has already been mentioned, Chekhov did not remain at this level in his battle with "introductions," but began to get along entirely without them. Take, for example, the beginning of his long story, "My Life": "The manager said to me: 'I am keeping you on only out of respect for your esteemed father; otherwise you would have been fired long ago' " (IX, 104). Here there is absolutely nothing of the traditional "beginning," "introduction," etc. It is a characteristic segment of the life of the main hero, the first of a great many similar elements from which the life of the hero as a whole is formed and whose story is therefore called "My Life."

In all probability, the dominant characteristic of his early work — always short stories — was the cause of the author's persistent concentration for many years on the improvement of literary devices directed towards condensing the "beginning of the plot" as much as possible, because there was simply no room for it in the outlets in which he was published — newspapers and humor magazines. Having mastered the art of a short introduction, Chekhov valued this achievement, became its principal supporter, and remained faithful to it even after every limitation on his work had been lifted.

2

Apropos of the second structural element, that is, the development of the theme, it must be said that here Chekhov's persistent demand for compactness stands out very sharply, as is quite understandable: at this stage the author must most often be on guard against the dangers of extending the description and making it too detailed, and of allowing repetitions and superfluous comments. It is quite natural that it was to this stage that Chekhov's inventiveness in the art of condensing the narration was directed. It would not be out of place to illustrate the laconism of his compositional devices here. The peculiarities of these devices are most spectacular in those instances where the author confronted the problem of chronologically depicting a process extending over a period of years. For the sake of illustration let us take an example:

It is necessary that the life of Startsev, the hero of the story "Ionych," pass before the reader. At first he is presented as a young country doctor —

a fresh, naive, trusting person with a romantic personality. Then he slowly begins to lose his color; he turns grey and sinks into the mire of a dull Philistine life. The spirit of greedy and senseless money-grubbing seizes him; he finally loses the image and likeness of a human being and even is given a specifically Philistine nickname: "Ionych." This entire slow lifelong dying of a man's humanity had to be shown on the background of a colorless, dull, pitiful, Philistine environment which drags everyone imperiously into its own morass.

This entire extended multiphased process which by its own nature would seem to demand a great accumulation of large and small characteristics is realized in a few short pages with a truly commanding persuasiveness!

One can say that the main literary device which Chekhov uses here is the arrangement of signposts along the path of Doctor Startsev's life, between which the writer leaves a broad space which the reader may fill in as part of his creative cooperation in the work.

These signposts follow various lines which often intersect: signposts along the path of the doctor's career; signposts along the path of the evolution of his tastes; signposts along the development and fate of his romance; signposts along the path of the lives of those individuals who form his milieu, etc.

Here are the signposts which signify the success of Startsev's career:

> (1) Startsev went to town to enjoy himself a bit and to make some purchases. He walked at a leisurely pace *(he did not yet own any horses)* and all the while he sang:
> "When I had yet to drink
> Tears from the cup of life" (IX, 287).

A little more than a year passes. How the hero spent this time is not mentioned, but it is stated almost in passing that:

> (2) *He already owned a pair of horses and had a coachman named Panteleimon in a velvet waistcoat."* (293).

Another four years pass, and there is a new, third signpost along the path of Startsev's career.

> (3) Startsev already had a large practice in the city. Every morning he *hurriedly* received his patients at Dyalizh, and then he left to make house calls in the city. *Now he drove not with a pair of horses, but with a troika with bells. . . .* (297)

A few years later we see the final phase of Startsev's transformation marked by the last signpost:

> (4) Startsev has grown even stouter, he breathes heavily and now walks with his head thrown back. When he rides in the troika with bells, fat and red in the face, and Panteleimon, also fat and red in the face with his thick beefy neck, sits on the box, extending his arms stiffly in front of

himself as if they were made of wood, and shouts to those he meets "Keep to the r-r-right!" it is an impressive picture, and it seems that *it is not a mortal being driven, but a pagan god.*" (IX, 302)

In this way the detailed depiction of the growth of Dr. Startsev's material success and the simultaneous destruction of his moral and spiritual being was replaced by Chekhov with a step by step view of his "mode of transportation." One could not, however, complain of an insufficient expressivity in the sum total of the portrait of Dr. Startsev as received by the reader.

But in other instances Chekhov found it possible to manage even without such signposts! Take for example the description in "Ariadna" of Shamokhin's love for the heroine after he gained her affections and when, as he put it, his love "entered into its final phase, its waning phase:" "I became her lover [says Shamokhin]. At least for about a month I was crazy, feeling only delight. To embrace her young, beautiful body, to take one's pleasure of it, to feel each time upon waking her warmth and to remember that she is here, she, my Ariadna—oh, one cannot get used to this very easily!" (IX, 79). It would seem that all of this was intentionally thought up to prepare the reader for a vivid story of the flowering of this passionate, intoxicated love, with the various shades of its further development.

No, the reader does not get a single line of this story! The words "one cannot get used to this very easily!" are followed immediately by "but nevertheless I did get used to it and gradually began to relate sensibly to my new situation" (IX, 79).

3

Of the three classical elements of structure—the beginning of the plot, the development of the plot, and the finale—it seems that Chekhov was most concerned with the finale. Evidently the popular saying "The end crowns the matter"[4] was for him a living experience in the process of his work. It is not without good reason that in his statements on matters of structure, considerations about the finale occupy the foremost place. The sharp changes in Chekhov's poetics over the course of years are observable best of all in his finales: both the theory and practice of the writer's early years not only differ from those of his later period, but they are often in direct contrast.

Chekhov's statements regarding his work on finales are characterized by their complete decisiveness. One of them which became quite popular, thanks to its unique aphoretical expressiveness, is particularly valuable in that it refers to the structure of both his short stories and his plays. When he finished working on *Ivanov*, Chekhov wrote the following in a letter to his brother Alexander: "I was writing a play for the first time, ergo, mistakes are unavoidable. The sujet is complicated and not at all foolish. I end every act as I do short stories: I carry each act calmly and quietly, but in the end I give the playgoer a slap in the face" (XIII, 372). Chekhov did not attempt to explain further what he had in mind with such an energetic formula, so it follows that he was certain that the addressee would not err on that account. And so it was: in 1887, when Chekhov wrote that letter, the characteristic feature of the finales of his short stories was tangibly clear: it was the *surprise effect*.

Here there is a situation deserving attention, but one which, however, is not immediately evident. We will recall that a surprise effect in a finale is strongly associated in our mind with the humorous stories of Chekhov's early period as, for example, "The Orator," who makes the mistake of extolling in his panegyric not the deceased, but rather a living person who happens to be present at the funeral; "A Horse Name" which turns out to be only indirectly related to horses; "Failure" where the groom, taken by surprise, is blessed with a portrait of Lazhechnikov [I. I. Lazhecznikov (1792–1869) – a writer known for his historical novels] instead of an icon; "The Drama" where the writer uses a heavy paper weight to kill the lady driving him insane with a reading of her drama, and so on *ad infinitum*.

What emerges from Chekhov's letter is that he deliberately applies this same literary device of an ending in his sombre drama! Moreover, in the letter, where he gives his brother only the most schematic idea of a literary genre which was new to him, he attempts to emphasize that fact: it turns out that he uses the same device for a dramatic work as for a humorous work.

It is certainly wrong to be surprised by this. In fact our erroneous impression can be explained by the fact that in Chekhov's early work there is a predominance of humor which is strengthened further in our mind in that we remember this sort of thing better. The effective surprise endings of the non-humorous genres do not play a lesser role in Chekhov's early works than they do in his humorous works. We recall such stories as "In Court" with its sudden assault on the reader's nerves in the finale where it comes to light that the defendant accused of murdering his wife is escorted by his son. Or the short story "The Beggar" in which he depicts the self-satisfied Pharisee of a lawyer, who believes that his own cliché admonitions have brought about the reeducation of Lushkov, a drunkard and beggar, but who discovers that it was not his own doing but that of Olga, the cook, who railed at him but in her heart wept over him and in his stead did the work which Skvortsev had given him to do as a repayment. We might also recall two other early short stories by Chekhov: "Without Title" and "The Bet" which stand apart in his literary legacy by their philosophical character, which is reflected both in style and theme. In the former story we hear of the abbot of a monastery which was isolated from the sinful world. One day, having visited the city, he related to the brethren how the life of the city dweller passes in the depths of sin and temptation, and how great the power of the devil is there. And then comes the ending: "When he left his cell next morning, not a single monk remained in the monastery. They had all rushed to the city" (VII, 11).

In the second story, a young lawyer bets a banker two million rubles that he will voluntarily remain in prison fifteen years; but then, having won the bet for all intents and purposes, he loses it deliberately by escaping from prison, and leaves a note which ends with the following remarks: "To show you my contempt for what you live by, I am abandoning the two million which I once dreamt of as paradise, but which I now scorn. To deprive myself of any claim to this money, I am leaving this place five hours before the agreed-upon time and thereby shall lose the bet . . ." (VII, 209).

It is clear that in both of these two philosophical stories the entire structure is bound up in its "surprise" ending. In particular, regarding "Without Title" (which in its first version was called "An Eastern Tale"), Polonsky [Y. P. Polonsky (1819–1898), Russian poet and editor] wrote to Chekhov immediately after reading the story: "The ending is not merely unexpected, but it is also significant." He was correct in this. In the more dramatic and perfect stories of the early Chekhov, we do not notice, however, that the denouement contains an element of surprise. The reason for this is that we usually associate surprise with amusing, funny, humorous stories; and when there is no laughter, we get the impression that there is no surprise. But, isn't the denouement of "Vanka" — the naive address on his letter to his grandfather — a typical final surprise? And isn't the denouement of "Sleepy" also a surprise? And don't we feel something of sudden tragic enlightenment when, in "Anguish," the cabman Iona turns with his tale of deep sorrow to his horse, the only, patient listener? And isn't the same thing true both in the author's intention and in our understanding: "I give the reader a slap in the face"?

It is necessary to take all of this into very careful consideration in order to evaluate correctly the abruptness of the change which later took place in both Chekhov's opinions about finales and in his creative practice. Only two years pass after he utters the aphorism regarding the ending of *Ivanov*, and he writes the following to Pleshcheev in a letter about "A Dreary Story": "A narrative story, like the stage, has its own characteristics. Thus, my feeling tells me that in the ending of a short novel or a story I ought to deliberately concentrate in the reader the feeling of the entire story, and to do this I must mention briefly in passing those people about whom I spoke earlier" (XIV, 407). Three years later, Chekhov writes the following in a letter to Suvorin: "I have an interesting *sujet* for a comedy, but still lack an ending. Whoever discovers new endings for plays will open up a new era. These damn endings do not come easy to me! Either the hero gets married or shoots himself — there is no other way out of it" (XV,

388). An exceptionally interesting situation! Chekhov already recognizes the necessity for a departure from the traditional "denouement," from the surprise effect ("he shoots himself"), that is, from the notorious "in the face," but in practice he still uses that very sort of denouement. However, he finally comes out the victor in this battle with tradition: even for a work of drama, where "he gets married or shoots himself" seemed somehow unavoidable to him, he creates a finale without either one: we are thinking about *The Cherry Orchard*. In his short novels as well as his stories, Chekhov succeeds not only in creating and elaborating, but also in strengthening the poetics of an ending without a "denouement." Was it conceivable before Chekhov that a story in which the "heroine" had gone through several love affairs would end as in "The Darling"?

> She lies down and thinks about Sasha, who is sleeping soundly in the next room. From time to time he mutters in his sleep: "I'll show you. Get out of here! Don't fight!" (IX, 327).

In the very nature of the finale there is a threatening danger for a writer, a danger which in spite of its relative variety — elevated and rhetorical, a bit sugary, spectacular, etc. — finally amounts to one thing: the danger of unoriginal "rounding." Chekhov used his own characteristic devices to do battle with this danger. One such device comes forward with special clarity in "A Case from a Doctor's Practice." A doctor comes to a sick woman who owns a factory, and is seized by an oppressive mood replete with strong social feeling. He leaves early in the morning.

> The singing of skylarks and the ringing of church bells was in the air. The windows in the factory buildings gleamed happily and on his way out of the yard and then down the road to the station, Korolev no longer thought about the workers, the pile dwellings, or the devil; rather he thought about the time, perhaps even in the near future, when life would be as bright and joyful as this quiet Sunday morning.
>
> (IX, 314)

It would seem that as far as logic, psychology, and even rhythm are concerned, one might put a period here: everything is said and a typical "ending" is made. But here the whole point is that the ending is "typical," is reminiscent of a curtain falling, is rounded in an elevated style, and using a semicolon instead of a period, Chekhov adds, clearly *adds* two unpretentious "lowering" lines: "and he thought of how pleasant this was to ride on a spring morning in a fine troika and how pleasant it was to warm oneself in the sunshine."

4

We have a classic example of a Chekhovian finale characteristic of the highest level of his creativity in "The Lady with the Little Dog" — one of Chekhov's masterpieces.

We have before our eyes a description of the story's two protagonists in one of the stolen moments of bitter "happiness" which seldom fell to their lot.

> He went up to her and took her by the shoulders to caress her and say something cheerful, and at that moment he caught sight of himself in the mirror.
>
> His hair was already beginning to turn grey . . . The shoulders on which his hands lay were warm and trembling. He felt compassion for this life which was still warm and beautiful, but probably already near the time when it would begin to fade and wither, like his own life had . . . And only now, when his head became grey, did he come to love well, in a genuine way—for the first time in his life.
>
> Anna Sergeevna and he loved each other like people very close, and akin, like man and wife, like tender friends; it seemed to them that fate itself had destined them for each other, and they could not understand why each was married to someone else. They were like two birds of passage, male and female, snared and forced to live in separate cages. They had forgiven each other for everything that they were ashamed of in the past, and they forgave everything in the present and felt that their love had changed them both.
>
> Formerly in moments of depression he comforted himself with any argument that came to his mind, but now he did not care any more for arguments, but rather felt profound compassion, he wanted to be sincere and tender . . .
>
> "Don't cry any more, my darling," he was saying. "You have cried enough, it is over now . . . Let's have a talk, we will come up with something."
>
> Then they talked for a long time consulting each other and spoke of how they might free themselves of the necessity for hiding, deceiving, and living in different cities while not seeing each other for long periods. How to free themselves from such unbearable fetters?
>
> "How? How?" he asked, clutching his head. "How?"
>
> And it seemed that in just a short while the solution would be found, and then a new, wonderful life would begin; and it was clear to both of them that the end was still far off and that the most complicated and difficult part was only just beginning.
>
> (IX, 370–71)

This ending deserves very close attention. Here, with direct, exact words, the very thing which is the real essence of Chekhov's finales, in almost all the works of his mature stage of creativity, is distinctly pronounced "aloud," the thing which he expressed elsewhere not so openly, sometimes only in an allusion.

Even if it is accidental, with no deliberate intention on the part of the author, that the quoted "end" of "The Lady with the Little Dog" ends with the word "beginning," it does not keep us from seeing that the same word could have been used in the finales of "The Duel," "The House with the Mezzanine," "The Betrothed," "My Life," "An Unknown Man's Story," and many other stories, which are still read with deep interest in spite of the fact that "the particular situations" from which they were created have almost completely disappeared into the past. These endings of Chekhov's stories announce that in the life process depicted by the author a certain stage was completed — and only that. The process continues, a new phase begins which is more important than the one depicted, but it is the reader himself who must create it: Chekhov places his courageous hopes on the creative cooperation of the reader, for whom he nonetheless has created all the necessary prerequisites for successful understanding.

In his excellent article "Chekhovian Finales", the late A. G. Gornfeld,[5] the well known scholar-critic whom Gorky held in high esteem, turned his attention to a peculiar feature of the finale in many Chekhov stories: the author breaks with his hero at the moment when the hero falls to thinking, becomes absorbed in thought after experiencing the events described. This, of course, is not a chance repetition of a device. The thoughts and reflections of the hero are a projection of the presumed thoughts of the reader. They are the sort of thing which comprise the goal of the author's efforts. It is natural that the most intensive work in the reader's mind be directed towards the crowning of the work, toward the completion of the work when all the images and events before the reader's eyes which constitute the segment of life portrayed have passed. Hence the attention Chekhov gave specifically to the finale. But if in his early years he concentrated in the latter all his resources to get an effect, in the most part for the emotional saturation of the reader's reaction, then in later years, while not ignoring this aspect of the matter, he nevertheless shifted the center of gravity towards arousing in the reader the deepest possible mental activity.

And so, turning attention to Chekhov's prose beginning with 1894, that is, in the last decade of his life, we find the following in the finales: In "Woman's World": "She [Anna Akimovna, the heroine] now *was thinking* that were it possible to draw a picture of the long day which she had just lived through, then everything that was bad and vulgar . . . would have been true, while her dreams . . . would have stood out from the whole . . . like something false or exaggerated" (VIII, 333). In "Rothschild's Violin" Bronza, the principal hero, reflects bitterly and resentfully just before his death: "Why is it that in this world there is such a strange order of things that life, which is given to man only once, passes without profit?" (VIII, 343). A student (in the story of the same name) "*was thinking* that truth and beauty . . . evidently always constituted the most important things in human life" (VIII, 348). In "A Case from a Doctor's Practice" Doctor Korolev, returning to the city early in the morning from a call to a patient "*thought* about the time, perhaps even in the near future, when life would be as bright and joyful as this quiet Sunday morning" (IX, 314). In "The New Dacha" the peasants *think* about their absurd relationship with the owners of the dacha: "What kind of fog is it which shrouded their eyes from what mattered most?" (IX, 341). This enumeration of Chekhov's works where the principal hero falls to thinking in the finale, trying to comprehend all that he has undergone, could be continued up to the very end of Chekhov's writings, including his swan song, "The Betrothed," at the end of which we read: "She went into Sasha's room and stood there for a moment. 'Farewell, dear Sasha!' she *thought*, and her new life, broad and spacious, was pictured before her, and this life, still obscure, full of mystery, attracted her and beckoned to her" (IX, 450). Out of all of these leitmotifs of finales, we will distinguish only one which is particularly remarkable. In the short story "On Official Duty," Inspector Lyzhin, under the influence of what he has undergone, surrenders to his customary thoughts about the connection of his personal life with the general order of things. Significant is the "addition" to these customary thoughts, engendered by the picture of harsh social contradictions raised before the eyes of Lyzhin, who started to feel his responsibility—keenly—to the victims of this general process: "He felt that this suicide and the peasant's misery lay on his conscience too; to tolerate the idea that these people, resigned to their lot, take upon themselves the heaviest and darkest burden in life—how terrible this was! To tolerate this, and to wish for oneself a bright, active life among happy, satisfied people and to dream constantly of such a life—would mean to dream of new suicides of people crushed by work and weariness . . ." (IX, 355). Regarding the sharpness and revelatory character of the given train of thought, the author interrupts at that moment: "Such were Lyzhin's thoughts, and such thoughts had long existed hidden within him, and only now were they displayed so broadly and clearly in his consciousness" (IX, 354). It is in these words that we find the key to Chekhov's finales as extremely important structural elements! He does not attempt to startle his reader or uncover before him some exotic, unusual area of life. Just the opposite: he attempts to take out of the shadows and put into light "old" but "*hidden*" thought, to direct it towards what is most familiar and constantly before the reader's eyes, to open his eyes even wider, to compel him to look more deeply into the depths of life, to help him to perceive this life which is taken for granted "broadly and clearly," *to begin to think.*

Notes

1. *Zaviazka*—that point in the *sujet* where the plot actually begins to unfold; sometimes called the "complication."

2. S. Shchukin, "Iz vospominanii ob A. P. Chekhove", *Russkaia mysl* (1911), 10, p. 44.

3. Numerals in parentheses in this essay refer to the volume and page number in Chekhov's *Polnoe sobranie sochinenii i pisem* (Moskva: Goslitizdat, 1944–1951).

4. Equivalent to the Latin *finis coronat opus*, not "the end justifies the means."

5. *Krasnaja nov* (1939), 8–9.

Warm Heart, Cold Eye

George P. Elliott*

She was a serious student with the steady gaze of one who will not be deceived, she wrote stories the surface of which was deceptively smooth and quiet considering how much was going on in them, and she was cross with me.

"What do you mean, my stories are too Chekhovian? He's the best, isn't he? You said so yourself. Besides, I *want* to write the way he does. What's wrong with that?"

"Manhattan isn't Russia."

"A lot of my characters aren't New Yorkers, originally at least." There was a brief loaded silence. She rallied. "Anyway, practically all of them are educated neurotics like so many of Chekhov's — you know, discontented and unreligious and liberal and they've read the right books but nothing seems to go right for them, love and so on. That's a lot to have in common, isn't it?"

"A whole lot," I said, "but they're Russians, they're different from us, they say and do things more dramatically." She didn't look convinced. "At least they do in all the 19th century novels and plays — more openly, more explosively, more revealingly. There, more revealingly. I bet if Chekhov were writing now, about educated Americans, he'd have to modify his style."

"Hm. Maybe there's something to that. Hm. — Maybe I'll go live in Russia."

I laughed as though she'd made a joke, but, when she stood to leave, her glance let me know what she thought of that laugh.

Twenty years later, she still lives in Manhattan, and both her stories and the people in them have changed. Her women are as liberated as their men are etiolated, but they are all constrained by a new respectability: those women, children, or men who are not into psychoanalysis one way or another are at least decently psychologized from head to sole. That is, they understand and explain themselves and each other, as she also does, in that liberalized-Freud synthetic which is fashionable these days. In this respect, of course, her world — our world — is not at all Chekhovian.

Even so, I think Chekhov speaks more clearly to Americans in the 1970s than he did in the 1950s and far more immediately than he spoke to any but a handful of Americans in his own lifetime or, indeed, in the first half of our century. (He was quite indifferent to having his work translated, saying, "If Russian writers are needed anywhere, it is only in Russia herself.")[1] It seems to me that a good many Americans now, and especially

*From *Chekhov and Our Age, Responses to Chekhov by American Writers and Scholars,* ed. James McConkey (Ithaca, N.Y., Cornell University Press, 1984), 45–70. Reprinted by permission of Mrs. Mary E. Elliot.

American writers, feel for Chekhov an affinity, a warmth of affection, a kinship, different from what we feel for the other Russian writers, including the two who are commonly seen as towering above him. Tolstoy and Dostoevsky castigate us for our sins; he talks with us about what's gone wrong.

As for myself, there is only one other writer, also a humane, various ironist, whose stories make me feel for him a friendship such as I feel for Chekhov, and that is Chaucer. Chaucer too was neither apart from nor above the people of all sorts and conditions whom he found so interesting, and he too was scrupulous not to get so entangled either with them or with us his readers as to interfere with our knowing them. But the world of Chaucer's stories is not only long ago, it is strange in ways for which I feel an acute, remote nostalgia, there being little in my actual experience to help me understand those ways. In the world he created after the model of the world he lived in, suffering was mostly unneurotic; in it, people were sinners who believed they knew what to do about guilt and who, open to grace, thought it possible to be happy. But in the world of Chekhov's stories, much of the suffering is neurotic in ways I understand intimately; in it, the reader gets to know some peasants and trades folk, but most of the people are educated in modern thought, and things are so arranged by and for them as to keep grace out and guilt in.

I am going to venture an extreme opinion. In Chekhov better than in any other writer of any age or nation including our own, we can see what educated, cultivated, enlightened Americans now are essentially like. I do not mean to imply that he mirrors the whole truth or that he is always right; some of the distortion of what he shows us is in the mirror itself. A couple of areas of such distortion are important enough to mention specifically. First, I am not entirely sure what he thinks of love, family, and mothers, but I think it fair to say that among all his educated, progressive characters there is not one happy love affair or marriage, except off in the wings, or one strong, devoted, good mother. In this I think he is wrong—though faithful, I must say, to a widespread opinion among the neurotics in whom he was so interested, being one himself. Second, though he is thoroughly successful at presenting a would-be revolutionary, he is not much help at understanding that important kind of new man, a radical ideologue, a true and consistent totalitarian. For that understanding, one must go to Dostoevsky. At the end of *Notes from Underground*, written in 1864 when Chekhov was a child, the Underground Man says: "Soon we shall contrive to be born somehow from an idea." And soon they did contrive it; the "idea" that the Underground Man is referring to is the system of Enlightened ideas for which the word *ideology* had been coined at the end of the 18th century. Chekhov, I believe, did not comprehend the differentness of born-again ideologues, of those who are a sort of parody of twice-born Christians. For us now, the most important such are those who are born of the Marxist idea, those whose hero and exemplar is Lenin. Chekhov died in 1904, just before these new, and unneurotic, men became so important that he could hardly have left them out of the picture, as we who have seen the Gletkins overrun vast tracts of the earth cannot ignore them.

The purpose of this essay is to persuade you that my opinion that we can see much of ourselves in Chekhov's work is, if not entirely true, at least a defensible exaggeration of the truth.

For convenience, I divide my argument into three sections: first, Chekhov's people are Russians; second, he looked at everyone, real or imagined, with a cold eye and a warm heart; and third, his world was not psychologized.

First, the Russianness.

Early in "The Duel,"[2] a fine novella marred but not spoiled by a poor ending, the central character, Laevsky, is talking with a new acquaintance named Samoylenko.

> ". . . I shan't hide anything. I'll tell you frankly, as a friend. Things are in a bad way with me and Nadezhda, a very bad way. I'm sorry to be confiding in you, but I must get it off my chest."
>
> Sensing the conversation's drift, Samoylenko lowered his eyes and drummed his fingers on the table.
>
> "I've lived with her for two years, and I don't love her any more," Laevsky went on. "Or rather, I've come to see that I never did love her. These two years have been a snare and delusion."
>
> While speaking, Laevsky had the trick of scrutinizing the pink palms of his hands, biting his nails or crumpling his cuff. He did so now.
>
> "You can't help me, that I realize," he said. "But I'm telling you because . . ."

Up to that "because," this passage could, with a little tinkering, be accommodated in a contemporary American realistic story; it is a mere slice of life, revealing nothing much. But then Laevsky goes on as Russians did but as no American is likely to and therefore as no American realistic writer should: ". . . because talk's the only escape for us failures and Superfluous Men." And what a difference it makes to the reader that the self-revelation that follows is delivered in the form of a credible conversation rather than as a fictitious confession (Philip Roth's Portnoy), as an unmailed letter (Saul Bellow's Herzog), or as a sort of interior monologue (a hundred writers' Anyman and Anywoman). Laevsky continues:

> "I have to base whatever I do on general principles. I must find an explanation, an excuse for my futile life in somebody's theories, in literary types — say in the fact that we, the gentry, are going to the bad, and so on. Last night, for instance, I kept consoling myself with the thought of Tolstoy — he's so right about things, so fiendishly right — and it made me feel better. He's a really great writer, old man — say what you like."

Laevsky is not posing when he labels himself a Superfluous Man, nor does Chekhov, despite his aversion to this sort of type-casting, put quotation marks around the phrase to disavow responsibility for it; for in actual life a Laevsky would have characterized himself as belonging to that 19th century Russian literary type, and Chekhov is responsible for assigning the word for him to use straight. And because Laevsky types himself as a Superfluous Man, Tolstoy's moral severity about the type really does make him feel better. Also, more dramatically, Laevsky's saying so one-ups Samoylenko.

> Never having read Tolstoy, but meaning to every day, Samoylenko was abashed.
> "Yes," he said. "All writers draw on their imagination, but he draws direct from nature."

To this Rousseauistic bromide, Laevsky responds with another one no less soporific, one which is still active among us ninety years later: ". . . How civilization does cripple us!" That is a bromide not because it is a lie— Chekhov in his own person believed it was true enough—but because it is uttered when and by whom it is uttered. Chekhov puts ideas in a character's mouth as a way of revealing and placing him, not as they are true or false. In Chekhov as in life, when a man of Laevsky's sophistication utters a cliché, he is lying even if the words he utters do not in themselves constitute a lie, and nothing makes it easier to lie with a truth than to have a lot of other people doing so too.

Laevsky speaks with a peculiarly Russian combination of self-contempt and self-honesty, futility and energy, which is enormously useful to a realistic writer; for it shifts much of the burden of characterization from the writer in a narrator's voice onto the character in his own voice. (An aside. Chekhov is the only great writer of realistic fiction also to write great plays—not James or Joyce or Lawrence, though they tried—as well as being the only great dramatist whose principal characters are bored neurotics—not Ibsen or Strindberg or Shaw, though they made gestures in that direction. I think the Russianness of his characters had something to do with this.) Laevsky continues:

> ". . . I fall in love with a married woman, she falls in love with me. It all starts with kisses, quiet evenings, vows, Herbert Spencer, ideals and common interests. How utterly bogus! We're really running away from her husband, but we pretend we're escaping from the futility of our life as intellectuals. . . . I'm just a miserable, namby-pamby neurotic. . . . As for love, living with a woman who has read Herbert Spencer and followed you to the ends of the earth—that's just as boring as cohabiting with any more common or garden specimen, you take it from me. There's the same smell of ironing, face-powder, and medicines, there are the same curl-papers every morning, there's the same old pretence."

Here, as throughout the story, Chekhov portrays a man who types himself a Superfluous Man but whose actual personality, as he reveals himself to us dramatically, is far more complex than that. He uses the label Superfluous Man, as an American might label himself a Libertarian or an Egalitarian, as a way to keep from knowing the far more difficult truth about himself, a truth which the writer makes it possible for the reader to know if he wants to.

At the end of *A Streetcar Named Desire*, Tennessee Williams gives Blanche a line which is moving in context and beautiful both in context and out: "Whoever you are—I have always depended on the kindness of strangers." But that sentence belongs to the realm of dramatic poetry ("Give me my robes, put on my crown. I have Immortal longings in me") far more than to the world of actual women in the South of the United States in the fourth decade of the 20th century. By contrast, and I do not mean this distinction to be in any way invidious but only clarifying, the speech Chekhov gives Sonya at the end of *Uncle Vanya*, though also moving in context, is not so lovely. Vanya is crying and has just said, "I'm so depressed, Sonya, you can't think how depressed I feel."[3] Sonya is speaking, half to him, half to herself: "We shall find peace. We shall hear the angels, we shall see the sky sparkling with diamonds. We shall see all the evils of this life, all our own sufferings, vanish in the flood of mercy which will fill the whole world. And then our life will be calm and gentle, sweet as a caress. I believe that, I do believe it. . . . We shall find peace. We shall find peace. We shall find peace." That speech, so gentle, so pretty, so untrue, belongs both to the imagined world of high dramatic irony and to the actual world of Russia in the 1890s—and also to the world of some unhappy, idealistic, self-tormenting young American women I have known in the past decade, and know now, and understand somewhat better because of that speech, the ironies and pathos of which, in context, wrench the heart. And I have also come to know Sonya's American cousin, esthetic and drug-impatient: Lucy in the Sky with Diamonds.

As for my second point, Chekhov's warm heart but cold eye, it is literarily the most important element of his special power to show us ourselves, but I find little to say about it. There it is. He neither prophet-like blames and exhorts nor god-like forgives and damns. Rather, he studies those fellow creatures his characters with intense interest and with an eye that will not be deceived, liking or disliking them individually as the case may be.

And you his reader are his fellow creature too, and he extends his unfailing courtesy to you. The perfection of this attitude is to be found in "Ward No. Six." The first paragraph describes the exterior of a small building in the courtyard of a dreadful provincial hospital. The narrator turns to the reader: "Unless you are afraid of nettle stings, let us take the narrow path to this shack and see what goes on inside."[4] The narrator is quite straightforward, he shares his opinions with you, he is full of good sense and acuity, he speaks with confidence, you soon trust him. Presently he shows you the warder, Nikita: "He is one of those dull, self-assured punctilious simpletons who believe in discipline above all things and who are therefore convinced that people need hitting. He hits them on face, chest, back or anywhere handy, being firmly convinced that this is the only way to keep order in the place."[5] You are introduced to the five inmates of the ward — *lunatics* or *madmen*, depending on the translation, but not *psychotics*. The narrator, who by now you are confident is Chekhov himself, tells you what he thinks about the most interesting inmate, Gromov:

> I like his broad face with its high cheek-bones, always pale and unhappy, mirroring a soul racked by struggle and ever-present terror. . . . I like him as a person polite, helpful and outstandingly delicate in his manner towards all except Nikita. . . . His speech is jumbled, feverish, delirious, jerky, not always comprehensible, but there is a fine ring about it, about his words and his voice. As he speaks you recognize both the lunatic and the man in him. It is hard to convey his insane babble on paper. He talks of human viciousness, of brutality trampling on justice, of the heaven on earth which will come to pass in time, of the bars on windows which constantly remind him of the obtuseness and cruelty of his oppressors. The result is like a chaotic, untidy, miscellany of old songs: old, but not yet stale.[6]

Chekhov has attached no labels to the mental disorders of the other four inmates, but Gromov is educated and frequently lucid; he has a name for his disturbance, so Chekhov must include it in the story. But the label he uses is minimally scientific, describing a symptom without pretending to explain the disorder. *Paranoia* was in use at the time Chekhov wrote the story, a rich and complex word, but he avoids it in favor of a term less technical but more accurate as describing what we see of Gromov, *persecution mania*. I find it instructive to think how much less clear Chekhov, Gromov, and you the reader would have been about Gromov's disorder had the word *paranoid* commonly been used in those days as it is among us. Recently I asked half a dozen graduate students of fiction writing what they thought *paranoid* meant; all but one agreed it meant fearful, being consciously full of fear; the sixth one tentatively suggested it meant delusions of persecution. Chekhov understands the layman's limitations and respects you enough not to flatter and mislead you by using a pretentious term you only partially understand — another large aspect of *paranoid*, though not all of it, being delusions of grandeur.

Then, nine pages into "Ward No. Six," Chekhov introduces you to the main character, Dr. Ragin:

> In early youth he was extremely pious, it is said, and he was preparing for a church career, proposing to enter theological college after leaving school in 1863, but his father, a Doctor of Medicine and surgeon, supposedly uttered a scathing laugh and announced categorically that he would disown the boy if he became a cleric. How true that is I have

no idea, but Ragin himself often confessed that he never had any vocation for medicine or for science in general.[7]

Yet Ragin's dreams and hopes are of an ever-improving medical science. From this point on in the story, Chekhov and you are out of it; you listen not so much to him as to what he says. Ragin is a study in what was called acedia in the Middle Ages or what an existentialist now would call anomie. He is educated, his will is weak and deteriorating, he neglects his duties as a doctor, he muddles himself with vodka and big ideas, he is a pluperfect slob: " 'As you well know, sir,' the doctor continues with quiet emphasis, 'everything in this world is trivial and boring, higher spiritual manifestations of the human intellect excepted.' "[8] Then Chekhov pushes him right through cliché into blather: "Life is a deplorable trap. When a thinking man attains adulthood and mature awareness he can't help feeling hopelessly ensnared. And it *is* against his will, actually, that he has been called into being from nothingness by certain chance factors."[9]

Dr. Ragin befriends Gromov, to whose often intelligent ideas and usually dead-right insults he responds with pleasure: " 'Now, what a nice young man,' thought Ragin as he went to his quarters. 'I think he's the first person I've been able to talk to since I've been here. He can use his brain and he is interested in just the right things.' "[10] The rest of the story is a careful account of the deliquescence of the doctor's will, at once pathetic and ugly, and it is worth noting that neither Ragin nor Chekhov, both doctors, ever gives his descent into lethargic madness a name; Ragin just doesn't care, but Chekhov the writer knows better. In fiction, a disease has far greater imaginative force if it has no name; down where the imagination has its being we are all Platonists, and a name gives a thing an existence of its own; *schizophrenia* becomes a thing which gets into your will, your self, and which chemicals can drive out; so, even, is *depression*. But Ragin is a man whom we are to imagine, and what happens to him his self has willed: no name, no thing independent of the will. In *Bleak House*, Dickens leaves unnamed the miasma that pollutes England and disfigures Esther, and in "The Death of Ivan Ilyich" Tolstoy does not name the disease that destroys Ivan Ilyich; in the reader's emotions and obscure understanding, these sufferings of the body become also disorders of the spirit. John Updike presents an example of *how not to*. In a recent *New Yorker* story,[11] he has a divorcing husband go to a doctor because he has a pain in his shoulder. The doctor tells him that "Arthritis, as you may know, belongs to a family of complaints with a psychosomatic component." The patient wants to know when he'll get over it. The doctor answers: "When your brain stops sending out punishing signals." That interchange sounds true to life and true enough, except for the moral word *punishing*, to modern medical theory; but what it does by way of overexplanation to that character's pain in the shoulder is to rob it of every ohm of fictional energy. In "Ward No. Six," Dr. Ragin's mental suffering as he approaches collapse becomes also a bodily one, and Chekhov enters his consciousness that we may know what he feels—the horror of what he feels, not the mechanics of how he feels it: "Layers of scum seemed to be forming inside him, and after each of his friend's visits he felt as if these deposits were mounting higher and higher until they seemed to be clutching at his throat."[12] When he finally goes over the threshold of control, Chekhov says: "Ragin suddenly felt the deposit of scum reach the level of his throat."[13] But Chekhov does not reduce Ragin to an inhuman puddle totally devoid of will. Ivanov's will was twisted but not broken; in the last action of the play, he puts an end to his torment, and also as it were transfers some of it to others, by shooting himself. Once Ragin is locked up in Ward Number Six and Nikita has beaten him too, his inert will seems to give one last spasm; he dies of a stroke, hurting no one else. Chekhov gives us his last thoughts, concluding with these: "But he didn't want any immortality, he only thought about it for a moment. A herd of deer, extraordinarily handsome and graceful, of which he had been reading on the previous day, darted past him. A peasant woman held out a registered letter, Michael Averyanovich said something."[14] Then, according to Chekhov, "Ragin plunged into eternal oblivion."

Now to my third main point, that it was to Chekhov's advantage as a writer that his world was not yet psychologized: What does that mean? Psychology was popping out all over the western world in the late 19th century; Herbert Spencer's *Principles of Psychology*, for example, had been published in Russian in 1876—Laevsky and Nadezhda could have been reading it together when falling in love. But for literary people, the overwhelming psychological phenomenon was Freud. To put it in a tidy, melodramatic way: the 20th century opened with the decisive event in its intellectual history, the publication of *The Interpretation of Dreams* in 1900, and realistic fiction and drama could never be the same again.

Portraying psychologized characters would not in itself have been a problem for Chekhov. For example, had the notion of birth trauma been fashionable in Laevsky's world, it would have been next to irresistible for his creator to present him as bemoaning his inability to remember the pains of having been born—for if only he could relive that primal experience things would be set right in him at last, and maybe, if he were very lucky, maybe he would even be able to remember the experience of living in the womb itself, that Eden from which we have been expelled and to which progress and socialism will return us when the state has withered away and we are freed one and all by science and provided with abundance and comfort world without end amen. No, psychology hasn't changed that familiar dream in any essential way, only added some frills to the manifest content. My argument is that Freudianized psychology generally and our hybrid of it specifically makes neurotics harder to see as people, in part because it alters the way they think of themselves but also because of all that explanation. Chekhov could see and present his neurotics with such exquisite honesty not only because of his own clarity of vision but also because they were not obscured to his view by various psychological labels, many of which are troublesome precisely because they are accurate. When the gentle Sonya uses ideals to cripple herself with, it is easier for Chekhov, as it is easier for us, to see the woman doing it because MASOCHIST is not blazoned across her chest—a bandage as tight as that alters the shape.

I am going to turn aside for a paragraph to mention some contemporary writers who have had to deal with or elude psychology in their work. First, here are three writers who I think handle the problem seriously but badly; there being a large audience for psychologizing, they have considerable prestige and success, both because of their own native gifts and because they do not see psychologizing, as I do, as an interference to creation (indeed, psychological narrative in its pure form, case history, seems to me a fail-safe contraceptive). Arthur Miller in *After the Fall* smothers the Marilyn Monroe character under so much plain-prose psychology about her sad state that she never takes on a life of her own. Psychoanalyzed Anna in Doris Lessing's *The Golden Notebook* wraps herself in so many layers of wool prose that her shape quite disappears. Most of John Updike's characters suffer from fuzz; for example, in the story I cited earlier, a man on the day of divorce is remembering his wedding day, and he thinks in standard Updike terms of his wife, ". . . she had been drawing near to marriage at the same rate as he, and with the same regressive impulses." Under the guise of providing an insight with a precise and commonly understood meaning, the action referred to is instead generalized (man and wife had the *same* impulse?) and the characters are fuzzed over (the same *regressive* impulse?). For me, the pages of these three intelligent, moral, serious writers are sealed with a gum the chief ingredient of which is over-explanation—and this is not even to mention the psychologizing in whole pulped forests of novels now on the racks or in such fashionable plays as *Equus*. But a writer need not succumb. When the protagonist in John Cheever's story "The Country Husband" goes to a psychiatrist, he presents the worst symptom of his disorder with these words, "I'm in love, Dr. Herzog," and what the doctor says in reply we are not told; instead, we are told what therapy the doctor recommends, woodworking; we last see the patient down in his cellar building a coffee table. The most successful good novel in the world these days is García Márquez's *One Hundred Years of Solitude*, and I think that a reason for its success both as fiction and in popularity is that it is set in a world into which psychology had not yet penetrated and is told with a flamboyance that effectively keeps psychology at bay. Getting away from psychology is, I think, one reason for the extreme self-consciousness of much recent fiction that is usually called "New" and that derives in good part from Borges. In my opinion, the two best "New" fictions by American writers are William Gass's short story "Order of Insects" and Lore Segal's short novel *Lucinella*. The heroines of both first-person stories are hard to get to know; Lucinella performs so many dazzling narrative stunts and the narrator of the Gass story lurks so far inside the story's structure that you have to work hard to make their personal acquaintance; however, it seems to me that once you do manage to connect with them, the rewards are the usual fictional ones, the main thing new about the characters being that they use subtle prose and narrative form-consciousness as ways of hiding out from psychology. There is also the problem, which Chekhov was spared, of hiding out from sexology. Like pornography, though for different reasons, sexology's way of looking at people behaving sexually has a tendency to turn lovers into puppets of compulsion and contrivance, which is at the very least indelicate. Satire has use for such indelicacy, but story is an art of fine discriminations. For example, the one time the story shows us Tristan and Iseult in bed they are clothed and a sword lies between them. If you want to see what sexology would make of them, read Updike's *Couples* and shudder. Chekhov was not prudish, he was fastidious; and he knew that among the many things realistic fiction has no use for, along with vampires, Utopia, and the state of the author's health, is naked, klieg-lighted, taped and measured copulation.

Lipa in the story "In the Hollow" is very poor, a drudge, but a rich merchant's son chooses her, despite her lack of a dowry, because she happens to be beautiful. She bears a child; her husband is imprisoned for counterfeiting; her father-in-law puts her child, his grandchild, into his will for a gift of land. Thereupon, her sister-in-law, in a rage of spite, pours boiling water on the baby and kills it; with this act, the sister-in-law comes to dominate the family; after the baby's funeral, she drives Lipa away—"you convict scum"—and takes over the management of the family's affairs. Lipa's response to all this is numb bewilderment, terrible grief, then resignation, but no resentment whatever, not even blame. She goes back to live with her mother again, as poor as before, and when we last see her, she has chanced upon her broken old father-in-law, Tsybukin, who has been driven out of his own home:

Then old Tsybukin came up with the crowd, and silence suddenly fell. Lipa and Praskovya had lagged behind a little.

"Good day, Mr. Tsybukin," said Lipa with a low bow as the old man drew level.

Her mother bowed too. The old man stopped, looked at them both wordlessly, lips shaking, eyes full of tears. Lipa got a piece of buckwheat pasty from her mother's bundle and gave it to him. He took it and started eating.

Now the sun had completely set—even from the top part of the road the fire had faded. It was growing dark and chilly. Lipa and Praskovya went on their way, crossing themselves for a long time afterwards.[15]

Tolstoy in his messianic Christian years wrote stories about such good souls, but none of those characters are fictionally as vivid and credible as Lipa; it is hard for a believing Christian to see a blameless, forgiving woman about whose head the word SAINT shimmers in letters of gold; it says so much about her that even a Tolstoy is likely not to see her herself and what she does. Similarly, the word MASOCHIST says so much about her to the psychologized that it might be hard even for a writer of Chekhov's gifts to see her herself. In fact, Chekhov uses in this story that best of all ways of knowing another: he lets you observe, totally without labels of any kind unless you yourself apply them, what Lipa says and does, and thereby he leaves intact in her that mystery of person which is essential to the life of an imagined character.

I submit that it was good for Chekhov's fiction and drama that he could represent the educated, cultivated people of his world as talking about how bored they were rather than about how guilty they felt. I of course do not know whether actual people in Russia in those days used the word *bored* anything like as much as Chekhov's characters do; however, I do know that in his letters he used *bored, boring, boredom* quite as liberally as his characters do, about himself, a book, the place where he was staying, the people around him, his own work (especially, for some reason, about his best stories and plays), and so far as I know, his contemporaries did not chide him for overusing the word except as part of the frequent criticism that his work was depressing and pessimistic. Corresponding Americans now, the people whom I am somewhat loosely calling *we* — we could not be accurately represented as saying *I am bored* very much because we do not in fact say it; perhaps (who can know?), we really are not as bored as they or have better ways to avoid boredom; for a writer what matters is that we think of ourselves as *feeling guilty* far more than as *being bored*. My hunch is that these expressions overlap a good deal in meaning. Maybe our boredom is less intense or pervasive than theirs — our frustration, tedium, mediocrity, inadequacy, irritability, lethargy, muddle, banality, slobbery. I am no more sure about that than about whether we feel guiltier than they felt. But I am confident that their boredom and our guilt feelings have some common sources but that *boredom* has a vague, amorphous quality which allows the floundering of its sufferers to be obvious to the reader, whereas *guilt feelings* has come to have something of a righteous quality. Those who suffer guilt feelings flounder at least as much as do the bored, but unlike the bored they are able to turn this very floundering into a source of self-congratulation and, what is worse for a writer, into self-obfuscation. A Chekhovian lady watching television soap operas would say, "How boring they are! How bored I am!" "True," says her American counterpart, "but at least I feel guilty for watching them." *Guilt feelings* is only one of many psychological labels which we apply promiscuously and with varying degrees of accuracy — Oedipus complex, penis envy, obsessive, compulsive, schizoid, projection, identification, reality problem, acting out, passive-aggressive, ego structure, sublimation, "I couldn't relate to the alienation of the father-figure"—but *guilt feelings* is the one that causes the most trouble for a writer. It has become the emotional mainspring of a new orthodoxy.

Psychology would bring up into consciousness many things which, for literary, imaginative, creative purposes, are best left obscure, best got at indirectly, and foremost among these things is pervasive guilt. Chekhov seldom talked about his intentions in his work, but in one series of letters about *Ivanov*[16] he explained at some length, very consciously, what he meant; he wrote these letters while in process of revising the play, which had not gone well at first. In his analysis of the character of Ivanov, he says, among other things: "He seeks reasons outside himself and can't find them, so he starts looking inside him, but can only find a vague feeling of guilt. This is a Russian feeling. A Russian always feels guilty when someone in his house dies or falls ill, and when he owes—or is owed—money." Maybe it was Russian in those days, but it has certainly been Americanized since. Later Chekhov says:

> The word "Russian" often crops up when I describe Ivanov. Don't let that annoy you. When writing the play, I kept only the essence of the thing in mind—that is, the typical Russian traits. The over-excitability, the guilt complex, the tendency to fatigue are purely Russian. . . .
>
> Of course I haven't used such terms as "Russian," "excitability," "tendency to fatigue" and so on in the play, trusting my readers and audience to pay attention and not need every i dotted and every t crossed.

Exactly. Chekhov the analyst knows that Ivanov is riddled with guilt, as does Ivanov himself, and Chekhov the artist is advising himself to have Ivanov talk about how bored he is, how depressed, how inadequate. But this is the first, and least, of Chekhov's five principal plays, and it was not for several years, in *The Sea Gull* and *Uncle Vanya*, that he followed his own advice faithfully and suppressed overt talk about guilt in his characters.

Among us, an Uncle Vanya would not talk much about how bored he is, loosely, evocatively, in a way that both reveals and conceals; he would instead talk even more than Ivanov does about how guilty he feels, in a way that reveals too much. For we don't just feel guilty; among us, feeling guilty has been erected into a moral imperative. One of the authorities of psychology, Bruno Bettelheim, recently put the dogma as extremely as it can be put, and his statement appeared in *The New Yorker*, our most influential organ of enlightened opinion. In the issue of August 2, 1976, toward the end of a long attack on Lina Wertmüller's film *Seven Beauties* and also on Terrence Des Pres' book *The Survivor*, Bettelheim, who was himself a survivor, makes this assertion, and nothing in the context modifies it: ". . . only the ability to feel guilty makes us human, particularly if, objectively seen, one is not." Bettelheim does not say, "To be human, you must have a conscience, and your conscience will make you feel guilty when you are in fact guilty and sometimes even when you are not, this feeling being important not for its own sake but in order to prompt you to take action to purge yourself of guilt and possibly to make restitution for damage done." He does not say, more elliptically, "If you cannot feel guilty, you are not fully human." He certainly does not say anything resembling what another survivor says—a Christian, unpsychologized survivor. Solzhenitsyn, no less absolutist than Bettelheim, in the essay "As Breathing and Consciousness Return" is speaking of the Soviet system: ". . . it demands of us total surrender of our souls, continuous and active participation in the general, conscious *lie*. To this putrefaction of the soul, this spiritual enslavement, human beings who wish to be human cannot consent."[17] Bettelheim says none of these things. He says: ". . . only the ability to feel guilty makes us human, particularly if, objectively seen, one is not." Hearing this, Sophocles would have scowled and spat, Lady Murasaki would have lowered her eyes and averted her face, Isaiah would have roared. But Chekhov would only shake his head and smile ruefully, for he would see how easily that statement could be mistranslated into "the guiltier I feel the more human I am."

In play after play and in story after story, he presents characters who are, without saying so, sentimental about feeling guilty; in them we may see one of our own vices portrayed without sociology, psychology, ideology of any sort. That is, as the sentimental always do, they allow an emotion in which they are indulging themselves to dictate the action they take whether that action is, rationally, appropriate or inappropriate; at the extreme, they even allow the emotion to substitute for action and wallow in guilt like a pig in a mud-hole. Bad as things already are in the guilt feelings line, they can get worse.

Here are two more examples of the energy and limpidity with which Chekhov speaks of complex matters, both passages taken from his letters about *Ivanov*: "Disillusionment, apathy, failure of nerve, exhaustion— that's what you must expect if you get over-excited, and such excitability is highly typical of young Russians. Take literature. Take the present day— socialism is a form of excitement." Socialism in those days was automatically thought of as revolutionary, something equivalent, now that there are so many varieties of socialism in the world, to what we mean by the radical activism of the 1960s and early 70s. How plainly and how lightly Chekhov points at the main thing about so many of his, and our, young radicals—"socialism is a form of excitement." But he points not accusingly so much as diagnostically.

In the following passage about Sasha, the girl who is out to catch Ivanov, Chekhov hits off a type superbly, and in the most natural language in the world:

> She's the type of female that males conquer by moaning and groaning and bungling—not by being brave and supple and having bright

plumage. She loves her men when they're going downhill. No sooner has Ivanov thrown up the sponge than up pops this young miss. It's just what she was waiting for—a great crusade, Lord save us! She'll bring him back to life, put him on his feet, make him happy. . . . It's her crusade she loves, not Ivanov. . . . But to Ivanov love's only one more snag, another stab in the back—that's what she doesn't know. What happens? Sasha gets to work on Ivanov for twelve whole months, but he still doesn't come to life—he only goes further downhill.

The least smudge of psychology, and that sketch would lose its sharpness. *Rescue fantasies*, for example, would thicken the lines around the mouth and eyes.

The time has come in this argument for me to bring some of the strands together. What do boredom and guilt feelings have in common, and what does being psychologized, as I am using the term, have to do with them? My key word now becomes *progressive*. Not for a moment do I intend *progressive* as a stereotyping label for Chekhov or his characters; rather, I shall use it shiftily, as he did *boredom*.

The less important aspect of *progressive*, as it applies to Chekhov's world, is its obvious meaning as the adjective of Progress—the enlightened improvement of man's condition through applied science and economic efficiency. Chekhov neither advocated Progress unambiguously as did some of his characters and as many people still do, nor did he repudiate it as did Tolstoy and Dostoevsky and as many are doing today. But faith in Progress is too clear-cut to be of much literary interest.

The other aspect of *progressive*, however, is far more important to Chekhov, being part of the social, moral, cultural realm, what can become the ideology *progressivism*. At the extreme, progressivism teaches the perfectability of society, salvation through politics. That was the original dream of socialism and still is the official Marxist dream. Some of Chekhov's characters believed in it, especially the narrator of "An Anonymous Story," whom Chekhov referred to as a socialist. Seized by the impatience which the dream of socialism generates, the narrator and central character of the story has decided to commit a political assassination. But once he has, as it were, the gun in his hand, what he sees it pointed at is no longer The Enemy but a man. Not being a Dostoevskian terrorist but a Chekhovian one, he can't pull the trigger but instead gets involved in all sorts of complicated ways with the son of his intended victim. A fine study of a man inside an ism.

However, most of Chekhov's characters believe, as he himself did, not that society can be perfected but that it can and should be improved—whether endlessly and generally improved or temporarily and locally is usually left ambiguous. The progressive may sometimes have vague paradisal dreams—"we shall find peace, we shall find peace"—but Chekhov always makes us know the personal torment and confusion those dreams are mixed with. Progressives are suspicious of every authority, even of one they themselves have legitimized, and they are unambivalently opposed to oppression; but nihilism scares them, whether in Russia in the 1860s or in America in the 1960s, and by and large they do not believe freedom and democracy will be entirely for the good. They revere science and high culture and think the masses of mankind ought to too, but such gestures as they make to bring this happy state of affairs about are usually ineffectual. But why go on? To describe Chekhov's progressive world is to describe the one we have been living in for the past generation or so, with a few important differences but many important similarities.

Chekhov's special genius was to reveal how this belief — liberal, enlightened, modern, progressive — complicates emotions and relationships in ways for which *neurotic* is the handiest word. Psychology as it was developing then and as it has developed now, particularly in the version common among us — Freud seriously modified by liberalism — is this belief's consciously systematized way of talking about man and his nature. Nabokov is famously cantankerous about repudiating Freud and all his epigones. Chekhov was still free to look at these modern intricacies of the psyche freshly, immediately, not through or around or despite a system of any sort. The fog of boredom in which so many of his people move, the mist of guilt feelings in which so many of us move, these miasmas emanate from a profound, obscure sense that something is wrong. Wrong, yes, but not just with you or me, though also with you and me; not just with that autocratic society or this democratic one, though also with them; not with this, that, or the other liberal, rational belief. Then with what? Chekhov does not say. Yet he is trapped in a labyrinth of unforgiveness as Kafka is. He is a realist: his first question is always *what is*?, not *what went wrong*? or *what should be*? A lot of his characters do some good in the world, a lot of them know how to laugh and enjoy themselves, a lot of them may not love well but they do love. He does not conceive of his characters as wearing a mask of ideas and ideals which he would strip off to expose the real person beneath; no, their beliefs are somehow part of them, modify their selves even as their selves modify the beliefs, varyingly, mysteriously.

In Chekhov, the way of seeing which later became systematized in psychology is opposed to the Christian way of seeing, and, in Chekhov as in life, one's way of seeing modifies one's way of being. Shakespeare lived in a world which saw humankind in the Christian way, and in all his works there is only one important character, Hamlet, who is commonly called neurotic. Among all Chekhov's important educated characters, only a few are not neurotic and nearly all of these few are Christians. This is by no means to imply that Chekhov means that *Christian* equals *good*; the villainous, evil family in the story "A Murder" are Christians. Neither is it to imply that he means something as large as that Christianity, or religion of some sort, is necessary for the good of civilization and the welfare of its members. But it is to imply that Chekhov saw in his enlightened characters and in himself an emotional scramble which he did not see in some Christians. The bishop in the story of that name (the next to last one Chekhov wrote) approaches his death in serenity; in "A Dreary Story" the professor, who shares most of Chekhov's progressive assumptions, approaches his death bitterly and nastily; but of the two stories the one about the professor is clearly the stronger; it is towards the professor, not the bishop, that Chekhov's creative energies flow most abundantly. In 1894 he wrote a little story, "The Student," about a young man in whom the experience of Easter releases a pure, deep, uncontaminated, unconvoluted joy such as no enlightened, progressive character in all Chekhov ever feels, or presumably ever could feel. Literarily this story ranks quite low in the Chekhov canon, far below the five principal plays, below a good fifty other stories. I have heard of only one literary person who thinks highly of this story, Chekhov himself; attacked for pessimism, he said "The Student" was his favorite among all his works. My guess is that, in addition to his using the story simply to defend himself with, this aberration of taste on his part was an expression of a nostalgia for a high good not available in a progressive world. In progressive eyes, that Christian world was unjust, repressive, superstitious, many bad things, in only one respect better than the enlightened one. But that one respect, Chekhov is saying, is more important than all others: in that world it is possible for a person to be happy. Among us, to ask "you are happy?" is tantamount to an accusation — the stock response is "who, me?" Progressives are much less uneasy, much more energetic, when talking about how bored they are or how guilty they feel. Chekhov was like that too, but he did not think it was a good way to be. He knew this way of feeling was a consequence in large part of a set of beliefs, but he held to these beliefs because he thought them true; like Ibsen, he had no personal use, only a literary one, for a "life-lie." Chekhov would rather not live than live by a lie; I take a certain pleasure in imagining the smile with which he would greet a cant sort of question of our time, "Are you comfortable with your belief-system, Anton Pavlovich?"

Notes

1. *The Oxford Chekhov*, translated and edited by Ronald Hingley (Oxford University Press, 1964–1975). Vol. IX, p. xvi. This is the most scholarly version in English of Chekhov's stories and plays. Hingley sometimes gives the language of Chekhov and of his characters a distractingly British cast, but he does not muffle it in translatese.

2. Vol. V, pp. 134–135.

3. Vol. III, p. 67.

4. Vol. VI, p. 121.

5. P. 121.

6. P. 123.

7. P. 129.

8. P. 135.

9. P. 136.

10. P. 143.

11. "Here Come the Maples," *The New Yorker*, 11 October 1976.

12. *Oxford Chekhov*, Vol. VI, p. 158.

13. P. 159.

14. P. 167.

15. Vol. IX, p. 187.

16. Vol. II, pp. 290–298.

17. *From Under the Rubble* (Little, Brown, 1975), p. 24.

On the Nature of the Comic in Chekhov
Vladimir B. Kataev*

Did Chekhov's interest in the "epistemological" theme, the means and varieties of his characters' orientation in life, extend beyond the self-consciously "serious" pieces such as "Lights," and the somewhat earlier pieces that this writer has called "stories of revelation"? To what extent is the intensification of this interest in the first half of the 1880s natural, in the sense that it reflects the internal tendencies of Chekhov's work?

It can be said that this interest was latently present in his artistic world from the beginning. To a considerable extent it determined what is most characteristic of Chekhov's humor, the main element of his early works, and one which persisted to the very end.

In Chekhov's world the comic generally arises from the simple coincidence, confrontation, superimposition, or juxtaposition of phenomena that belong to different, incompatible categories. What sort of confrontations are they, and what sort of phenomena are involved?

The answer is what we might expect: different conceptions of the world. They include conceptions both individual and collective; expressed in words, gestures, and actions; codified in social hierarchy; reflected in systems of ideas, rules, opinions, judgments, or in the speech patterns that give verbal expression to thoughts and feelings; crystallized in cultural manifestations, including the literary and rhetorical.

The clash of the incompatibly dissimilar strikes a spark of laughter. And in the densely populous and varied world of Chekhov's humor, such clashes are inevitable.

What guides the hero of the humorous works as he attempts to orient himself in the life that surrounds him? Most importantly, its duly consti-

*From chapter 4 of *Proza Chekhova* by Vladimir Kataev (Moscow: Izd. Mosk. un-ta, 1979), 45–56. Translated for this volume by David Woodruff. Reprinted by permission of the publisher.

tuted, generally accepted regulatory mechanisms, in the sense of received forms and conventional signs. They may be grade or rank, ceremony or ritual, received opinion or established order, an assortment of speech mannerisms or a favorite theatrical or gastronomical repertoire, the canons of mass literature or the verdicts of the press. From this multiplicity of ready-made signs systems (in the broad sense), which incorporate society's attempts to regulate living reality, Chekhov's heroes take their behavioral bearings and voluntarily or perforce regulate their lives. Each of Chekhov's hundreds of characters has his own system of available signs (be it correct or incorrect, orderly or incoherent, conscious or unconscious), which gives him membership in a certain social group with parameters of class, generation, profession, etc. And Chekhov has a brilliant feeling for this multiplicity of systems that are imposed on a man by his social position and that he assimilates and revises.

The diversity of the world in Chekhov's early stories is the diversity of various forms of apprehending the world and orienting oneself within it, as Chekhov grasped them and gave them artistic expression. At first this diversity and disharmony struck him as humorous. In time this attitude was to change, but from beginning to end Chekhov's artistic interest was engaged by one and the same range of phenomena.

"To Grandfather in the village" implies a system of orientation in the world. This system encompasses only two geographical concepts: Moscow, and the village where Grandfather Konstantin Makarych lives ("Vanka").

This is self-evident from the point of view of Vanka Zhukov, but absurd from the point of view of postal workers, who classify the world under different sign headings. Replying to an examination question about the tributaries of the Ganges, a floundering postal worker says, "The Ganges, that's a river in India, the river that flows into the ocean," and gets hopelessly muddled. There is nothing about the Ganges in post office regulations. But in answer to a question about Zhitomir he fires back without hesitation: "Tract 18, locality 121!" ("Promotion Examination").

For the dog Kashtanka mankind is divided into masters and customers. But its master has his own universe with its different poles and scale of distances: "You're against mankind the way a carpenter's against a cabinet-maker" ("Kashtanka").

The warm humor of Chekhov's stories about children ("Grisha," "Children," "The Boys," "The Run-away") has the same basis: in children's perception and thought familiar objects and actions are measured and valued on an unexpected scale. The world is seen afresh, and what is habitual and established in the adult world betrays its contingent nature: "Mama looks like a doll, but the cat looks like Papa's fur coat, only the coat doesn't have eyes or a tail . . . Papa is a very puzzling person! Nanny and Mama are understandable: they dress Grisha, feed him and put him to bed, but it's not clear what Papa's for. There's another puzzling person, the aunt who gave Grisha a drum. She appears and disappears. Where does she go? More than once Grisha looked under the bed, behind the chest and under the sofa, but she wasn't there . . ." ("Grisha").

When the adherent of one system of ideas is unable to master another, it is funny. This happens with the clerk Merdyaev, whose superior decides to make him read books and starts him on *The Count of Monte Cristo*. Despite all efforts, Merdyaev, who has lived his life in the orbit of other ideas, is unable to get through what the superior considers light reading. "I've started it four times," he says, "and I don't understand a thing . . . Some sort of foreigners" ("Reading").

The opposite situation, where one character resorts to several systems of ideas and values, is also a rich source of the comic for Chekhov.

Are there devils or not? " 'How shall I put it, my friend?,' the doctor's assistant answered, shrugging one shoulder. 'According to science, of course devils don't exist, because it's superstition. But to talk about it in the ordinary way, as I'm talking to you right now — well, they do . . .' " ("Thieves").

It is the same in "The Chameleon." If a dog is running loose, it and its master are subject to the strictures of the law: "I'll teach you to let dogs loose! It's high time to see about these gentlemen who don't want to obey regulations. When they fine him, the villain, he'll understand the meaning of dogs and such like stray beasts!" But if the dog belongs to a general, this strict guardian of regulation changes color on the spot, adopting a tolerant, extremely lenient system for evaluating what has taken place.

Many works of Chekhov derive their humor from the mixing of different sign systems. This may lead to total harmony, as in the story about the clerks who substitute photographs of civil servants for the suits and ranks of playing cards ("Vint"). Or it may lead to dissonance, like that occasioned by retired rear-admiral Revunov-Karaulov's stream of naval terminology at a lower-middle-class wedding ("Wedding with a General").

It is also funny when someone tries to show his easy mastery of a sign system that he has clearly grasped incompletely or incorrectly. This includes all the situations where Chekhov's characters "want to show their education and talk about things they don't understand." Thus in the speech of Chief Conductor Stychkin ("Happy Ending"), the petit-bourgeois calculation of the practical man combines with pretentious, distorted, at times meaningless turns of bookish speech and an elevated manner of conversation. "I am a man of the educated class, far from penniless, but if you look at me from a point of view, who am I? A landless peasant with no family of his own, like some sort of Catholic priest. And so I should wish exceedingly to join together in Highman's bonds — that is, to enter into lawful matrimony — with some worthy person."

In his humorous stories beginning as early as "Letters to a Learned Neighbor," Chekhov was supremely alert to inappropriate quotations, misplaced learned jargon, incorrectly used foreign words, and illogical logic; he made these absurdities of thought and deed yield comic effects.

The characters of the humorous stories live in a world strictly bound by regulation, where any action must fit in the grid of one sign system or another, be it a table of ranks, a schedule, rules, etc. To the little man, the hero of these works, this order seems the immovable foundation of the world, and if some sign system is abolished, as in the case of orthographic reform or the elimination of ranks, for him it has the force of a personal catastrophe. "If I'm not an ensign any more then just who am I? Nobody? Zero?" ("Abolished"). Or: " 'The philologist Grot argues somewhere,' muttered the teacher, 'that "gate" is neuter, not masculine. Hm . . . That means the Russian word for "red" in "red gate" would have to end in "e," not "a" . . . Well, not so fast! I'll put in for retirement before I'll betray my convictions about "gate" ' " ("To Paris"). And conversely, to attach oneself firmly to a system of reference points in the form of general ideas is like finding happiness or the meaning of life. Olga Plemyanikov ("The Darling") wastes away when she has no one whose ideas she can repeat, and flourishes when she can derive her orientation in the world from the ideas of each of those whom she loves in turn—the impressario, the lumber dealer, the veterinary, and the little schoolboy. It is precisely this motif that connects Chekhov's late masterpiece with his early humorous work.

Characters in the early works often find themselves at a loss when they try to evaluate and make sense of ordinary events:

> "So where shall I enter him? If he's dead, under prayers for the repose, but if he's alive, under prayers for the health. Try and understand my position!"
> "Hm! Put him down in both lists, dearie, and they'll sort it out up there. Not that it matters to him how he's entered, the wretched good-for-nothing."

Deacon Otlukavin's attempt to force life's unanticipated complexity into a sign system that admits only dichotomous distinctions ("prayers for the health" or "prayers for the repose") ends in failure in "Bother." For the moment this is funny, but later the characters in "Neighbors," "Terror," "The Story of an Unknown Man," and "The Three Sisters" will suffer despair in their attempts to understand something in this life, that is, to assign some event or phenomenon to a rational category.

Chekhov derives comic effects with particular frequency from the impossibility of orienting oneself with perfect accuracy in the hierarchical world of different ranks, grades, decorations, and conditions, and from the misunderstandings that proceed from this multifarious social variety and inequality ("Two in One," "Fat Man, Thin Man," "The Medal," "The Mask," "At the Bathhouse," and many others). Ranks and people are the constant theme of Chekhov's humorous stories—a theme that can also be interpreted in the broader and more universal sense of man's orientation in the world that surrounds him.

The frequent clashes in these works of phenomena from different literary and rhetorical genres have been beautifully demonstrated by V. N. Turbin.[1] The attention that Chekhov devoted to the interchangeability of genres, the constant penetration "behind the scenes" of genre, the attempts of Chekhov's characters to assimilate themselves to some genre, be it a serious article or at least a chronicler's entry ("First-class Passenger"), the depiction of an event in two genres (newspaper account and live narration of a recollected event, as in "Joy"), a glaring discrepancy in genres (the entries in "The Complaint Book") — all these are special cases or variants of the clashes and confrontations which are so frequent in the humorous stories. The particular method of investigating the world that Chekhov's work represents cannot be reduced, of course, to the question of genre, but it does include this question.

I have spoken of the juxtaposition in Chekhov's humorous stories of sign systems, that is, of *general* forms of mastering the world and orienting oneself within it. Another source of the comic is the absorption of people in their *individual* interests, modes of behavior, and trains of thought — the absolutization by each character of what is individually his own — and the incongruities and contradictions that proceed from it.

Again there are examples at every turn in the humorous works.

"The Impressario under the Sofa": for the impressario, the main thing is to hide from the jealous man who is after him, while for the actress it is to use the delicacy of the situation to get a raise in salary. Hence their totally different interpretations of what is moral and what is not.

"Lost": the humorous point is not simply that the friends get lost and in the failing light end up at the wrong cottage, but that the host is entirely given over to anticipations of seeing his wife and eating and drinking and talking till midnight, while his guest wants only to sleep.

In exactly the same way a comical crime is committed in "The Drama" only because the hero, a writer, wants desperately to get away, even to the cellar, to escape the heat and the need to make conversation, while his guest insists on reading him her drama.

An animalistic specimen is represented in "The Siren" — the gourmet civil servant, who is capable of talking inspiredly for hours about food, while contrasted to him is the district philosopher Milkin, "dissatisfied with his surroundings and seeking the meaning of life," who listens to the stories about preparing various dishes with a disdainful smile. Chekhov is laughing equally at both characters, whose lives are absorbed in such different pursuits.

At first glance there is an enormous distance between these humorous pieces and "The Duel," "The Black Monk," "Three Years," "My Life," or "Ionych," where people seem to speak different languages, the characters cannot make contact with each other, and each one has his own "definite view on things" in which he is totally engrossed. But this theme of mutual incomprehension absorbed the attention of both "Antosha Chekhonte," the pseudonymous author of the early stories, and the mature Chekhov.

The simple juxtaposition of different sign systems or "views on things" is in itself a rich source of humor in Chekhov's world. Nevertheless it is not the sort of humor that is peculiarly Chekhov's, the humor that proceeds from the clash of the semiotically rigid and formalized with that which has no name in human speech, which "music alone, it seems, is capable of conveying," which though spoken is ineffable. In the article mentioned above, V. N. Turbin has analyzed this phenomenon in relation to literary genres, but all he says there can be applied to the entire range of sign systems that occur in Chekhov's works.

"To Grandfather in the village" is already funny in itself. But the tension between a false, illusory notion and the real human pain and suffering of the half-literate Vanka Zhukov aims at a more complicated response on the reader's part.

> "There are two kinds of lace, Madam, cotton and silk! Oriental, British, Valenciennes, crochet, torchon—these are the cotton. Rococo, soutache, and cambray are silk. For goodness sake, wipe you eyes. They're coming."
>
> And seeing that the tears were still flowing, he continued, louder still:
>
> "Spanish, rococo, soutache, cambray. Fil d'Ecosse stockings, silk, cotton."
>
> ("Polinka")

Through the store clerk's uneducated speech and the stream of incomprehensible and therefore funny names, we glimpse the love story of two people who are humorous but who arouse our sympathy at the same time, Polinka the milliner and Nikolai Timofeich the clerk. A rather specialized sign system—the jargon of the haberdasher and the seamstress—overlies something entirely different that stands behind the external action and the spoken words.

Iona Potapov, who has buried his son ("Misery"), needs more than simply to tell someone of his sorrow. It seems to him that the only way he can properly express his misery and cry himself out is in defined, ritualized forms—that is, forms that are semiotically fixed.

> Soon it will be a week since his son died, and he still hasn't really spoken about it with anyone. He needs to tell it properly, in good order. He needs to say how his son got sick, how he suffered, what he said before his death, and how he died. He needs to describe the funeral and the trip to the hospital to get his son's clothes. He still has a daughter Anisya living in the village. And he should speak of her as well. He certainly has plenty to talk about! The listener should gasp and sigh and lament. The best thing would be to find some women to talk to. They're foolish, but they start howling after two words.

This simple ritual, the fixed sequence of events established by custom, could still be carried out at the unhurried pace of village life. But in the hustle and bustle of the capital, neither the gentlemen passengers nor the yardkeeper nor his fellow cabman listen to Iona. Each is absorbed in his own affairs. As will become usual for Chekhov's heroes, Iona does not understand the true reason for his suffering (" 'And I didn't make enough for oats,' he thinks. 'That's where the misery comes from. A man who knows his business — who's had enough to eat and whose horse has too — will always be content' "). He finally accomplishes the ritual, though it takes a most absurd form: his collaborator in performing it is his horse. If a note of irony sounds here in relation to the hero's mistaken ideas and absurd behavior, it dissolves in the author's lyric emotion.

The bitter humor of "Vanka" and "Misery" will sound again more than ten years later in the story "At Christmastime." A mother's unspoken yearning for her daughter who lives far away is opposed to the idle words of a self-intoxicated clerk who thinks anything in the world can be expressed in the lexicon of military regulations. The tears of Yefimya, for whom one look at the letter from the village is enough to understand everything, without words, are opposed to the solid orderliness of the offices and procedures of Doctor B. O. Moselweiser's hydrotherapy establishment, where her husband works. In both cases the contrast is between anguished, weeping, inarticulate, and unorderly but real life, and the self-satisfied assurance of established signs and those who use and cherish them.

This general foundation, which underlies the funniest as well as the most tragic of Chekhov's stories and the interpretation and treatment, now comic, now sad, of situations that are basically the same, is responsible for the profound internal unity of Chekhov's work throughout his career. Humor never disappears entirely[2] because both the humorous and the "serious" pieces have essentially one theme and are concerned with one range of phenomena.

In the humorous stories of 1884–87 Chekhov found himself as an artist. Ultimately these stories do not aim at simply amusing the reader at any cost, but at giving a comic interpretation to Chekhov's profound and fundamental theme of man's orientation in the world around him and his attempts to understand it and to find truth.[3] Once again: at the basis of Chekhov's humor there lies not merely keen observation, apt detail, rich language, etc., but precisely the over-all governing conception, by which it is essential that the "philosopher" Milkin appear next to the "siren" and Moselweiser next to Yefimya. It is exactly the same in the "serious" pieces where Chekhov's conception is revealed in the juxtaposition of the feverish certainty of the proselytizing Ananyev with the "brain fatigue" of the dubious Sternberg, and many similar oppositions in the later works.

Chekhov's world is populated by a variety of endlessly disagreeing people with varied beliefs (for reasons natural and artificial, objective and subjective). It is not simply the differences among people, but their self-absorption and mutual incomprehension, the lack of reliable, adequate points of orientation. These epistemological problems became fertile ground for Chekhov's humorous masterpieces of the second half of the 1880s.

But in these years Chekhov's deepening commitment to "the province of the serious" became a fact of his artistic development. He might have answered a reader who had grown used to Antosha Chekhonte's mocking mask by citing the words that Doctor Ovchinnikov, the hero of "An Awkward Business," utters (in a different context): "You're smiling! You think it's all just petty details, trifles, but you have to understand that there are so many of these trifles that together they make up the whole of life, as grains of sand can make a mountain."

Deeply absorbed in the "province of the serious," Chekhov did not speak merely of trifles that grow into problems. It is precisely these problems that make up the life of ordinary people, and their life was Chekhov's chief concern as a writer.

Notes

1. V. Turbin, "Toward the Phenomology of Literary and Rhetorical Genres in the Work of Chekhov," in *Problems of Poetics and the History of Literature*, Saransk, 1973, p. 204–16. (V. Turbin, "K fenomenologii literaturnykh i ritoricheskikh zhanrov v tvorchestve Chekhova," in: *Problemy poètiki i istorii literatury*.)

2. On the relation of laughter and "seriousness" in Chekhov see: Z. S. Paperny, "Chekhov," in: *The Short Literary Encyclopedia (Kratkaia literaturnaia entsiklopedia)*, Moscow, 1975, 8, columns 489–90.

3. It may not be inappropriate to point out once more that this article is concerned not with the content and form of Chekhov's humorous works in all their variety, but only with the nature of the comic in Chekhov.

On Specific Stories

Chekhov's "An Attack of Nerves" as "Experimental" Narrative

Phillip A. Duncan*

The naturalist aesthetic of Chekhov's stories of the late 1880s and the early nineties has long been recognized. Much of Chekhov's writing in this period seems to reflect Emile Zola's injunction to the naturalist author: "Return to nature and to man, to direct observation, exact anatomy and the acceptance and the depiction of what is."[1] Chekhov perceived the human animal in its various Russian disguises and he saw life as it was, sometimes madly hilarious, sometimes poetic but very often dismal, monotonous and without hope. And many of the stories are cast in that spare, economical statement that Zola called the protocols of human events. This is, for example, the world of "A Tedious Story" in which illusion has been eroded away and banal people, empty social forms and useless things encumber our vision of life's essential void. If this pessimism does not express the mood of Chekhov himself, it certainly translates the depressing conditions that he found in the society he described. Chekhov's probing of contemporary Russian life has been called "clinical" and his presentation "objective," an analysis, in other words, which reflects the physician–author's assimilation of the natural sciences and scientific method expressed in the now familiar admission: "I do not doubt that my involvement in medical science had a serious influence on my literary activity; it expanded significantly the sphere of my observation and enriched my knowledge. Only one who is himself a doctor can understand its true value for me personally and for my work as a writer. It had a guiding influence on me. . . . Knowledge of the natural sciences and scientific method always kept me alert and I tried where it was possible to conform to scientific fact and where not possible, I preferred not to write at all" (XVIII. 243–44). What was the character of this "serious influence" that the medical sciences had on Chekhov's literary activity? Was it limited to searching out the physiological sources of human conduct? Or did it involve, as Leonid Grossman contends, the conscious or unconscious

*From *Chekhov's Art of Writing, a Collection of Critical Essays*, ed. P. Debreczeny and T. Eekman (Columbus, Ohio: Slavica Publishers, 1977), 112–22. Reprinted by permission of the publisher and the author.

transfer of Claude Bernard's experimental method in medicine to the field of creative writing as Zola had professed to do?[2] Nicholas Moravcevich has recently argued that there is no concrete evidence that Chekhov was acquainted with Bernard's *Introduction to the Study of Experimental Medicine*, although some indirect evidence does exist.[3] While positive proof is lacking, it seems unlikely that a medical student endowed with Chekhov's curiosity would have been unaware of perhaps the most revolutionary and lucid medical treatise of the nineteenth century, one so widely known among Russian intellectuals that when Dmitri Karamazov is interrogated by medical experts he mutters "Bernard" under his breath.[4] It is even more difficult to believe that Chekhov, given his inclination for the natural sciences and his literary interests, did not read Zola's essay on the experimental novel, based on Bernard's work, published in the *Herald of Europe*.[5]

By the mid-seventies, Zola's uncompromising novels had made him a favorite of the Russian reading public.[6] Petr Boborykin, who might be called Zola's herald and principal champion in Russia, wrote that "not a single novelist has been so fortunate as Zola in our newspaper and journal criticism. More than all his contemporaries he has given authority and a governing tendency to literature."[7] As a result of his popularity and, to paraphrase Boborykin, the authoritative governing tendency he had given literature, Zola was retained as a regular collaborator on the *Herald of Europe* beginning in 1875. In September 1879, Zola's essay on the experimental novel appeared in these pages some months before its publication in France. Zola argued that the new novelist would be able to conduct a mental experiment using human beings in a reconstructed, mental environment based on his observation of nature. The purpose was to demonstrate how individuals, possessed of character traits which are the legacy of past generations, responded to the influence of specific social and physical environments or the reverse. The reaction to Zola's concept of the novel as a function of science was almost universally negative and even sarcastic. How could the Frenchman pretend that evaluations made in the head of the novelist and transcribed were the equivalent of experimental processes which occur in the controlled environment of a laboratory? No such exact equivalent is, of course, possible.

Zola's new novel was generally dismissed as a striking but fanciful novelty. By the late eighties, however, it was evident that his idea of the experimental novel had left its stamp on a certain critical perspective which renewed Valerian Maikov's demand for "objective," non-tendentious literature. Mikhail Protopopov called it "scientific objectivism" — a philosophical position and a literary style which characterizes a number of Chekhov's stories in the middle period. Protopopov named Zola its most important contemporary champion.[8]

In the late 1890s Dmitri Ovsianiko-Kulikovsky became convinced that Chekhov's stories were scientific statements of another kind. Many, he argued, were eminent examples of literary laboratory experiments. About the middle of the 1890s, Ovsianiko-Kulikovsky adopted a theory of literature based on Zola's concept of the experimental novel which he elaborated in his article "Observational and Experimental Methods in Art." He divided writers, as did Zola, into objective and subjective artists. Only objective writers he thought worthy of his serious attention. He divided them into writers who were content to remain observer–writers and those who took a further step and became experimenter–writers. The experimenter–writer, as Zola had already defined him, launched his protagonist in a specific milieu (established by the observer component of the author's consciousness) in order to observe the interaction of an individual and his environment.[9] Along with Gogol and Tolstoy, Osvianiko-Kulikovsky considered Chekhov a master of experimental writing in Russia and a late Chekhov story, "Ionych," to be an exceptional example of experimental writing in which a pernicious environment gives definition to a relatively unformed personality.[10]

For Ovsianiko-Kulikovsky, the focus of experimental writing was quite small. The observer–writer might represent life richly, but the experimenter–writer was highly selective, concentrating on only one or a few traits of character in order to give, as Ovsianiko-Kulikovsky said, a one-sided illumination of human conduct. Ovsianiko-Kulikovsky examines this aspect of experimental writing in his analysis of Chekhov's "A Tedious Story," the longest of the stories collected under the title Gloomy People. The critic notes that we seem to see in this narrative what he calls a rich, many-sided presentation of the life and character of Nikolai Stepanovich. Thus the work appears to be of the observational type, but on closer examination, it is apparent that "A Tedious Story" belongs to the category of experimental writing. Ovsianiko-Kulikovsky can discover in the hero in the final analysis only two basic mental traits: (1) An exceptional capacity for scientific analysis associated with a vague belief in humanity and its potential for progress; and (2) a profoundly gloomy, misanthropic view of contemporary life which results in deep sorrow and almost complete solitude. The consequence is the loss of illusion, alienation, and khmurost'. Ovsianiko-Kulikovsky believes that what Chekhov has done in Gloomy People is to select only one of all possible temperamental phenomena and examine its expression in a cross-section of society "like a chemist," as he puts it. Chekhov is not studying social or personality types — the professor, the postman, etc., but a psychological state, "gloominess," which in the mind of the professor appears in one form and in the postman in another. In the "artistic laboratory of the poet," concludes Ovsianiko-Kulikovsky, Chekhov studies "gloominess" in various temperamental environments.[11]

Less than twenty years later, writing on Chekhov's Naturalism, Leonid Grossman accepted Chekhov as an experimental writer without reservation: "Systematically, with a surgeon's lancet," he said, "Chekhov made deep incisions into puffy human material in his experimental laboratory. . . . With the patience of a scientific investigator, Chekhov pursued his experiments into the exact observation of reality."[12] Further: "His insistence on the scientific method in literature, the systematic incorporation of physiology in the novel, the entire complex of exact methods of observation, the detailed investigation of human life, the rich gathering of minute facts — this renowned experimental method was so very appropriate to Chekhov's creative nature."[13] It goes without saying that Grossman credits the influence of Zola's theory of the novel.

A recent student of Chekhov, Alexander Roskin, notes the authority of Bernard's treatise on experimental medicine among the teaching faculty at the time Chekhov was studying medicine. Roskin argues that "echoes of the argument of the *Introduction* are heard in many of Chekhov's judgments concerning art,"[14] and adds: "the theoretical views of young Chekhov concerning literature were close to and often fully coincided with the positivist opinions of Claude Bernard and Zola."[15]

Thus, there has been a relatively persistent tendency to associate Zola's "experimental" structure with the fabric of certain of Chekhov's short narratives. Chekhov himself has neither confirmed nor denied a debt to the experimental novel. While it would be temerous to argue a conscious adoption of Zola's proposed novelistic formula for some of the stories, it is conceivable that Zola's statement reinforced and helped define a natural inclination in Chekhov's composition. To be sure, there is no question here of a scientific experiment such as might be conducted in a research laboratory. At one point in his manifesto, Zola himself recognized the experimental novel as impossible to compose in his time.[16] The writer's scientific equipment was still too inadequate. The new novel would remain an ideal to which later authors might aspire. In the meantime, Zola's "records of laboratory experiments" remained a literary rather than a scientific form. The author, with what he could command of the natural sciences (especially physiology) and the social sciences, was limited to a social, psychological and physiological study animated by positivist determinism. The author's judgment substituted still for the independent and arbitrary consequences of laboratory reactions. The "record" of the author's judgment *imitated* a scientific experiment and thus, seemed to be the record of an experiment on human subjects.

What is the experimental novel such as Zola's contemporaries sought to construct it? It is designed to give the impression of a provoked observation, one which attempts to search out those forces which shape things, people and events. In formulating the experimental novel, the author first identifies a specific social and physical environment which serves as a reagent in the experiment. Then a new element is introduced into this fixed environment: an unformed personality or one that may be well developed but is, as yet, a mystery to the reader. The inbred character traits of this subject and his physiological structure are incorporated as the second active agent in the experimental process. The interaction of the

unknown or undefined personality and a stable exterior situation constitutes the experiment. Normally, environmental circumstances prevail. The
subject, frequently betrayed by a hereditary or some other endemic
weakness, falls victim to the environment. Alain Pagès, in a recent article,
says that this environment forecasts the future of the hero—a destiny
without hope, immobile.[17] The world of the experimental novel is in fact
circular, one which purges itself of the intruder or which claims him for its
cast of stereotypes.[18] There are variants, of course, and even some
exceptional cases where the will of the hero prevails.

The experiment, that is the story line, is essentially simple, reiterating
the same conflict and thus the short story genre is well suited to
experimental writing. Repetition is usually a feature. Logically, more than
one shock is necessary to bring the psychological and (possibly) the
physiological process to a definitive term. The whole must, of course,
project a certain scientific aura. Ideally, the psychological processes will
be bound to a physiological condition so as to bring the former more surely
within the reach of the novelist–natural scientist. While the author chooses
the environment and his protagonist, he insists on the fiction that the
experiment is not chosen but issues from conflicting forces inherent in the
milieu. The experiment, says Zola, is latent in the social context and not
imagined by the author and the denouement of the process is preordained
and inevitable but imperceptible to the reader at the outset.

Several of the stories of *Gloomy People* follow this outline to some
degree, but one of the best examples is "An Attack of Nerves." The first two
paragraphs serve as an exposition for the story. An intruder, Vasilev, is
introduced. Clearly, he tries to avoid the ugliness of the world. He has
never been to S. Street and its houses of prostitution and is very reluctant
to go now with his friends. He appears to be an idealist (and this idealism
is confirmed later) for he complains that these women know nothing of
"pure" love. In the first paragraphs, too, Chekhov sketches briefly the
social environment that will oppose Vasilev's naive, idealistic preconcep-
tions. Vasilev sees these unfortunate women as victims of fatal circumstances "who all acknowledge their sin and who hope for salvation" (VII.
173) and he is determined to understand them and to save them. So, the
"experiment" begins. Vasilev is off to S. Street to confront life as it really is,
to crusade against it and be defeated by it. As Vasilev proceeds, he is struck
by what he calls the "equilibrium" of his friends, their apparent normality
and the ease with which they deal with problems. They live instinctively
and act out of self-interest. He, on the other hand, is an idealist who insists
on imposing an ethical system on human conduct, and his insistence on
ethical purity generates the crisis which Chekhov describes in his story—a
crisis which is intensified by the fact that Vasilev is conceived as excessively
sensitive. "He possessed an extraordinarily fine, delicate scent for pain in
general," reports the author (VII. 190). By the time this fragile hero has

left the eighth house, his heart is pounding slowly, but violently and the nervous crisis is building. By the time he leaves the ninth, he realizes that he is in an "alien, incomprehensible world" (VII. 185). He is seized with fear and the attack of nerves begins: "It was a dull, vague, indefinite pain akin to anguish, to an extreme form of terror and to despair" (VII. 191). After about thirty-six hours, Vasilev's condition worsens and he is taken to the psychiatrist by his two companions. There, in a scene confirming his circular destiny, he hears the same questions he has heard previously, because he has had such attacks before, and is given a prescription for the same remedies which he has taken in the past.

"An Attack of Nerves" has all the typical features of an experimental story.[19] The stranger is matched against an inflexible environment and meets with defeat and despair after repeated attempts to influence it — a contest which permits the reader to follow the consequently deteriorating nervous state of the hero. A psychological weakness, Vasilev's extreme sensitivity and predisposition to nervous tension and mental imbalance, is a major factor in his failure to dominate the environment or, at least, to come to terms with it comfortably as do his comrades. Vasilev's experience in the story is a fragment of a circular pattern. We can predict that his future, like his past, will involve a series of disenchantments and frustrations that precipitate a series of mental crises. He will never bring reality to correspond to the perfection which he imagines. The process does seem inevitable, given the nature of the social environment and of the protagonist. The action appears to stem more from the inescapable conflict of two antipathetic forces than from the imagination of the author. The repetition often associated with experimental writing is present as well. The repeated entries into the houses, all really identical, provide the sequence of shocks which breaks down Vasilev's mental stamina and illuminates Vasilev's redemptive mission against the backdrop of the women's indifference and complacency. Also, the role of science is emphatic. Vasilev's physiological and mental conditions are linked. A number of pages are devoted to Vasilev's medical and psychiatric examination and the doctor eventually attempts a chemical cure for Vasilev's neurosis. And, finally, the story seems to be conceived as a demonstration of the influence on human conduct of certain social and natural forces.

It is difficult to see in this narrative (and certain others of this period) the gratuitousness which Aleksandr Chudakov attributes to events in Chekhov's stories generally beginning with this period. The motivation of the two friends, on the one hand, and of Vasilev, on the other, for visiting the houses of prostitution is never in doubt. Vasilev's psychological and philosophical conformation is rapidly, but clearly defined. The girls and the mores of S. Street are predictable, consistent and quite sufficiently elucidated. In the confrontation of Vasilev and S. Street it soon becomes clear that the environment is impervious to the ministry of Vasilev. Given his nature, he will be inevitably and profoundly affected. The only "accidental" element in the story is the degree to which he is affected. The consequences could have been more serious or less serious. In any event, some sort of nervous crisis is well-prepared and the reader accepts as altogether natural Vasilev's response to his experience.

Where Chekhov offers anecdotal or psychological facts without adequate preparation (as Chudakov argues), does this mean that such facts are accidents and of inexplicable origin or that Chekhov's optic does not permit insight into the veiled and ineluctable patterns in which the individual protagonist becomes entangled? One could even argue that, having presented the "experiment" (the imitation of an experiment) with as much understanding as the experimenter might be expected to possess, Chekhov leaves the reader to decipher stages of the experimental process that could not be predicted. The process may indeed be inevitable but were it entirely foreseeable there would have been no justification for the experiment. It must be remembered, in other words, that "experimental" prose fiction is the *record* of an experiment, not an analysis. Alain Pagès has summed up the aesthetic of experimental fiction in the following statement: "It is oriented . . . toward the impartial account . . . it reveals, but it does not comment; it exposes, but it does not explain."[20]

A number of the stories of *Gloomy People* follow the pattern of "An Attack of Nerves" but with varying degrees of "experimental" orthodoxy: "Volodia," "Sleepy" and, in important respects, "A Misfortune" and "A Tedious Story." The fact that these stories incorporate other features such as impressionistic description and the romantic grotesque does not comprise their character as "experimental" stories any more than it does in the case of Zola's novels. All of the stories of *Gloomy People* share one characteristic index: they are, as Ovsianiko-Kulikovsky said, studies of *khmurost'*. Indeed, these ten stories are "chapters" in a projected but unwritten novel which was to examine the paths to suicide in Russia.[21] In each, Chekhov records the encounter or encounters which create and intensify mental anguish and frustration, often discharged in a violent catharsis near the end of the story. It is a process which corresponds roughly to what Zola called in the experimental novel the revelation of the mechanism of human thought and passion.

There are marked similarities in the prose writings of Zola and of Chekhov at the end of the eighties, even the susceptibility of both authors to the impressionist and symbolist temptations. A critical issue for each, however, is verity. "Literature is called artistic when it depicts life as it actually is," Chekhov argued in one of his letters; "its aim is absolute and honest truth" (XIII. 262). He was perhaps less willing than Zola, in the final analysis, to appeal to the methods of science in seeking truth. He said once that "the hot-head of today . . . wants to discover physical laws for the creative impulse, to seize upon a general law and the formulae by which the artist, who feels them instinctively, creates a piece of music, landscapes, novels, etc." (XIV. 216). But he went on to affirm the existence of natural laws which govern not only the environment but even artistic creation:

> These formulae probably exist in nature. We know that there is a, b, c, do, re, mi, fa, and sol in nature. There is the curve, the straight line, the circle, the square, green, red and blue. . . . We know that these factors in some particular combination produce a melody or verse or a picture, just as simple chemical bodies in some particular combination produce wood, or stone, or the sea; but the only thing we know is that there is a combination and that the structure of this combination is unknown to us. Anyone who has assimilated the scientific method is deeply aware that there is something in common between the piece of music and the tree, that both are created as a result of equally true and simple laws.
>
> (XIV. 216)

The preceding assessment came in 1888, the year he composed "An Attack of Nerves." While he did not believe that such laws were knowable at that time, like Zola he acknowledged their existence and clearly expresses physiological and environmental determinism in Vasilev's collision with the society of S. Street. As a result, the "general law and formulae" which govern the world of "An Attack of Nerves" bear a strong resemblance to the general law and formulae of Zola's experimental novel.

Notes

1. Emile Zola, "Le Roman expérimental," *Oeuvres complètes* (Paris: Cercle du livre précieux, 1968), X, 1235.

2. Leonid Grossman, "Naturalizm Chekhova," *Vestnik Evropy*, 49:7 (July 1914), 218–47.

3. Nicholas Moravcevich, "Chekhov and Naturalism: From Affinity to Divergence," *Comparative Drama*, 4:4 (Winter 1970–71), 221.

4. Fedor M. Dostoevsky, *Sobranie Sochinenii*, 10 vols. (Moscow: GIKhL, 1958), X, 208. Thomas Winner states unequivocally: "Chekhov was intimately acquainted with Zola's *Le Roman expérimental*, as well as with Claude Bernard's *Introduction à la médicine générale* [sic]. . . ." *Chekhov and His Prose* (New York: Holt, Rinehart and Winston, 1966), 90.

5. "Eksperimental'ny roman," *Vestnik Evropy*, 14:9 (Sept., 1879), 406–38.

6. See my article "Echoes of Zola's Experimental Novel in Russia," *Slavic and East European Journal*, 18:1 (Spring 1974), 11–19, especially footnote 2, for additional bibliography.

7. Petr D. Boborykin, Preface to Paul Alexis, "Emil' Zolia (Biograficheski ocherk)," *Nabliudatel'*, Nov. 11, 1882, p. 153.

8. "Ob'ektivny metod v literaturnoi kritike," *Russkaia Mysl'*, 12:10 (Oct. 1891), 125–45.

9. *Sobranie sochinenii*, 9 vols. (St. Petersburg: "Obshchestvennaia pol'za," 1911), VI, 71–75.

10. "Etiudy o tvorchestve A. P. Chekhova," *Sobranie sochinenii*, V, 124–37.

11. "Etiudy," pp. 120–24.

12. Grossman, "Naturalizm Chekhova," p. 218.

13. "Naturalizm Chekhova," p. 229.

14. *A. P. Chekhov* (Moscow: GIKhL, 1959), p. 197.

15. *Chekhov*, p. 206.

16. Zola, *Oeuvres*, II, 1182.

17. "En partant de la théorie du roman expérimental," *Les Cahiers naturalistes*, 20:47 (1974), 82.

18. This proposes an alternate interpretation of the "endless" structure which Alexander Chudakov argues is typical of Chekhov's stories. *Poetika Chekhova* (Moscow: "Nauka" 1971), 224–27.

19. For further analyses of characteristic experimental fiction see Lyle Powers, "Henry James and Zola's *Roman expérimental*," *University of Toronto Quarterly*, 30 (October 1960), 16–30 and J. H. Matthews, "Zola's *Le Rêve* as an Experimental Novel," *Modern Language Review*, 52 (April 1957), 187–194.

20. "En Partant," pp. 77–78.

21. Roskin, *Chekhov*, p. 209.

Vestiges of Romantic Gardens and Folklore Devils in Chekhov's "Verochka," "The Kiss," and "The Black Monk"

Joseph L. Conrad[*]

Anton Chekhov's short stories are not usually considered in terms of literary romanticism, yet many aspects associated with traditional romantic fiction can be found in his prose. In the three stories under consideration Chekhov did not merely adopt the conventions of romanticism: he began by including certain typical features, and then used them to produce situations that are more realistic, and certainly more in keeping with his own time, than those found in tales of the 1830s. A brief review of the essential characteristics of traditional romantic prose may be helpful before proceeding to discussion of those elements as found in "Verochka," "The Kiss," and "The Black Monk."

Romantic tales focus the reader's interest on an unusual event and its impact on the hero's psychology. That event occurs at a time in the hero's life when he finds himself in conflict with his environment. In the exemplary *Novellen* of the German romantic movement, the natural world is marked by a certain duality: temporal and spatial, organized and chaotic, spiritual and physical. It is a place where the egocentric protagonist searches for an unattainable ideal (cf. landscapes in the major works of Ludwig Tieck, Friedrich Novalis, E. T. A. Hoffmann, and Joseph von

*This essay was written specifically for this volume and is published here for the first time by permission of the author.

Eichendorff). But the vision of that ideal (e.g., Novalis's "blaue Blume," truth, eternal beauty, and/or ultimate perception of one's "true self"), is to be fleeting at best. The hero's search for an alternative to stifling routine brings him to reflection that results in understanding of his situation, however short-lived that understanding may be. Other important aspects of traditional romanticism include an interest in history (primarily the medieval period), distant lands, supernatural phenomena (especially the devil), and an integral role played by music.

Central to most romantic works is an unusual landscape that is often represented by a garden filled with exotic flora. Its description emphasizes the hero's sensory perceptions. Nature's components such as trees and bushes, birds and animals, the moon and stars, and even murky mists are described by verbs and adverbs normally restricted to human actions. In this way natural phenomena and supernatural or demonic forces are personified, thus making the unusual event seem more personal, for both the protagonist and the reader.[1]

In Chekhov's early stories there are few gardens as such, and it is not until "Verochka" (February 1887) that we find a description approaching that of a romantic landscape.[2] Told by an omniscient narrator, the story unfolds as the protagonist's reminiscence of an unexpected event that he experienced some years before. As Ivan Alekseich Ognev was preparing to return to the city after a summer spent on the estate of his friend Kuznetsov, an interesting comparison occurred to him, namely, that "people and their faces and words flicker in life and are drowned in our past, leaving nothing more than insignificant traces in our memory."[3] This passage would seem to be misleading, for the experience that Ognev had was indeed central to his understanding of his character. Seen in retrospect, however, it confirms Ognev's comparison, as will be demonstrated below.

The description of the garden outside Kuznetsov's house is a crucial element that establishes both the mood and the personalities of Ognev and Verochka, Kuznetsov's daughter. It includes the evening quiet and warmth, the smell of mignonette, tobacco, and heliotrope,[4] and a thin tender fog (*tuman*) suffused with moonlight. Bits of fog move "like apparitions" along the tree-lined paths: "The moon stood high above the garden, and below it transparent patches of fog were moving off somewhere to the east. It seemed the whole world consisted only of these black silhouettes and meandering white shadows . . ." (71). Consisting almost entirely of clichés inherited from romanticism (exotic flowers, personified fog and moonlight), this rather dreamlike landscape concentrates on Ognev's sensory perceptions: the heat, the silence, the fragrant aroma of the unusual blossoms, and the vision of the slow-moving fog.

Bathed in moonlight, the scene becomes a curious chiaroscuro that establishes a mood for the introduction of Verochka. But it also clearly reflects Ognev's personality, for the unromantic, and quite ordinary,

Ognev can think only of "artificial decoration, where clumsy pyrotechnicians, in an attempt to illuminate the garden with white Bengal light, let white smoke into the air along with the light." This view is typical of his character: Ognev is a statistician concerned with impersonal data. It comes as no surprise to the reader that he has not noticed that Verochka has fallen in love with him over the course of the summer.

A second descriptive passage suggests the gentle nature of Verochka: "As if covered by a veil, all nature was hiding behind a transparent dull haze, through which its beauty shone forth happily. The fog, somewhat thicker and whiter, was unevenly settling down around the tree stumps and bushes or meandering across the path in patches, pressed close to the ground, as if trying not to block the expanse . . ." (73). Like the meandering fog, Verochka timidly steps into view, for she intends to accompany Ognev to the station. Thus the scene has been set for what the reader thinks will be a romantic encounter.

But that meeting is to be quite different from the reader's expectation: Verochka's passionate declaration of love does not have its desired effect; instead, it causes Ognev to react in panic and serves as a catalyst for his process of self-examination. The narrator tells us that in Ognev's soul "something bad and strange (*chto-to nekhoroshoe i strannoe*) was taking place," and that he quickly understood that he was "seeing and hearing something which, from the point of view of nature and personal happiness, was more serious than all his statistics, books, and truths (*istiny*)" (78). Coming as a revelation, this experience unleashes in him an inexplicable (and unexplained) sensation of guilt. His frustrated exclamation: "Lord, there's so much life, poetry, meaning in all this, even a stone would be touched, but I . . . I am stupid and awkward!" (80) does not, however, signal a lasting change in his perception of his true nature; it is only a momentary insight, and one that he soon represses.

The garden, whose description was used so successfully to set the scene and mood for Verochka's entrance, recedes from view during her declaration of love. But nature has yet another important role to play. When, angry at his own weakness, Ognev returns to have one more look at her house from the garden, the thick smell (*gustoi zapakh*) of the mignonette and heliotrope are still present, but the fog has disappeared. We read: "The bright moon was watching from the heavens, as if cleansed, and only the eastern sky was becoming clouded over and frowning" (*vostok tumanilsia i khmurilsia*; 81). Thus nature judges his failed response to an unparalleled opportunity for happiness. Unable to reshape his destiny, Ognev returns to his lodging in resigned acceptance of the fact that he is unfit for love as a fundamental human experience.[5]

In this story Chekhov has introduced a natural world with the garden as its center, which — through its sensual description, semi-exotic flora, and personifying allusions — recalls those of romantic literature. Having set the scene for a declaration of love, he focuses the reader's attention not only on Ognev's recognition of his impotence in the face of the emotional demands of human interaction, but on his suppression of that insight as well. Recalling Ognev's earlier philosophical comment that people, their faces, and their words "leave only insignificant traces in [one's] memory," the reader sees that the Kuznetsovs, father and daughter, are indeed such traces from Ognev's past.[6] But the fact that the story is told (largely from Ognev's point of view) as a reminiscence indicates that his attempt to ignore that important insight into his human fallibility has not been successful: he is still haunted, several years afterward, by a sense of guilt over his inability to respond to Vera's declaration of love.

A second stage in Chekhov's use of the romantic heritage can be illustrated by "The Kiss" ("Potselui"; December 1887), where the contrast between the real and the ideal is central. In this story there is regular interaction between the routine details of military life and the hero's fanciful imagination, which is stimulated by sensory perceptions associated with the garden. As we will see, the garden itself is brought inside, both inside the drawing room and inside the mind of the protagonist, Staff-Captain Riabovich.

The opening lines establish a properly realistic background; they read like a military report indicating the precise date (20 May) and time of evening (8:00 P.M.) when Riabovich's artillery brigade arrives at its bivouac. Yet no sooner has this specific information been given than the scene undergoes a transformation: "A rider in civilian dress, on a strange horse (*strannaia loshad'*) appeared from behind a church . . . the horse approached not directly but sideways, as it were, making little dancing movements as if it were being lashed on the legs."[7] The horseman delivers a formal invitation to tea from retired general von Rabbek, and in a moment the rider and his strange horse disappear behind the church. "The devil knows what that means!" some of the officers exclaim. Though the officers may not be aware of the danger of invoking the devil by name, readers familiar with romantic literature may be certain that something extraordinary is about to take place.

The scene itself, with its unexpected arrival of the strange horseman, suggests an apparition such as are found in romantic tales from the 1830s. In every way it challenges the regulated nature of military life: the rider is in civilian dress, his strange horse seems undisciplined, and they both appear and disappear "from behind the church." The role of the church is at first puzzling; it is mentioned six times at the beginning, once in the middle, and four times at the end of the story. In a sense, it functions as a frame. And if we think of the dual nature of the church as a place of religious awe and simultaneously dark and mysterious, we may surmise that Chekhov intended it to occupy a place more significant than that of a mere landmark. The rider appears from behind the church, just as pagan forces lurk behind the fervor associated with charismatic believers. Thus the church may be either an ambiguous shield or a source of the mysterious rider.[8]

In a similar way, the landscape is initially undistinguished but soon becomes suggestive of danger. The officers are told that they can reach von Rabbek's estate by one of two paths: "a lower one, going down behind the church to the river and then along the bank to the garden itself . . . or the upper one—straight from the church along the road which . . . leads to the master's barns" (407). That the landscape seems to betray a kind of dual personality is suggested by its description: "At the first barn the road divided in two: one branch went straight ahead and disappeared in the evening mist, the other went to the right, to the master's house. . . . Stone barns with red roofs, heavy and sullen-looking, very like barracks in a district town, stretched along both sides of the road" (407).

At the general's house, even the mild, unassuming Riabovich notices that appearances are more important than reality (cf. the romantic concern with *Schein* vs. *Sein*). To be sure, the general and his wife follow the formal conventions of gracious hosts. But when she engages the guests in polite conversation, her "beautiful majestic smile" vanishes instantly from her face each time she turns away from them.[9] Moreover, there is an air of something foreign about each: von Rabbek bears a strange, un-Russian surname and his wife is likened to "Empress Eugénie." Further distortions of the ordinary occur: a group of men in the dining room are "wrapped in a haze of cigar smoke," and "some sort of thin young man with red whiskers" (red hair and whiskers are associated with the devil in traditional European folklore) is talking loudly in English, but with a continental accent (*kartavja*).

Riabovich, who considers himself to be "the shyest, most modest, and most colorless (*bestsvetny*) officer in the whole brigade!" begins to observe the others. The result is anything but positive: the drawingroom, the unfamiliar faces, the crystal decanters of brandy, and the steam from the glasses "become fused into one huge impression planting anxiety (*trevoga*) in Riabovich and a desire to hide his head." (Though he does not realize it, this attack of anxiety is a warning of what is to come.) Recovering his mental equilibrium, he singles out a young lady in a lilac dress, only to note an insincere smile that appears and disappears on her face as she ardently discusses something alien (*chuzhdo*) to her. The narrator tells us that "the more Riabovich looked and listened, the more he liked this insincere, but excellently disciplined family" (410). The lack of sincerity seems to capture his fancy and makes him susceptible to the exciting emotional experience he is about to have.[10]

That experience is prepared by unusual sensory perceptions linking the world outside to that within the drawing room: piano music, a melancholy waltz, flows from the room out the open windows, and the smell of young poplar leaves, roses, and lilacs floats inside. Transplanted into the drawingroom, the aromas of the garden become linked in

Riabovich's perception with the women: the various scents seem to come "not from the garden, but from the women's faces and their gowns." References to the lilac blossoms and the "young lady in lilac" (*baryshnia v sirenevom*) recur often (twelve times) as a leitmotiv maintaining the connection between nature, the lilacs in the garden, their intoxicating scent intruding into the rooms, and the sexual stimulation provided by the unknown woman's perfume.

Sensuous nature reappears just before Riabovich is to experience the kiss that initiates his idyllic summer dreams and eventual despair. As he wanders through a darkened room he notices that the smells of poplar, lilac, and roses are coming through the open windows there as well. At this moment he hears hasty steps and the rustle of a dress; a woman's heavy-breathing voice whispers "Finally!" and he feels "two soft, perfumed . . . feminine arms" embrace him. A warm cheek touches his and a kiss resounds. This description emphasizes Riabovich's sensory perceptions; three of five senses are represented: aural, olfactory, and tactile; a fourth, visual perception is partly present (he sees light from the next room through a crack in the door). The final phrase (*razdalsia zvuk potseluia*) seems an almost bizarre expression for the culmination of a passionate embrace. And its effect is equally strange and magical for it leaves a fifth sensation, that of taste, as a light, mint-flavored, and pleasant chill on his cheek, which signals the beginning of the struggle between fantasy and reality within his mind and soul.[11]

That Riabovich does not yet understand the event's significance is revealed by his mistaken thought: "This adventure (*prikliuchenie*) bore a mysterious and romantic (*romanicheski*) character, but it was not difficult to explain" (412). Yet despite careful scrutiny of each female present, Riabovich cannot identify the mystery woman; rather he creates a composite figure and then begins his idealized, imaginary life with her. Thus, as in the romantic tradition, Riabovich's situation is transformed from the ordinary to the extraordinary; his is an experience that changes his life permanently.

The landscape description as the officers leave the party seems ominous:

> . . . They went along the path which descended to the river and then ran along the edge of the water, bending around the shoreline bushes, pools, and the willows hanging above the water. The riverbank and path were barely visible, and the opposite bank was completely drowned in darkness. Here and there on the dark water were reflections of stars; they trembled and became scattered — and this was the only way that one could guess that the water ran swiftly. It was quiet. On the other bank sleepy sandpipers were moaning (*stonali*) but on this side, in one of the bushes, . . . a nightingale began to pour forth its call loudly. The officers stood next to the bush, touched it, but the nightingale kept on singing. (414)

The threatening dark, the rushing water, the pitiful sound of the birds on the other side of the river, accompanied by the nightingale's insistent call (a warning sign in Slavic and European folklore), should give Riabovich reason for concern. He does not take notice of them, however; and the remainder of the story pulses between his romantic imagination and military routine.[12]

The leitmotiv "strange," found first in the unusual invitation and the undisciplined horse, figures prominently in Riabovich's imagination as he longs for a repeat invitation. It returns to close the episode. When the unit passes by the von Rabbek estate once again, the river and its banks are the same as before, but there is no aroma of the trees and bushes; even the warning call of the nightingale is missing. The garden's former magic has evaporated, and Riabovich now thinks that it would indeed be strange if he were to meet his unknown woman again. As he approaches the river and watches the rivulets extend the moon's reflection and break it into pieces, his mood of resignation turns to one of despair. Watching the river's constant flow, he now recognizes the contrast between cyclical nature and individual human existence, which is destined never to be repeated. Summarizing his romantic experience and life itself, he exclaims: "How stupid. How stupid." This judgment demonstrates that his existential dilemma is significantly more profound than that of Verochka's Ognev, for Riabovich now perceives his life as "unusually barren, miserable, and colorless . . ." (423). Here the reader may remember his self-characterization as "colorless" (bestsvetny), a description that has a secondary suggestion of "flowerless." Riabovich has been unable to find his ideal, the unknown woman with whom he has spent the summer in imaginary wedded bliss. Was she perhaps the young lady in the lilac dress? If so, then he is indeed without his crowning flower.[13]

If "Verochka" and "The Kiss" may be considered as Chekhov's early approaches to the romantic literary heritage, it is "The Black Monk" ("Cherny monakh"; January 1894) that is his most romantic tale.[14] In this story the garden consists entirely of exotic flowers and bizarrely shaped trees; it is a garden and orchard complex that is not the background, but the springboard for the enigmatic apparition of the medieval monk in black.

Andrei Vasilyich Kovrin, who suffers from nervous fatigue, is spending the summer on the estate of his guardian, Egor Pesotski. To the attentive reader, the description of the estate and grounds is a psychological minefield: Pesotski's huge, imposing house has tall columns in front and plaster lions, regal symbols of strength, but whose facade is peeling off. There is an old park, described as "sullen and stern-looking," laid out in the preromantic English fashion; its regular lines suggest a conformity alien to the Slavic soul. Stretching for over a kilometer to the river it seems to be infinite. But it ends there in a steep, clifflike clay bank that has pines with "bare roots like hairy paws" (*s obnazhivshimisia korniami, pokhozhimi na mokhnatye lapy*) growing out of it. The water glistens "inhospitably" (*neliudimo*) below; sandpipers fly overhead with a pitiful cry. Kovrin's reaction to all this is "you could almost sit down and compose a ballad."[15] Surrounding the house there is a garden with an unusual collection of flora. We are told that Kovrin "had never seen such amazing roses, lilies, camelias, such tulips of all possible colors from bright white to black as soot, as were found at Pesotski's . . ." (227).

There are two strongly opposite aspects to this landscape. Dominated by the overbearing house with its decaying imitation lions, limited by the hostile river, its threatening cliff and hairy-pawed pines, and the mournful cry of the sandpipers in the distance, the extended park certainly seems forbidding. By contrast, the immediate grounds and the orchard produce a joyous feeling in Kovrin. The brilliant white and soot-black flowers themselves suggest a certain duality. Thus Chekhov has produced a natural vista with its own split personality as preparation for the egocentric Kovrin to see the apparition of his alter ego, the Black Monk.

But this portion of the grounds is in fact overshadowed by the exotic orchard that is the centerpiece of the estate:

> The decorative part of the garden, . . . produced a fabulous (*skazochny*) impression on Kovrin sometime ago in his childhood. What strange creations (*prichudy*) there were here, refined deformations (*urodstva*), mockeries (*izdevatel'stva*) of nature! Hedges made of fruit trees, pear trees with the shape of the pyramid-like poplar, globe-shaped oaks and linden, parasols of appletrees, archways, monograms, candelabras and even the year 1862 formed of plum trees . . . There were also beautiful, well-shaped saplings with trunks straight and strong like palm trees, and only if you looked at them directly could you recognize that they were gooseberry or currant bushes. But what more than anything else produced a happy mood and vital look, was the constant movement. From early morning to evening people with wheelbarrows, hoes and waterbuckets swarmed around the trees, bushes, walkways and flowerbeds like ants. . . . (227)

The exotic shapes (cones, globes, pyramids, etc.) suggesting early eighteenth-century English gardens, and the fluidity of movement found in this landscape serve to activate Kovrin's imagination and, in connection with other stimuli, provide the basis for his vision. Pesotski's garden, while based on the fanciful shapes of English gardens before the introduction of romantic irregularity, serves at the same time the function sought in romantic gardens themselves: stimulation of the imagination, products of sensations of grandeur, of sadness, and of gaiety, that are intended to lead to sublime meditation.[16]

As the story progresses there is an ever-increasing tension between the irritable Pesotski and his neurotic daughter Tania: Kovrin is caught between them.[17] Far from being helped by quiet country life, he experiences the same nervousness and restlessness as in the city. As he walks in the orchard seeking peace, it seems to come alive and its elements foreshadow Kovrin's visitor:

> It was cold. There was already the strong smell of smoke. In the large orchard . . . thick, black, acrid smoke was spreading, surrounding the trees, and saving [them] from the frost. The trees stood all in a row, their rows were straight and direct, just like ranks of soldiers, and that pedantic regularity and the fact that the trees were all the same height and had completely identical crowns and trunks, produced a picture at once monotonous and even dull. . . . the workers wandered around in the smoke like ghosts. Only the cherry trees, plums and a few types of apple trees were in bloom, but the whole garden was drowning in smoke. . .
>
> (227–28)

The thick black smoke rising from the disciplined trees would be ample preparation for Kovrin (and the reader) to experience the monk's appearance. However, these details are not the only elements associated with his vision. As Kovrin studies Italian (a quintessentially romantic and exotic language to the Slavic ear) music (Gaetano Braga's "Walachian Legend") is being played on the violin to the accompaniment of Tania's soprano voice. The song tells of a mentally disturbed girl in a garden who hears the music of the heavenly spheres. This music, and Kovrin's vague memory of a legend of a medieval Syrian monk whose image appeared and multiplied into the infinite distance to be reported in exotic locales (Africa, Spain, India, the Far North, and even on Mars and in the Southern Cross constellation), come together to produce Kovrin's hallucination.[18]

The monk appears when Kovrin is alone and walking toward the inhospitable river and its sullen pines. Out of the waves of rye rustling in the wind and accompanied by the dull murmur (*glukhoi ropot*) of the pines, Kovrin sees a dark whirlwind moving so fast toward him that he has to jump aside to avoid being hit:

> A monk in black clothing, with a gray head and black eyebrows, his arms crossed on his chest passed by . . . His bare feet did not touch the ground. Having passed by a few feet, he glanced at Kovrin, nodded his head and smiled at him, both affectionately and somewhat slyly (*laskovo*; *lukavo*). But what a pale, terribly pale and thin face! Beginning to grow again he flew over the river, silently landed on the clay bank and going through the pines, disappeared like smoke. . . .
>
> (296–97)

The park, the music, the evening twilight, combine once again to produce the monk's second appearance, conjured up mentally by Kovrin as "that dark spectre" (*temnoe prividenie*; 241). He materializes out of the pines, silently, all in black and looking like a beggar, with the same affectionate and sly look on his face.

The peculiar combination of friendly but sly or cunning glances might well be read as an indication of the monk's dual personality. But it is also a combination found in the traditional devil of Russian and European folklore. In fact, Chekhov's Black Monk has many features in common with that devil, who, though he may appear in the form of a cat, dog, or some other animal, has been frequently reported as a monk, dressed in black. He has also been seen as a whirlwind or waterspout gliding across the surface of land and water. Moreover, he is associated with violin music, which is often his cue to appear. Finally, like Chekhov's Black Monk, the devil is intent on seducing his victims, and often tempts them at night with hopeful visions of happiness. In the end, however, he leaves them suffering bitterness and discontent.[19]

Despite Chekhov's claim that his Black Monk stemmed from a dream he had, and despite his fondness for Braga's "Serenade" and his strong interest in the new science of psychiatry,[20] it may well be that the image of the devil/monk sprang from Chekhov's own psyche as part of the collective folklore conscience. This interpretation can be supported not only by the monk's outward appearance, by his means of locomotion and seductive behavior with Kovrin, but also by certain almost subliminal details in the description of the landscape and the monk's personality. For example, in addition to "*chernyi monakh*" (black monk), among the most common euphemistic terms employed by the Russian people for the devil (*chert*) is "*lukavyi*" (the sly one); we have already seen that this trait is one of the features of this monk's personality. The oft-repeated adjective used for the hairy pine roots, "*mokhnatyi*" ("hairy, furry, mossy"), is another common folk epithet for the devil. Moreover, the devil, as an inhabitant of hell, is reputed to have a sulphuric odor (compare the pots producing acrid smoke in the orchard; *dym* (smoke) is mentioned eleven times in the course of the story), and he is usually associated with rivers, whirlpools, and frightening forests.[21]

Kovrin's "dark spectre" is certainly not a savior genius. His conversation is almost mundane in its bald attempt at intellectual seduction: he speaks of eternal life, the verities, and the "highest goal": enjoyment (*naslazhdenie*; 242), which he says is to be found in knowledge or heightened awareness (*poznanie*). As his alter ego, the monk unfetters Kovrin's imagination, and Kovrin is temporarily happy to have found the secret of life. In an instruction reminiscent of Schopenhauer, the monk tells him: "Heightened moods, excitement, ecstasy, all that which distinguishes prophets, poets, martyrs for an idea from ordinary people, is contrary to the animal side of man, that is, his physical health. If you want to be healthy and normal, join the herd" (243).[22] This is comforting, for Kovrin considers himself to be "one of God's chosen and a genius" (257).

The monk's persona is quickly accepted by Kovrin, and he appears often, during the day as well as at night. But after Tania and Pesotski have taken Kovrin to be treated, the monk ceases to visit him, and the landscape no longer has its effect. Kovrin walks into the garden, not noticing the luxurious blossoms, and proceeds to the park where the "sullen pines, with their hairy roots" no longer whisper to him but stand "motionless and mute, as if they did not recognize him" (243). He is now sane, but life has no meaning for him. Following the course of many a romantic hero, he finally understands that he is a mediocrity; from this point on, he accepts the fact that, in his opinion, "every man must be satisfied with what he is" (256). The monk/devil appears one last time to claim Kovrin's soul and to reproach him for not believing his tempting words about eternal life:

> A tall black column, like a whirlwind or water spout, appeared on the other side of the bay. With a terrible velocity he moved across the bay in the hotel's direction, becoming smaller and darker, and Kovrin could barely step aside to make way for him. The monk, with his bare gray head and black brows, passed by and stopped in the middle of the room. . . . "If you had believed me then, that you were a genius, you would not have spent these past two years so sadly and without reward."
>
> (257)

An attack of internal bleeding leaves Kovrin dying while calling out for "Tania, the big garden with the dewy luxuriant flowers, the park, the pines with their hairy roots, the field of rye, his own wondrous knowledge, his youth, boldness, joy, and life which had been so beautiful." "The Black Monk," which began with fantastic romanticism dominant, ends with realistic detail akin to that of Chekhov's own fatal disease, tuberculosis.

To summarize, in these stories we find many features common to literary romanticism (emphasis on the supernatural, music, insanity, existential despair) and especially landscapes (gardens, orchards, and parks), which transmit the protagonists' experiences. To varying degrees, the egocentric hero's acute sensory perceptions, stimulated by exotic flora and haunting music, combine to produce an effect not unlike that found in romantic literature of a half-century earlier. Ognev, while seeming at first to be an unusual romantic hero in that he is very ordinary, experiences an insight that reveals to him the essence of his nature; but, because that insight would endanger his routine, he quickly represses it. Riabovich, the "meekest of men," reaches heights of fancy unusual in such a timid soul, but then must pay for his recognition that life is ultimately meaningless by suffering existential despair. And Kovrin, convinced that he is a genius, grows delirious from his heightened awareness, and dies spitting blood but with a blessed smile (*blazhennaia ulybka*) in the belief that his illusion is reality. While normally thought of as a writer whose themes and characters are far removed from those of the first third of the nineteenth century, Chekhov has drawn on traditional romanticism to demonstrate three levels of consciousness responding to an unusual event that disturbs a previously uncritical life, and he leaves his readers with greater understanding, not only of the protagonists' woes, but of our own problems in an increasingly disorienting world.

Notes

1. The philosophical and literary innovations of German (and English) romanticism provided the stimulus for the appearance of corresponding developments in the literatures of Russia and the other European countries. For informative surveys, see: Marshall Brown, *The Shape of German Romanticism* (Ithaca, N.Y.: Cornell University Press, 1979); *The Romantic Period in Germany. Essays by Members of the London University Institute of Germanic Studies*, ed. Siegbert Prawer (London: Weidenfeld & Nicolson, 1970); and Marianne Thalmann, *The Literary Sign Language of German Romanticism*, trans. Harold A. Basilius (Detroit: Wayne State University Press, 1972).

For an introduction to Slavic romanticism, see: Dmitrij Chizhevskij, *On Romanticism in Slavic Literatures* (The Hague: Mouton, 1957), and Dmitrij Tschiževskij, *Russische Literatur des 19. Jahrhunderts. I. Die Romantik* (Munich: Eidos Verlag, 1964). Specific discussion of this literary movement in Russia can be found in Lauren Leighton, *Russian Romanticism. Two Essays* (The Hague: Mouton, 1975); John Mersereau, Jr., *Russian Romantic Fiction* (Ann Arbor, Mich.: Ardis, 1983); and *Problems of Russian Romanticism*, ed. Robert Reid (London: Gower Publishing Co., 1986). See also Charles Passage, *The Russian Hoffmannists* (The Hague: Mouton, 1963), and Norman Ingham, *E. T. A. Hoffman's Reception in Russia* (Würzburg; Jal Verlag, 1977).

2. For the evolution of Chekhov's landscapes from his early through late tales, see Joseph L. Conrad, "Anton Chekhov's Literary Landscapes," in *Chekhov's Art of Writing. A Collection of Critical Essays*, ed. Paul Debreczeny and Thomas Eekman, 82–99, (Columbus, Ohio: Slavica Publishers, 1977).

3. The text is taken from A. P. Chekhov, *Polnoe sobranie sochinenii i pisem* (Moscow: Nauka, 1974–83), *Sochineniia* 6 (Moscow 1976):70. Passages cited are identified by volume number here with subsequent page numbers within the text. All translations are my own.

4. Mignonette is native to northern Africa; its fragrant flowers are greenish yellow or greenish white. Heliotrope is native to Europe and northern Asia, and its blossoms are white, pinkish, lavender, or red; it is the source for valerian drops, once used as a sedative for nervous disorders.

5. The protagonist's surname, Ognev (⟨ *ogon'*, "fire," "ardor") is ironic in that he is quite impassionate, and certainly lacking in ardor. "Verochka" represents a transitional stage between Chekhov's early, satirical anecdotes describing an unusual event, which may even destroy the protagonist (cf. "Death of an Official" ["Smert' chinovnika"], 1883), and later philosophical tales in which the protagonist is left in despair, unable to suppress the insights gained as a result of his experience. Here, while nature is used as a mood-setting and characterizing background, it is also a silent, if disapproving witness to the outcome of the event.

6. This story may also be read as an early attempt by Chekhov to come to terms with Turgenev's superfluous men, especially Rudin and N. N. ("Asya"). See my "Čexov's 'Veročka': A Polemical Parody," *Slavic and East European Journal (SEEJ)* 14, no. 4 (Winter 1970):465–74.

7. *Sochineniia* 6 (Moscow 1976):406

8. The horseman, found again as a leitmotiv near the end of the story, seems like the devil incarnate (or at least his envoy). If he is indeed a manifestation of the devil, it may not be reaching too far to suggest that he reappears in the form of the mysterious woman who kisses Riabovich in the black darkness of the room. This is not clearly indicated by Chekhov,

and the mystery is never solved. But in folk belief, the devil often attempts to seduce a man by appearing as a beautiful woman (just as he tries to tempt a lonely wife by appearing as a handsome man).

9. The year 1887 was one during which Chekhov found himself under the strong influence of Tolstoy's style. That influence is visible here: in an aside recalling Tolstoy's interpretive technique, the narrator explains that, from the hostess's look, ". . . it was evident that she had seen numbers of officers in her day, and that she was in no humor for them now, and if she invited them to her house and apologized for not doing more, it was only because her breeding and position in society required it of her" (408). Many other instances of such authorial interpretation of gestures, glances, and thoughts can be found in this story as well.

10. Petr Bicilli called attention to the similarity between the shy, fanciful Riabovich and Gogol's Akakii Akakievich, in *Tvorchestvo Chekhova. Opyt stilisticheskogo analiza* (Chekhov's work: an attempt at stylistic analysis) (Sofia: Universitetska pechatnitsa, 1942), 127.

11. For discussion of Chekhov's use of the senses, see my "Sensuality in Čexov's Prose," *SEEJ* 24, no. 2 (Summer 1980):103–17.

12. Though failing to guess which woman kissed him, he spends the summer in pleasant daydreams about married life with her. But at one point his fanciful dreams are rudely jolted: when he tries to discuss his experience with his fellow officers, the unit's womanizer dismisses its significance with a joke: "Probably a psychopath!" (420). This experience causes him to retreat further within his emotional shell.

13. Rufus Matthewson noted that this story treats the "rise and fall of a fantasy, the birth, life, and death of an illusion." Truly Riabovich has lost his capacity for happiness, and the capacity for "illusion, the power to love, and perhaps even to live," and thus his is a premature, spiritual death. See Matthewson's "Intimations of Mortality in Four Čexov Stories," in *American Contributions to the Sixth International Congress of Slavists*, vol. 2: *Literary Contributions*, ed. William E. Harkins, 261–83 (The Hague: Mouton, 1969).

14. Interesting studies concerning "The Black Monk" include David Matual, "Chekhov's 'Black Monk' and Byron's Black Friar," *International Fiction Review* 5, no. 1 (1978):46–51; and L. M. O'Toole, who in *Structure, Style, and Interpretation in the Russian Short Story* (New Haven, Conn.: Yale University Press, 1982), analyzes its axes of space, time, and psychological health (pp. 167–79). For discussion of recent Soviet criticism, see V. B. Kataev, *Proza Chekhova. Problemy i interpretatsii* (Moscow: Izdatel'stvo Moskovskogo universiteta, 1979), 192–203.

15. *Sochineniia* 8 (Moscow 1977):226–27. The narrator's suggestion that Kovrin thought of writing a ballad may either fit well within the romantic tradition or be a form of irony, especially when viewed in light of the details of this landscape.

16. For further commentary and many illustrations comparing early eighteenth-century gardens with those of the romantic period, see H. F. Clark, *The English Landscape Garden*, 2d ed. (Gloucester: Alan Sutton, 1980), and Laurence Fleming and Alan Gore, *The English Garden* (London: Michael Joseph, 1979).

17. The psyches of Pesotski and Tania each border on schizophrenia: Pesotski's frustrated attempts to combine the English design of the park and orchard for commercial purposes with his innate love of natural beauty (cf. the variety of exotic flora in the garden) bring him close to nervous collapse more than once. And Tania, at first seeming to be a normal young woman living in harmony with her environment, soon shows signs of hysteria and other manifestations of nervous tension.

18. The story resulted from a combination of factors: at the time of its composition (July 1893) Chekhov had been beset by attacks of anxiety and had experienced an unsettling dream in which he saw a black monk. Another stimulus for this story was reported by M. P. Chekhov to have been Anton Pavlovich's fascination with Braga's popular romance. M. P.

Chekhov, *Vokrug Chekhova* (Moscow: Moskovskii rabochii, 1960), 247–51; for additional details, see the notes to the story in *Sochineniia* 8:488–96.

Braga (1829–1907) was an Italian cellist and prolific composer of cello concertos, chamber music, operas, symphonies, and salon pieces; his most popular, "Leggenda Valacca," was also known as "La serenata," and in English, "Angel's Serenade." According to his brother, Chekhov found it had something "mystical, full of beautiful romanticism" (*Vokrug Chekhova*, 248), but His Master's Voice recording company described its melody as "cloying" (*The New Grove Dictionary of Music and Musicians*, ed. Stanley Sadie [London: Macmillan Publishers, 1980], 3:153).

19. For a short summary of various apparitions of the devil through the ages, see Kurt Seligmann, *Magic, Supernaturalism and Religion* (New York: Pantheon, 1948), 150–61. For specifically Russian sightings, consult F. A. Riazanovskii, *Demonologiia v drevne-russkoi literature* (Moscow: 1915; reprinted, Leipzig: Zentralantiquariat der Deutschen Demokratischen Republik, 1974), and E. V. Pomerantseva, *Mifologicheskie personazhi v russkom fol'klore* (Moscow: Nauka, 1975).

20. In a letter denying A. S. Suvorin's suggestion that he was describing his own psychological tensions in this story, Chekhov replied (25 January 1894) that he had "simply wanted to describe '*mania grandiosa*'" (*Pis'ma* 5 [Moscow 1977]:266).

21. Chekhov's Black Monk belongs to a long tradition of reported occurrences of such phenomena; it is still with us today in the form of sightings of so-called Men in Black (MIBs) who have been described as operators of UFOs or military or civilian secret agents who visit those who do research on UFOs. According to recent testimony, the MIBs come unannounced, sometimes alone or in twos or threes, and they know more than a stranger could know about the person who has the experience. They are dressed in black clothing, which may be soiled or clean. They move in an unusual way, seeming to glide along the earth. For stimulating discussion linking today's MIBs with the traditional devil, see Peter M. Rojcewicz, "The 'Men in Black' Experience and Tradition: Analogues with the Traditional Devil Hypothesis," *Journal of American Folklore* 100, no. 96 (April–June 1987):148–60.

In this connection it is interesting to note that, according to a recent Gallup Poll, 57 percent of college-educated Americans, and 46 percent of noncollege graduates, say they believe in extraterrestrials (cited in *Harper's* Index, April 1987, p. 13).

22. The monk's pronouncements have much in common with those of the German philosopher, and thus the story may be read as Chekhov's polemic with Schopenhauer. See E. I. Kulikova, "Ob ideinom smysle i polemicheskoi napravlennosti povesti Chekhova 'Chernyi monakh,'" in *Metod i masterstvo*, vypusk 1, *Russkaia literatura*, no. 1, ed. V. V. Gura (Vologda: Vologodskii gosudarstvennyi pedagogicheskii institut, 1970), 267–81.

Chekhov's "A Woman's Kingdom": A Drama of Character and Fate

Robert Louis Jackson*

"A Woman's Kingdom" ("*Bab'e tsarstvo*," 1894) was received well by Chekhov's contemporaries, but it was generally seen as a genre picture of the world of workers, merchants and lawyers. Some critics viewed it as an

*From the *Russian Language Journal* 39, nos. 132–34 (1985):1–11. Reprinted by permission of the editor, Professor Munir Sendich, Michigan State University.

incomplete work, the beginning of a "large novel" that was broken off just when it had become interesting: What happens to the 26-year old heroine, Anna Akimovna? Did she get married? These critics obviously did not perceive Chekhov's art of embodying the story's ending in the story itself. Indeed, concerned as they were with the superficial side of the story, they missed its point, or inner content. Modern criticism has not advanced substantially beyond earlier criticism. A recent critic finds in the heroine "a remarkable type of woman from the merchant milieu,"[1] while another rightly admires "A Woman's Kingdom" for "passages of excellent characterization," but finds it "not an entirely successful story."[2] In our view, "A Woman's Kingdom" is one of the most profound and successful of Chekhov's stories, an artistic masterpiece in every respect.

What is the focal point of interest in this story? To answer this question is to define the story's inner content and to address the question of its unique form. We may broadly characterize "A Woman's Kingdom" as a drama of character and fate (an ancient European theme), but one that involves the rich moral and religious symbolism of the Gospel at its deepest level.

Chekhov's fundamental statement concerns the idea of freedom and responsibility. Man's freedom, Chekhov recognizes, is conditional, not absolute; but it is as much a part of man's fate as the force of heredity and environment. Man must have the courage to be free. The renunciation of personal freedom and accountability for Chekhov is a renunciation of responsibility not only before oneself, but society; it is essentially an immoral act that has profound social implications. In "A Woman's Kingdom" moral failure is expressed, psychologically, in the heroine's predisposition to superstition, gambling and fatalism; socially, it is expressed in a capitulation to the bourgeois ethos of the rising capitalist class.

The 26-year old Anna Akimovna, a young woman of working class origin who has inherited a factory and mansion from her uncle, is the arena where conflicting forces of heredity, class, environment, ideology and elements of personality struggle for supremacy. At the opening of the story, as she faces the philanthropic activities of Christmas day, Anna seems equally drawn to, and repelled by both the lower-class world of her origins and the upper-class world in which she must now function as proprietor. She finds her role as "king's daughter" (*korolevna*) terribly burdensome with its unwanted power and responsibility, and she yearns to return to the simple and uncomplicated workday world of her childhood. "She should have been a working woman, and not a proprietress" (*khoziaika*).[3] Yet she is full of the social prejudices of the class to which she now belongs. Though she finds her elegant mansion "alien" (*chuzhoi*) with its sycophantic petitioners who despise her for her humble origins, she is also repelled by the "alien people (*chuzhie liudi*) with beastly faces," people in rags, frozen, hungry, and drunk, who appeal to her as the "sweet mother-benefactress" (*matushka-blagodetel'nitsa*). The working people at the factory look upon this elegant young woman as "already alien to them, incomprehensible." In turn, Anna Akimovna was "always afraid of being regarded as a proud upstart (*vyskochka*) or crow in peacock's feathers."

Anna understands the uselessness of philanthropy. Indeed, she feels guilty and ashamed in the face of exploitation, poverty and degradation around her. But she is caught between her conscience, her instinctive sense of right and wrong, on the one hand, and, on the other hand, her squeamishness, passivity, fear of ridicule, moral weakness and fear of life.

As the story opens, all these conflicting forces seem, at least upon first glance, to be in balance within Anna. She is free. "A Woman's Kingdom" is the account of what she does with this freedom at a critical moment in her life. Chekhov structures his story around this moment. "A Woman's Kingdom" has the strict form of a neo-classical drama. There is a classical unity of time, place and action. The story takes place in twenty-four hours, encompassing Christmas Eve and Christmas day. There are four scenes, "On the Eve," "Morning," "Dinner" and "Evening," that is, Christmas Eve and Christmas day. With the exception of Anna's visit to the house of the poor provincial secretary of gentry origin, Chalikov (a parody of Dostoevsky's Marmeladov), the entire action of the story takes place in Anna's mansion: upstairs and downstairs. Upstairs and downstairs constitute the story's vertical axis. In Chekhov's design, Anna's movements upstairs and downstairs have a symbolic as well as real function; they signal the tensions in her conflict as it develops in the course of the story.

Strictly speaking, very little happens in the twenty-four hours of action in the story. There are no love trysts, no violent incidents, no clashes between good and bad people, and no struggles for power, either on stage or off stage. Yet a momentous drama is underway inside Anna.

A thin but important thread of plot accompanies this internal drama, and, indeed, forms the horizontal axis along which it moves. "Here is a thick bundle of money" (*vot tolstyi denezhnyi paket*), reads the first line of the story. The fate of that bundle becomes a focal point in Anna's drama of character. To whom shall she hand over that money in the form of charity? Shall the money be divided equally among the workers? Shall she give it to Chalikov whose name she abritrarily picks from a packet of letters? Or to Pimenov, a young handsome foreman, whom she accidentally meets in Chalikov's house and for whom she develops a secret liking? When Anna hands over the money to the rapacious bourgeois lawyer Lysevich at the end of the third scene, the die is cast: she has resolved the crisis of her life. In the course of twenty-four hours the destiny of the heroine has been determined. That is, she discovers, indeed shapes a potential fate, embryonic in her character but not yet crystallized in consciousness, which Chekhov makes visible to the perspicacious reader in the opening paragraphs of the story when Anna is trying to figure out how and to whom to distribute the "disgusting money" (*protivnye den'gi*) for Christmas.

The origins of this money are unclean. Anna received it as "damages" in some court case involving her property. She is morally uneasy about it. Christmas philanthropy, or charity, of course, is an appropriate activity in which to expiate one's sense of guilt. But rather than give this money to the workers ("you don't give a worker anything for nothing or he'll demand it next time"), her idea is to give all the money to one person, and thus stun him with good fortune. "This idea seemed original and amusing to Anna and diverted her. She drew a letter from the pile at random and read it."

Anna's distrust of the workers tells us a good deal about her social prejudices. But something more important is revealed in this opening episode. Charity is a random and impersonal affair. For good reason, those who receive it consider themselves lucky, fortunate, happy (it is noteworthy that *schast'e* in Russian means both happiness and luck). Not without reason does Anna think: "The wretch (who receives the money) would be thunderstruck by the money and perhaps would feel happy for the first time in his life." As she later puts it, the money would be received, as it were, like a gift "from heaven."

The giver, Anna, seems to assume here a godlike role, one in consonance with her role as *"matushka-blagodetel'nitsa."* Yet, in fact, this episode reveals her passive, fatalistic psychology, her slavish inclinations. She refuses to make a choice — a firm, considered decision with respect to the distribution of the money. Instead, she "drew a letter from the pile at random." Thus, her act of gambling constitutes, like all gambling, a symbolic surrender of will to fate; in social terms it will constitute in the story a surrender to people who have no compunctions about taking advantage of the weakness and passivity of others. At the very beginning of the story, Chekhov then subtly signals Anna's abdication of freedom and responsibility by an important gesture: the random selection of a letter. Her irresponsibility at this moment is underlined by her lighthearted mood *(ei stalo veselo)* — a mood that recurs later, immediately after she gives the money to Lysevich.

The theme or motif of chance and fate with its problematic of freedom and responsibility is central to Anna's psychological drama in the three remaining scenes. Christmas morning (scene 2), Anna wakes up late. She has missed the morning mass ("it's God's punishment," remarks her servant). Anna prefers her dreams. But she finally gets up, dresses. "The remnant of a distant childhood feeling — joy that today is Christmas," fills her soul, and "she felt light, free and pure in spirit, as if her soul had been washed or plunged in the white snow." Typically these memories of childhood and Christmas bring with them thoughts that once again signal her basic inclination toward dependency and abdication of responsibility. "Christmastide is here," she says merrily to Masha, "now we'll find out our fortunes" *(Vot i sviatki . . . teper' budem gadat').* Anna's interest in fortune-telling (again the motif of gambling) is, not surprisingly, linked with her interest in finding a husband who will take her burdens.

After a brief discussion of the distinction between upstairs and downstairs (one floor is the world of the masters and the other the world of the dependents), the narrator writes: "Anna descended to the lower floor," that is, the "woman's half" of the house. Here in the "woman's kingdom" is to be found not the masters but the people who have no control over their destinies; service people, petitioners, servants and working people who are at the receiving end of philanthropy and who are preoccupied with chance and fate: with lottery tickets, fortune-telling, card games and match-making. Old Varvarushka, we are told, "had already sewn herself a shroud for the hour of death, and . . . the same storage chest which held the shroud also concealed her lottery tickets." Anna, "the king's daughter," goes downstairs to learn her fate and to play the unpleasant role of philanthropist. Here everybody on Christmas day kisses her hand and genuflects. But Anna behaves here not like a king's daughter, but a dependent. Pantelei the coachman is on his knees. He has been dismissed for drunkenness and is asking forgiveness. "Forgive me, Anna Akimovna," he exclaims. "Aunty dismissed you, ask her," Anna replies. "What about Aunty now," says Aunty Tatyana, "you're the mistress here and you give the orders" *(ty tut khoziaika, ty i rasporiazhaisia)*. Socially Anna is the *khoziaika*, but psychologically she is a true inhabitant of the world of dependents.

In Chalikov's house, at the end of the first scene, Anna meets the handsome foreman Pimenov, who also repairs watches. At that first meeting she thinks of giving him the fifteen hundred rubles. She meets Pimenov a second time downstairs on Christmas day and asks him if he would repair her little broken watch. The significance of this gesture on the symbolic plane of the narrative is clear: Anna, like the watch, has stopped. She wants to be wound up. She does not really want, nor does she have the courage, to pursue Pimenov; that is, to take her life in her own hands. Characteristically, she "wanted to tell Pimenov to come to visit her without ceremony, but was unable to do so; for some reason her tongue did not obey." Anna's weak impulse to act is intercepted by a deeper instinct that warns her away from any situation or relationship that might be demanding.

At this same Christmas day gathering, Anna wanted to treat kindly the school teacher who came to greet her Christmas morning; she wanted to protect him from the harassment of the factory director, Nazarych. But she was afraid of the director, and when the teacher became flustered she simply turned away awkwardly and wearily. The narrator notes at this point that Anna "went upstairs to her own part of the house." Here she ponders the cruelty of holiday ceremonies. But her sentiments are contradicted by her weakness and passivity, her objective capitulation to the cruelty and feudal social behavior of the upper class.

Upstairs is where she does all her dreaming and fantasizing, where she feels beautiful and extraordinary; but it is also where she feels lonely and "superfluous in this world." She bewails the fact that she has not gotten married. Her reasoning here again reveals her essentially passive nature:

> But she was not to blame for this. Fate itself had flung her from a simple worker's setting where, to believe her memories, she had felt so comfortable and at home, into these vast rooms where she was completely unable to imagine what to do with herself . . . "If only I could fall in love," she thought . . . Then she remembered her father and thought that if he had lived longer he would surely have married her to a common man, for example, to Pimenov. He would have ordered her to marry him — and that would be that.

Typically, Anna blames fate for her situation, and consoles herself with the thought that her father would have ordered her to marry him. And that would be that. In short, everything would be accomplished without suffering, effort or personal decision.

Against this background, the exchange upstairs between Anna and her lackey Misha at the end of scene 2 is noteworthy. Mishenka remarks: "You are my mistress *(gospozha)* and benefactress and you alone can guide me in marrying, as you are just like my own mother to me . . . But order them not to snicker and tease downstairs." Just as Mishenka views Anna as a superior mother figure who can guide and protect him, so Anna dreams of her father who would marry her off to Pimenov. Mishenka does not want to marry the downstairs Masha; and Anna, as she is soon to realize, does not really want to marry Pimenov. She, too, is looking for a guide, a father figure. And it is not Pimenov (the "shepherd," as his name implies in its Greek roots) whom she chooses to guide her, but the devilish Lysevich.[4] Her encounter with Lysevich and discovery of the truth about herself forms the inner content of scene 3, "Dinner." This episode, of course, takes place upstairs.

In scenes 1 and 2 we are introduced for the most part to Anna's working class world and surroundings, as well as to the inhabitants of the "woman's kingdom" downstairs. Figuratively speaking, we are downstairs most of the time. Here we see Anna primarily in relation to her roots, her past, her working class background. It is a world of which she nostalgically yearns — it is precisely the security of childhood that she wants — but has become alien to her. Yet if there is any hope for Anna it lies in a genuine moral and social identification with the workaday world from which she emerged. Anna in the first two scenes seems inwardly balanced between opposing alternatives. But in scenes 3 and 4 her passive inclinations shift the balance toward psychological and moral capitulation.

Anna's dinner with Lysevich and Krylin, the third act, as it were, in Anna's drama, constitutes the turning point in the destiny of the heroine. We are introduced to the spiritually void and amoral monied world of the rising bourgeoisie, an active class accustomed to giving orders. We are introduced above all to the cynical and corrupt Lysevich who epitomizes the world of the masters. He overcomes Anna with the cynical flattery of the archdeceiver. He appeals to her to be depraved like "a *fin de siècle* woman," to smother herself "in musk, eat hashish, and, most important, love, love, love." Anna responds with swooning words that underscore the intrinsic passivity of her nature: "For myself, personally, I cannot conceive of love without a family. I'm alone, alone like the moon in the sky, and moreover on the wane, and no matter what you're saying there, I'm certain, I feel, that this wane can be filled only by love in the usual sense. It seems to me that this love will define my obligations, my work, illuminate my view of the world. I want the peace of my soul, tranquility, from love."

The Chekhovian irony in these words is unmistakable. Here, as elsewhere in his work, Chekhov insists that love is not going to shape our obligation or work; rather it will itself reflect the fundamental nature of the lover. It is right to desire a husband, wife, or children, but not like "the moon in the sky." This moon will only bring sterility.

Lysevich with his lies, flatteries and verbal pyrotechnics (the episode deserves the most detailed analysis as a Chekhovian parody of some literary and cultural currents of the 1890s) draws Anna across the moral barrier into his unprincipled and spiritually empty world. She gives him the fifteen hundred rubels. It is a moment of capitulation and betrayal. The concluding lines of scene 3 after her betrayal are noteworthy: "She quickly threw off her dress, of which she had already tired, put on a dressing gown, and ran downstairs. And as she ran down the staircase, she laughed and stamped her foot like a mischievous child. She felt a strong yearning to play pranks."

Anna's sense of unrestraint, her prankish mood, her childlike behavior here points to her complete renunciation of freedom and adult responsibility; it signals the momentous shift that has taken place in her life. Her flight downstairs at this point is both literal and figurative: it is a flight into the world of dependents, a passive world of cards, games, and superstition, a world dominated by the powerful figure of the fortune-teller Spiridonovna. Just as Lysevich, upstairs, is for Anna the incarnation of fate, so Spiridonovna, downstairs, is the incarnation of fate in the woman's kingdom. The philosophy of both Lysevich and Spiridonovna presupposes a world that is anarchic, amoral and without any meaning.

The conversation downstairs is about husbands and the difficulty of finding them. Anna wants very much to be married. "She felt she would have given half her life and all her fortune just to know that there was someone upstairs who was closer to her than anyone on earth," the narrator says. "And the instinct of health and youth flattered her and lied to her that the true poetry of life had not yet begun, but still lay ahead; she believed it, and leaning back in the chair (at this, her hair loosened), began to laugh, and looking at her the rest of them laughed, too; and it was a long time before the reasonless laughter died down in the dining room."

With these words the ideologist of the woman's kingdom, the "devout" *(bogomolka)* Spiridonovna, arrives, and the card game of Kings *(igrat' v koroli)* begins with its chance-inspired rise to, and fall from power. We may note here that when Anna visited the poor provincial secretary Chalikov, in scene 1, that Dostoevskian figure had fallen to his knees and cried out in a sobbing voice: "Mistress Glagoleva! . . . The benefactress! . . . The holy little hand! . . . A dream! A beautiful dream! . . . Providence has heard us! Our savior *(izbavitel'nitsa)* has come, our angel! We are saved! Children, on your knees!" Anna, repelled by Chalikov's disgusting behavior and filthy house, characteristically does not wish to play the role of mistress *(gospozha)*, providence, savior, angel or benefactress. She departs, leaving him only with a little money.

Chalikov's actions form a parallel to Anna's own search for a savior. Her real psychological status is made apparent to all in the game of kings in which she participates in the last episode of the story, "Evening." "The first to become king was Spiridonovna, the fortune teller, and Anna as a soldier paid her tribute; then Aunty became king, and Anna fell down to the 'peasants' or 'oafs' *(popala v muzhiki ili 'tiut'ki')* which provoked general excitement." Important here is not only Anna's symbolic fall, but her actual participation in the card game, her inclination to gambling, her passivity.

Discussion of finding husbands is simultaneous with the game of kings. Spiridonovna asks Anna why she does not get married. Anna believes that "nobody" will take her. Spiridonovna remarks: "But, could it be she made a vow to stay a spinster?" . . . "You're to blame yourself." Indeed not fate, but Anna herself is to blame. Like her opposite number, the verbal prestidigitator Lysevich upstairs, Spiridonovna recommends that Anna as a free rich woman, her own queen, marry "some sort of broken-down and simple-minded little man . . . and have fun." "Life is a carnival *(Èhk, ne zhizhn', a maslenitsa!)* . . . Have fun . . . have fun til you're forty . . . and then hurry and pray it off." Anna, bounced about in the capricious conversation that accompanies the game, capriciously agrees to marry a common man. The name of Pimenov is mentioned. But at the moment she agrees to being matched with Pimenov she "jumbled the cards on the table and ran out of the room." For once, jumbling the cards, Anna seems conscious of her inner inclinations or disinclinations. She not only runs out of the room, but upstairs where she sings "ballad after ballad in a whisper, more and more about love, farewells, lost hopes, and she imagined how she would stretch out her hand to him and say prayerfully, with tears, 'Pimenov, take this load from me' *(snimite s menia etu tiazhest')*. And then, as if her sins were forgiven, her soul would become light, joyful, and it would be the beginning of a free and maybe happy life." But Anna prefers beautific dreams to reality. As the holiday excitement wears off, she comes to her senses. A remark of the lackey, Mishenka, invidiously comparing Pimenov with Lysevich, fills her with uneasiness. And now, "for the first time in the whole day, she understood clearly that everything she had been thinking and saying about Pimenov and about marriage to a simple workman was rubbish, nonsense and caprice." Sobbing with shame and boredom she recognizes that Lysevich and Krylin were closer to her than Pimenov and all the workers taken together, while the dreams and talk about Pimenov were "a lie, an affectation" (fal'shivoe mesto, kak natiazhka).

What has happened to Anna during Christmas Eve and Christmas day? A series of meetings and incidents in a period of particular stress for her — the philanthropic activities of the holiday season — led, as it were, to a crystallization of character, a discovery of self. In the terms of Chekhov's dominant metaphor in the story, we may ask: figuratively speaking does she, in the final resolution of her trials and tribulations, go upstairs or downstairs? The answer, it is clear, forms a paradox: in a social sense, Anna goes upstairs where she makes her peace with the new bourgeois rulers of Russia; in fact she is most comfortable in their world. She subordinates herself to the Krylins and Lysevichs. Yet in a psychological sense, Anna goes downstairs; that is, she definitely joins the woman's kingdom, the world of the dependents. Her alternative choice that was open to her was to go upstairs psychologically; that is, to master her fate, to take responsibility for her life, to resist the blandishments of the Lysevichs and Krylins and, in so doing, go downstairs socially; that is, identify herself at least on the moral plane with the world of the poor and the oppressed. Anna, fearing life and overwhelmed by the alienating power of new industrial Russia (her visit to the factory constitutes one of the finest pages in Chekhov) chooses not to take the alternative path. Marriage to Pimenov, a man who stood between the worlds of upstairs and downstairs, would have meant for Anna a step in the direction of mastering her fate, a step in the direction of acceptance of conflict and of the responsibilities that go with personal freedom. This step she was incapable of taking. In the final analysis, she nominally rules a kingdom of which she is in reality a dependent.

An important question arises: does Chekhov portray Anna as a person who was fated to succumb psychologically and morally to evil? Does Chekhov emerge in his story a determinist? Certainly in the time-context of the story — twenty-four hours — it may be said that Anna seems fated to succumb to Lysevich. Anna's inclination to abandon her freedom, as we have noted earlier, is signalled by her random selection of a letter and other gestures. But in the broader time-context of Anna's life and personality, Chekhov perceives the fatality of Anna's actions as the result of a long maturation of character, the subtle and free interplay of conflicting forces, acts, choices, attractions and repulsions all of which *ultimately* (and in the context of the stormy, paradox-ridden development of Russian capitalism) adds up to the unity of Anna's character and fate. But here the word "ultimately" is important. The concept of incurring the fate appropriate to one's character is an ancient one. But in everyday life the notion of a clear and manifest unity of character and fate is a construct, an abstraction; that is, in the life of an individual there is rarely a single point in time when that ideal unity, the result of a long pattern of development, manifests itself and decisively alters or confirms the course of a destiny. In tragic drama, however, such moments of self-discovery not only exist but form the center and circumference of the action. Chekhov's "A Woman's Kingdom," though neither a tragic drama or a tragedy in a generic sense, nonetheless markedly resembles this genre in its structure, devices and inner development.[5] The presence of Chekhov the dramatist is felt everywhere in this story. Twenty-four hours in the life of Anna, then, constitute for her a decisive point in time, a moment of self-discovery. These same twenty-four hours, encapsulated for the reader in an hour or less reading, provides for him one of those moments of recognition, so familiar to the ancients, that "a man's character is his fate" (Heraclitus).

At the deepest level of "A Woman's Kingdom" the essentially Greek drama of character and fate merges with the Christian drama. Here, as in many of Chekhov's finest stories, Biblical event and imagery form an organic part of the semantic structure of the work. The Christmas setting is neither an accidental nor dressy background for "A Woman's Kingdom"; it serves, rather, to amplify the story's dramatic and ideological tensions on the universal plane of Judeo-Christian moral, spiritual and religious experience.

After Anna's moment of betrayal, the handing of fifteen hundred rubles to Lysevich, and after her symbolic plunge downstairs into the world of fortune-telling and superstition, she goes upstairs. Here in an access of self-pity and sentimental dreaming, as we have noted, she imagines herself saying, "Pimenov, take this load from me." Anna's words, uttered in a day-dream immediately after her act of betrayal, parodies the words of Jesus in the Garden of Gethsemane[6] just before his betrayal by Judas and the crucifixion. Anna's wish to be saved by Pimenov is an empty one.[7] She lacks the courage to approach or marry him; even more, soon after her imaginary appeal to Pimenov, she realizes that "Lysevich and even Krylin were closer to her than Pimenov and all the workers put together." Anna's cry for help to Pimenov, of course, is uttered in a sweet daydream. Moreover, it comes not before but *after* she has renounced freedom, responsibility and conflict. Unlike Jesus, she is not suffering. She has already yielded to the money lenders and to temptation.

The disciples of Jesus sleep while he prays in the Garden of Gethsemane. Anna sleeps through the Christmas morning mass; troubled by the thought that she should be in church, she dreams all the while of "a huge garden on a hill." Is there a suggestion here on the part of Chekhov that she was dreaming of the Garden of Gethsemane and anticipating her own temptation? Was she unconsciously reflecting on her reluctance to play the role of Christian philanthropist (a role which she plays nonetheless) and her distaste for the poor and the working class? When Jesus, coming from the Garden of Gethsemane, finds his disciples "sleeping for sorrow," he awakens them with the words: "Why sleep ye? Rise and pray lest ye enter into temptation" (Luke 22:46). Anna, dreaming of a "huge garden on a hill," does not pray to avoid temptation. She sleeps.

From another, and important, point of view Anna's failure to attend Christmas morning mass is symptomatic of her deeper, essentially non-Christian preoccupations. Her concern with Christmastide *(sviatki)* centers wholly on its festival side: the practice of fortune-telling *(gadan'e)*, card playing and other amusements and distractions. The Church fathers, as S. V. Bulgakov notes, insistently condemned these amusements and placed them on the level of pagan rites and customs. "But Christmastide means chiefly holy days *(no sviatki — èto sviatye dni)* and therefore everything that does not correspond to this holiness must be extirpated. . . . Contemporary Christmastide fortune-telling, though it sometimes starts as a joke, almost always ends by bringing great harm to the soul."[8] Anna's failure to attend Christmas morning mass, her preoccupation with fortune-telling and other pagan customs, all are linked with her proclivity toward passivity and gambling (renunciation of choice), moral compromise and betrayal. The merging of psychological, moral-spiritual and religious landscapes in the characterization of Anna at this point in the story is one of Chekhov's most brilliant accomplishments.

On the mythopoetic plane of the story, then, Chekhov opposes the "kingdom of Christ," with its doctrine of freedom, responsibility and sacrifice, to the pagan "woman's kingdom" with its superstition, lottery tickets, fortune-telling and slavery to fate. Jesus is a man of humble origins who, in the face of temptation, remains faithful to his origins and mission. He challenges the money lenders and identifies himself with the poor and oppressed. Chekhov opposes the figure of Jesus, on the parodistic plane, with the figure of the pretender (and bourgeois philanthropy) the "sweet mother-benefactress" Anna Akimovna Glagoleva. Anna's patronymic and surname are significant in the context of the story. *Akim*, or *Iakim*, is rooted in the ancient Hebrew word for God, while *Glagoleva* — from *glagol* (word, speech) — echoes such expressions as "to live in a godly way" *(zhit' po glagolu)*. But Anna does not live in a godly way. She is a pretender who knows she is a pretender; a "king's daughter" in social position, she is more "a crow in peacock's feathers," an "upstart," a betrayer of the true faith in her gestures, actions and inactions. Her response to the poor and oppressed (she speaks of "feeding animals"), her contempt for workers, her laziness and narcissistic self-indulgence and squeamishness all lead her to a betrayal of her humble origins, to a renunciation of her freedom, to moral-spiritual decay. On the symbolic plane of the story's discourse, her capitulation to the rapacious bourgeois Lysevich is a capitulation to the prince of darkness.

Notes

1. Gleb Struve, preface to "A Woman's Kingdom," in Anton Chekhov, *Seven Short Novels*, trans. by Barbara Makanowitzky, with an introduction and prefaces by Gleb Struve (New York: W. W. Norton & Co., 1971), p. 158.

2. Thomas Winner, *Chekhov and his Prose* (New York: Holt, Rinehart and Winston, 1966), p. 126.

3. All translations are from "A Woman's Kingdom," Barbara Makanowitzsky's excellent translation in Anton Chekhov, *Seven Short Novels, op. cit.* pp. 159–95. In places I have altered the translation for stylistic reasons.

4. The name Lysevich is not without symbolic meaning. *Lysyi* means "bald." A Russian saying goes, *"Na lysoi gore, pod Kievom, ved'my shabash spravliaiut"* (On a bald hill, near Kiev, the witches celebrate sabbath). The allusion here is to Calvary (from Lat. *calvaria*, "a bare skull"). Significantly, one also speaks of *lysyi bes* (the old, bald devil). On the symbolic or mythopoetic plane of the story, the demonic Lysevich might be said to be opposed by the "shepherd" Pimenov.

5. "A Woman's Kingdom," however, in typical Chekhovian drama would doubtlessly emerge as tragicomedy; indeed, the comic element is latent in the drama.

6. "Father, if Thou be willing remove this cup from me: nevertheless, not my will, but thine, be done. . . . And being in agony, he prayed more earnestly; and his sweat was as if it were great drops of blood falling down to the ground" (Luke 22:42, 44).

7. It should be noted here that originally in the eastern churches the holy day celebrating the birth of Christ was known under the name of *Bogoiavlenie* (God's appearance). "This holiday had a special character," S. V. Bulgakov points out, "and was devoted not to the recollection of the birth of Christ or baptism of Christ, but in general to the appearance of Christ in flesh." Bulgakov, *Nastol'naia kniga dlia sviashchenno-tserkovno-sluzhitelei* (Kharkov, 1900), p. 473. Anna's appeal to Pimenov, psychologically an appeal to her father, is appropriate on this Christmas day, a day consecrated to "God's appearance."

8. *Ibid.*, pp. 474–75.

Narrative Technique and the Art of Story-telling in Anton Chekhov's "Little Trilogy"

John Freedman*

[*Editor's note: This essay was named "Best Article of the Year" for 1988 by the editors of the* South Atlantic Review.]

The elusiveness of Anton Chekhov's art has caused no end of confusion among critics and readers ever since he began to publish serious

*From the *South Atlantic Review* 53, no. 1 (January 1988): 1–18. Reprinted by permission of the publisher.

literature in the latter half of the 1880s. The socially oriented critical industry of Russia of the late nineteenth century was alternately baffled and outraged by what it perceived to be an unprincipled, immoral writer. In time, Chekhov came to be known as the bard of twilight Russia. Soviet critics throughout much of the twentieth century have been wont to see in him an unabashed optimist and even a budding revolutionary. Recent times have generally seen a more sober atttitude in his work, although there still exists no general consensus.[1] Two examples demonstrate well the extremes to which Chekhov criticism has sometimes gone in the past. In 1926 Janko Lavrin wrote about Chekhov's "meek, evasive smile" and "sad voice" (3), and in 1909 Leon Shestov opined that "Chekhov was doing one thing alone: by one means or another he was killing human hopes" (4–5).

More recently, Georges Nivat has returned to the idea of Chekhov's cruelty. After noting the contradictory nature of Chekhov criticism, he writes: "On parle de sa 'bonté,' de son 'humanisme,' de ce qu'il [Chekhov] appelait lui-même le 'talent humain de la compassion'; mais on doit bien constater que l'oeuvre tchekhovienne est une de plus cruelles qui soit" (98). And, while no one entirely repeats Lavrin's excesses any more, such epithets as "sweet," "gentle," and "melancholic" still abound in descriptions of Chekhov's art.[2] It should not surprise us, then, that the young, though perceptive Vladimir Maiakovskii entitled his 1914 article about Chekhov "Two Chekhovs."

The source of this confusion lies primarily in the nature of Chekhov's writing, in which he always maintained a distinction between his own opinions and those of his characters.[3] A close look at a series of stories that the so-called mature Chekhov wrote in 1898 — the "little trilogy," as it is frequently referred to, consisting of the stories "The Man in a Shell," "Gooseberries," and "About Love" — will allow us to define better the nature of Chekhov's story-telling art. In so doing, we may resolve some of the confusion concerning the writer's apparent split personality.

Each of the three stories is a frame story narrated by a different teller: "The Man in a Shell" by Burkin, a teacher at a gymnasium; "Gooseberries" by the veterinarian Ivan Ivanych Chimsha-Gimalaiskii; "On Love" by the miller and petty land-owner Pavel Konstantinovich Alekhin. In all three cases, Chekhov's narrator[4] sets the stage for his story-teller and then almost entirely disappears during the course of the frame story. Upon completion of each narrated story, he intrudes once again to wrap up the story as a whole with maximum efficiency. In each of the frame stories there is a bare minimum of interruption from the narrator and the listeners. Each teller becomes, as it were, the independent author of his own story. The trilogy as a whole is marked by four distinct and widely varying voices: Burkin, Ivan Ivanych, Alekhin, and the narrator. There is a progressive movement of the tellers' points of view: from third-person (story one), to split third/first-person (story two), to first-person (story three). This movement causes a parallel shift in the attitudes of the tellers toward their subjects. Burkin, as we will see, displays a thinly-veiled animosity for the "hero" of his tale; Ivan Ivanych displays something bordering on a love-hate relationship both to his brother and to himself; Alekhin tells of a love for Anna Alekseevna that is both passionate and tender. Any involvement, regardless of its position on a scale of positivity or negativity, will produce a skewed picture of events and personalities. Naturally, then, each story contains its own point of view, its own inconsistencies, its own peculiarities, and the point of view of one teller does not necessarily belong to any other teller — including the narrator — or to Chekhov himself.

"The Man in a Shell" is most often interpreted as a story about Belikov the Greek teacher, and in many respects this view is justified. However, to see Belikov as the focal point not only limits the story's scope but distorts its intention. Certainly Belikov is a "man in a shell." However, it is also frequently indicated that he is not the only one. "The Man in a Shell," like the other stories in the trilogy, begins with a folkloric prelude-story, a *priskazka*, in which Burkin and Ivan Ivanych encounter Mavra, who herself is a "woman in a shell." This meeting prompts Burkin to tell his story about Belikov, and he begins his narrative by indicating that there are not a few people in the world who, like hermit crabs or snails, try to hide in their shells. Upon completing his story, Burkin exclaims no less than three times how many men in shells there are, to which Ivan Ivanych replies, " 'Isn't that the way it is' " (53).[5] Hints abound, then, that Belikov is not the only one who must be considered a man in a shell.

The teller in each story is a prominent figure in his own right: Burkin spins such a skewed tale that he cannot but be considered an active focus of the reader's and narrator's attention; in "Gooseberries," there is an overt indication that Ivan Ivanych is worthy of our careful attention when he states that the focal point of his story is not his brother's story but his own; Alekhin in "About Love" is both teller and actor in his own tale. Upon reading the group of stories as a whole, then, one wonders why critical discussion has seldom centered around Burkin as a character. Many critics never even mention him, assuming that he is Chekhov's unmediated voice, and quoting his words as though they are Chekhov's own. This failure to note Burkin's independent voice has distorted the story's ultimate significance.

Belikov's story is revealed entirely through Burkin's eyes, so that in order to appraise the legitimacy of Burkin's frequently harsh judgments it is necessary first to determine whether these observations are well-founded. Several moments indicate that they are not. Burkin tells his story in an omniscient mode, claiming to be privy to Belikov's thoughts at moments when no one could possibly have access to them. Burkin clearly perceives himself as a literary narrator and uses the common tricks of the trade to embellish his story. Perhaps it is this element of the story as much as any that has induced readers to accept Burkin's tale as Chekhov's. Let us then focus on a few isolated moments in the story that may allow us to distinguish between the points of view of Burkin and of the actual narrator of the story as a whole.

Early on Burkin provides us with a good reason to believe that his account of Belikov's life may not be strictly objective. He explains to Ivan Ivanych that Belikov oppressed everyone with his cautiousness and suspiciousness: " 'With his sighs, his whimpering, the dark glasses on his pale little face, you know, like a polecat's face, he weighed us all down . . .' " (44). Burkin has an axe to grind and it is evident that we cannot expect from him an uncolored view. This in itself, however, does not yet provide sufficient reason to question the objectivity of his story. If in fact Belikov tyrannically imposed his will on others, his poor reputation among the townspeople would be justified. But the story reveals that Belikov was hardly a willful character. In fact, he was a meek, frightened recluse who almost never ventured out of his own private world. The romance which arises between him and Varenka is entirely the result of meddling on the part of the townspeople, Burkin included. His outrage at seeing Varenka ride a bicycle in public with her brother is less aimed at condemning Varenka than at protecting the privacy and stability of his fragile world, since he now knows that he is linked with Varenka in public opinion. His uncharacteristic outburst at Kovalenko's apartment is also more an effort to preserve his own anonymity than it is an overt attempt to exert control over others. In short, a disparity begins to arise between Burkin's Belikov and the Belikov who ostensibly gave rise to the story. This disparity is highlighted when we contrast Kovalenko's casual dismissal of Belikov with the difficulty Burkin and the other townspeople experience in interacting with him. As noted above, Burkin complains that Belikov's narrow-mindedness oppressed the entire town. He goes so far as to say that Belikov held the town hostage for fifteen years, during which time the town ladies were afraid to arrange theatrical gatherings and the clergy was afraid to eat meat during Lent or to play cards. In fact, Burkin says, " 'We were afraid to talk out loud, to send letters, to make acquaintances, to read books, to help the poor, to teach others how to read and write' " (44).

Despite Burkin's assertions to the contrary, such exaggerated fear could not have been induced by the likes of a Belikov unless the townspeople themselves were Belikovs of a sort. Prior to this passage Burkin attempts to characterize the teachers at the gymnasium as decent, thoughtful, and well-educated, but their meddling in Belikov's "romance" with Varenka is cruel. One need only consider the confrontation between Kovalenko and Belikov to see the extent of Belikov's "oppressive" nature. Belikov is frightened by Kovalenko's crude retorts and in order to preserve his insular existence, he threatens to report the conversation to the authorities. Unlike the other teachers or the rest of the townspeople, however, Kovalenko is undaunted, and before giving him a shove out of the door, he tells him to make his report. It is the humiliation of the rebuff—not the fall down the stairs—that ultimately brings about Belikov's rather Gogolian death.

Curiously, the plausibility of Belikov's "reign of terror" was called into question by one of Chekhov's contemporaries, although he did not develop his observation. After listing Belikov's nasty characteristics in detail, Evgeni Liatsky writes: "However, reader, does this really make sense? Is it conceivable that a gymnasium faculty and their director, consisting of educated people who have read Shchedrin, would submit to the influence of this pale caricature of Shchedrin's Judas for fifteen years?" (146).[6] But the critic is content to explain away this inconsistency as merely a small flaw in the story.

Certain of Burkin's comments that cause a careful reader to question his reliability are connected with his observations of the "outsiders" in the story, the Ukrainian Kovalenko and his sister Varenka. Both of these characters are drawn superficially. Varenka particularly is presented mockingly as a stereotypical "Little Russian" who is " 'always singing Little Russian songs and laughing' " (46); she is said to be " 'not a maiden, but marmelade,' " and is frequently referred to as a " 'new Aphrodite' "; none of these descriptions are borne out by the subsequent portrayal of her in the story. Kovalenko himself is superficially portrayed as a rather gruff, self-assured, loud man, presumably in contrast to the more refined Great Russian inhabitants of the town (who are, Burkin assures us, a thoughtful lot, well-versed in Turgenev and Shchedrin). This inability to comprehend someone from outside the town's narrow confines borders on crude nationalist chauvinism at one point when Burkin says: " 'I have noticed that *khokhlushki*, top knots [a derogatory Russian term for Ukrainians], only cry or laugh; they don't have any in-between moods' " (52). Burkin is incapable of seeing these people as individuals, and the true narrator of the story certainly does not expect his reader to accept these observations as truths. They serve instead to undermine the reader's confidence in Burkin's authority as an observer.

As has been noted more than once, Burkin claims to be privy to information that only an omniscient narrator could possess. One particularly striking instance of this occurs when he undertakes to describe Belikov's paranoia even while lying in bed at night: " 'When he went to bed he would pull the covers over his head. It was hot and stuffy. The wind knocked at the door and the stove hummed. Sighs, ominous sighs, could be heard coming from the kitchen. . . . He was terrified there beneath the covers' " (45). That these details are Burkin's own narrative creations is easily discerned from other moments in the story. For instance, Burkin describes Belikov's state on the morning following one of these hypothetical nights: " 'When we would go to school together he was drawn and pale and it was obvious that the bustling school to which he was going was terrible for him; that it was repulsive to his entire being; and that it was difficult for him, a solitary man by nature, to walk along beside me' "

(45). Belikov's few utterances are entirely devoid of substance, and he does not share with Burkin his personal thoughts or feelings. Hence, it does not appear that Burkin has the right to speak of what Belikov was thinking the previous night while lying beneath the covers. In fact, Belikov's pale and drawn appearance may represent the discomfort he feels in the company of his hostile neighbor. This, of course, does not occur to Burkin.

Burkin's description of Belikov's occasional social visits to his colleagues also leads us to doubt that he could have learned of Belikov's inner thoughts from the teacher himself. Says Burkin, " 'He would call on some teacher, sit down and silently stare as though he were looking at something. He would sit there like that silently for an hour or two and then leave' " (44). This is hardly the picture of a man who would share his private moments with an unfriendly neighbor. Only after the idea of marriage has been planted in his head and he comes to think he is enamored of Varenka does he actually venture to engage Burkin in a conversation of any substance. But even then the conversation never ventures beyond the subject of Varenka, and his speech mannerisms (he speaks with a feeble, twisted little smile) and actual statements ("I must admit, I'm afraid.") once again indicate that Belikov does not present a threat to the town's stability.

In fact, Belikov is an outcast who is ostracized by the townspeople. When the idea of marrying him off to Varenka arises, everyone joins in the machinations with malicious joy, and no opportunity is missed to foist this unwanted, unthought-of event on Belikov, who is no match for the likes of the town busybodies. Burkin describes Belikov on an outing to the theater with Varenka as "a hunched-over little man, who looked as though he had been pulled out of his apartment with pincers" (47). This is hardly the picture of a man who holds a town hostage.

The details of this story that point to an interpretation of Burkin and his fellow townspeople as the real oppressors are myriad. Let it suffice to conclude with an observation of Burkin's upon returning home after Belikov's burial: " 'We returned from the cemetery in good humor. But not a week passed before the same severe, tedious, senseless life began anew' " (53).

It is evident, then, that our perception of Belikov is heavily colored by the picture Burkin draws of him, and as the details are examined it becomes clear that Burkin's fictionalization of Belikov actually becomes a major element in the story. We may certainly assume that the Belikov who prompted this story shared some characteristics with the one whom Burkin creates for us—his meekness, his fear of spontaneity, even his occasional petty cruelty—but the ferocity attributed to him by Burkin is fabricated. Burkin, and thus the element of story-telling itself, is as much an object of observation in this story as Belikov, and this fundamentally alters the basic premise of the story.

This inability to disgintuish between Chekhov's narrative voice and that of his characters has also caused particular confusion in interpretations of "Gooseberries."[7] In this story the good-hearted, sentimental Ivan Ivanych tells the story of his brother Nikolai who devoted his life's labors to acquiring an estate on which he could grow his own gooseberries. For Nikolai the idea of the estate and particularly that of the gooseberries are emblems of bourgeois success that naturally bring with them happiness. As Ivan Ivanych develops his narrative he becomes increasingly carried away by the moral that he perceives to exist in his story, since, for all his hopes, efforts, and transgressions, the "happiness" that Nikolai achieves is nothing but a lie. The gooseberries are hard and sour, and his pathetic, run-down estate, squeezed between two factories, one of which calcinates bones and the other of which makes bricks and turns the nearby river brackish, is far from being an idyll of the Russian countryside.

While Nikolai does not recognize that the realization of the dream is a fraud, Ivan Ivanych does, and as he warms to his subject he seeks to turn his story into a homily. At one point he interrupts his narrative to say: " 'But he's not the point. I am. I want to tell you about the change that took place in me . . .' " (61). This is the sort of red herring frequently employed by Chekhov to mislead those of his readers who were forever seeking tendentious statements in their literature. Shortly thereafter Ivan Ivanych launches into his now famous pronouncement that happy people are only happy because the unhappy bear their burden silently. Developing this notion with frequent rhetorical questions and exclamations, he finally implores Alekhin: " 'There is no happiness and there shouldn't be. And if there is any sense or purpose in life, then this sense and purpose are not at all to be found in our happiness but in something more rational and great. Do good!' " (64).

On the other hand, Chekhov's narrator offers several other, more fruitful, hints that Ivan Ivanych's story is not what he thinks it is. When Ivan Ivanych completes his tale, the narrator describes the three men's surroundings and states of mind. Ivan is said to have told his whole story with a "pitiful, imploring smile"; the two listeners, Burkin and Alekhin, are said to be very "dissatisfied" with Ivan's story; and finally, Burkin is unable to fall asleep because of a mysterious, unpleasant stench that is in fact emanating from Burkin's burned-out pipe. Together, these details indicate that something is amiss with the story that has just been told. When juxtaposed against the narrator's neutral observations, the hyperbole of Ivan's narration takes on an almost grotesque tinge. That is, the contrast between the idealistic, impassioned, but misplaced harangue against "happiness" is suddenly revealed to be as much a "lie" as was his brother Nikolai's achievement of "happiness." Milton A. Mays cleverly puts it this way: "Ivan Ivanych's story is a "bad smell' in the context in which he tells it, and his 'truth' traduces reality" (67).

Even within the frame story itself there are hints that Ivan Ivanych's moralistic diatribe is not to be taken at face value. Ivan frequently arouses the careful reader's suspicions by committing slips of the tongue or by contradicting himself. He misquotes an excerpt from a dialogue in Pushkin's "Geroi" (Hero), transforming the lyrical statement of an individualized character-poet into a generalized, aphoristic phrase. Whereas Pushkin's character proclaims, " 'I value more an ennobling deception than a multitude of base truths' " (189), Ivan Ivanych quotes, " 'We find more dear a deception which ennobles us than a multitude of truths' " (61). His erroneous atttibution of a statement by one of Pushkin's characters to Pushkin himself is a fittingly ironic twist.

After delivering a lulling, lyrical description of his youth in the country at the outset of his narration, Ivan expresses a nostalgic longing for the country. But later he reacts critically to his brother's desire to set up house on his estate and calls the exodus of the intelligentsia from the city to the country nothing more than selfishness and sloth. This inconsistency is uttered in the first paragraph of Ivan's story and should clearly induce the reader to doubt his reliability.

There is also a more organic — perhaps it might be called psychological — flaw in Ivan's character that serves to undermine his reliability. Following his fervent soliloquy on the nature of happiness, during which he supposedly exposes the false nature of the concept, he passionately asks why man must wait for time to free him of his shackles. He implies that decisive action and a radical reevaluation of attitudes would make it possible to overcome the lethargy of social change and to institute a new order. But he no sooner expresses this idea than he ironically reveals his own incompetence and impotence: He is "too old," he says, and no longer capable of pursuing the struggle. He pleads with Alekhin to "do good" while he is young and able, justifying his own apathy with the impotent phrase " 'Oh, if only I were young!' " (64). By the end of the story, then, the careful reader is wary of accepting what Ivan Ivanych says at face value, and it becomes evident that Chekhov's intent in writing this story is not to instill in it "instructive" qualities.

The third story of the trilogy, "About Love," presents somewhat different complications from the first two since there is a fundamental shift in the relationship of the story-teller to his tale. In "The Man in a Shell," as we have seen, Burkin recounts an essentially third-person narrative about Belikov. In "Gooseberries" Ivan Ivanych spins a tale that is approximately half third-person narrative (the elements of plot that touch upon his brother Nikolai) and half first-person (his essentially plotless portrayal of himself in relation to his brother's experience, most of which is taken up with his moral and philosophical concerns). The frame story in "About Love" is told entirely in the first-person. The teller in this case is the subject of his own tale. However, the relationship of each of the story-tellers to verisimilitude is constant: Alekhin, as will become apparent, is no more a reliable source of information than were Burkin or Ivan Ivanych. David E. Maxwell's observation that Alekhin frequently speaks in the subjunctive mood is illuminating in that it indicates his story may have no basis in fact (49). As a result, the narrative irony of "About Love" is of a subtler nature than that of the other stories. In "The Man in a Shell" and "Gooseberries" the reader is able to achieve a measure of perspective by means of the distance that exists between the tellers and their tales, but that distance is lost in "About Love." In the final story the reader must rely on key phrases and omissions in the narrative to reconstruct the gulf that exists between the event as it may have happened and the event as it is related by Alekhin.

As does Ivan Ivanych in "Gooseberries," Alekhin inadvertently gives his listeners reason to doubt his full credibility early on. After his short prelude story about the beautiful Pelageia, Alekhin acknowledges the inscrutability of love and says, " 'Each case must be individualized, as the doctors say' " (66). Burkin readily approves, initially reinforcing in the reader's mind the apparent truth of the matter. However, Alekhin immediately reverses himself and launches into a generalization about love: " 'We Russians, cultivated people, have a predilection for these questions which remain unsolved. People usually poeticize love, embellish it with roses and nightingales, but we Russians embellish our loves with fatal questions . . .' " (67). He appears to be unaware of the inconsistency in his statements.

In light of the problems of point of view and teller's credibility raised in the previous stories, the reader's primary problem here is to achieve a reasonable understanding of Anna Alekseevna, the object of Alekhin's love. This problem is highly complex, since with one exception (to be discussed later) our only information about her comes from Alekhin, whose love for her makes him far from an objective observer. Can we accept Alekhin's account of the alleged love affair at face value? I think not.

Alekhin's first meeting with Anna provides us with a major insight into the probable nature of his relationship with her. Images of childhood (Alekhin's included) and motherhood are constantly repeated. The second time he mentions Anna, Alekhin notes that she has just given birth to her first child. He then describes how she first appeared to him: " 'I saw a young, beautiful, good, intelligent, charming woman, a woman such as I had never met before. And immediately I sensed in her a being close to me, already familiar, as though I had already seen this face, these friendly, intelligent eyes sometime in my childhood, in a picture-album which lay on my mother's chest of drawers' " (69).

Alekhin's first impression of Anna, then, is closely intertwined with his memories of childhood and his own mother. As will subsequently become apparent, Anna's relationship to Alekhin is in fact quite maternal, and does not have the sensual nature that he comes to experience, and that he attributes to her feeling for him. The lonely Alekhin, isolated in the country with his mundane cares of running an estate, is smitten by the vision of a beautiful young woman who arouses in him a feeling of warmth, comfort, and a longing for maternal love.

As this vague and undefined feeling develops into a true sensual passion, Alekhin begins to question the nature of the relationship between Anna and her older husband, ultimately concluding that it is an unhappy marriage. But this is likely to be wishful thinking on Alekhin's part. Following is his account of the first evening he spends with the Luganoviches: " 'Both husband and wife tried to make me eat and drink more. From a few insignificant details, for instance, the way they made coffee together, and the way they understood each other without finishing their sentences, I was able to conclude that their life was peaceful and successful, and that they were glad to have a visitor. After dinner they played a duet on the piano . . .' " (69).

These "few insignificant details" are apparently insignificant only for Alekhin, for they actually suggest the closeness that may well exist between the couple. This is not an isolated picture. The husband and wife are frequently mentioned together as a close unit ("both of them," "both husband and wife," "the Luganoviches," etc. [71]). Anna is frequently referred to as either "the wife" or the "young mother." It is through this interplay of words between the true narrator and the character Alekhin that the ironic distance in the story looms large. Chekhov's narrator allows his character to speak of a love that he believes to have existed (and which presumably did exist for him), while by carefully selecting Alekhin's vocabulary and the scenes that he relates, Chekhov also allows his reader to arrive at a very different interpretation of the affair.

Alekhin introduces several instances that he believes corroborate his conclusion that Anna shared his love. The first occurs in his account of their friendship. After his first visit to the Luganoviches, Alekhin does not see them for nearly six months. One evening he meets Anna by chance at the theater. She tells Alekhin: " 'I must confess I was a little taken with you. For some reason you frequently came to mind during the course of the summer, and today when I was getting ready for the theater it seemed that I would see you' " (70). She concludes by laughing and telling him that his tired appearance makes him look old. On the following day Alekhin accompanies them back to their summer home where, Alekhin relates, " 'I had tea at their place in quiet, domestic surroundings while the fireplace crackled and the young mother often went out to see whether her little daughter was sleeping' " (70). Within the context of Anna's placid family life her comments made at the theater are probably little more than polite, endearing, perhaps lightly flirtatious conversation.

Over a period of years the friendship between Alekhin and the Luganoviches grows and Alekhin develops a particularly close relationship with the children, almost as though he himself were one of them. He even describes himself once as a child in relation to Anna: " 'I used to carry her packages for her, and for some reason I carried those packages with such devotion and ceremony as though I were a little boy' " (71). Alekhin's utterance of "for some reason" is far from incidental, although he does not seem to recognize its significance. Hence, the relationship between Anna and Alekhin far more resembles that of mother and son than that of two lovers. Their long conversations (none of which is reproduced in the story) are often marked by silence, which Alekhin interprets as their mutual fear of acknowledging their love. He begins to speak of "our love" and "our lives," although nothing has transpired to justify this romantic link. Claiming a (novelistic) omniscient knowledge of Anna's thought processes, he reasons that Anna would have run away with him were it not for social constrictions and family concerns, but neither Anna's words nor her behavior provide any reason for such assumptions.[8]

Toward the end of Anna's stay in the country the relationship sours. Alekhin tells us: " 'Anna Alekseevna began to go away more often to her mother's and her sister's. She was frequently in bad spirits, she appeared to recognize that her life was unsatisfactory and ruined, and she didn't want to see either her husband or her children. She was already taking a cure for nervous prostration' " (73).

Anna's dissatisfaction with her life reflects on her relationship with Alekhin as well. Their conversations more and more come to be marked by silences and she frequently responds to Alekhin's comments harshly and sarcastically. Alekhin describes it this way: " 'She displayed some sort of strange irritation with me' " (73). The phrase "some sort of," as the previously mentioned "for some reason," is an indication that Alekhin fails to understand what the narrator, the reader, and, presumably, Anna herself do understand. Anna's irritation is "strange" only for Alekhin, whose perception of the "affair" is very different from hers.

In order to find a satisfactory explanation for Anna's dissatisfaction, we may turn to one of the central themes of the trilogy as a whole: the indolence and boredom of life in the Russian countryside. While this theme was openly dealt with in the first two stories, it is alluded to much more subtly in "About Love." Chekhov's narrator in "Gooseberries" had already exposed the futility of Alekhin's life in the country, and thus the reader comes to Alekhin's story with a ready understanding of his situation. While the narrator in "About Love" has little more to add on this account, the idea that Alekhin has squandered his talents buried in the country is supported by Anna's responses to him, by occasional comments that Alekhin makes about himself, and by an observation shared by Burkin and Ivan Ivanych. Certainly the oppressive atmosphere that poisoned the lives of the people in "The Man in a Shell," seduced the simpleton Nikolai and brought Ivan Ivanych to a state of impotent indignation, and caused Alekhin to squander his talents had a similar effect on the "young, beautiful, good, intelligent, charming" Anna. The difference is that while none of the other characters of the stories had the good sense to combat this killing life, Anna does. Her trips to her mother and sister are quite probably an attempt to escape the prison-like atmosphere of the country, and her irritation with Alekhin is more apt to be an ill-formed expression of disgust with a capable man who has allowed himself to wither away aimlessly.

For Alekhin the climax of his tale is the final proof of Anna's love for him, while the careful reader is left far from convinced. The scene takes place at the train station as Alekhin, Luganovich, and the Luganovich children see Anna off. Alekhin follows her into the train car where he finally confesses his love for her. The tearful scene is striking in that, with one exception, the only "actor" is Alekhin himself. Here is the scene as Alekhin tells it:

> It was necessary to say good-bye. When our eyes met in the train car our emotional strength abandoned us both. I embraced her, she lay her face on my breast, and tears began to flow. While kissing her face, shoulders, hands wet from tears, — oh, how unhappy we were! — I confessed to her my love and with a bitter pain in my heart I understood how senseless, insignificant and deceptive everything was which had stopped us from loving. . . .
>
> I kissed her one last time, took her hand, and we parted — forever. The train was already moving. I took a seat in the next car — it was nearly empty — and I sat there weeping until we reached the next station. Then I went home to Sofyino on foot. . . .
>
> (74)

Alekhin kisses Anna, Alekhin embraces Anna, Alekhin confesses his love to Anna. Nothing here suggests that Alekhin can justify his claim that "our emotional strength abandoned us both." Anna's only response is to rest her head on Alekhin's chest and perhaps to shed a few tears, although it is not entirely clear that even this is so. The phrase "tears began to flow" is an impersonal construction, so that we cannot say for certain whose tears they were. They may be Alekhin's and not Anna's.[9] In any event, that Anna rests her head on his chest and perhaps even sheds a few tears is hardly proof that she passionately loves him and is suffering from the same tragedy as he is. There is more than ample proof in the text that she feels an affection for this family friend, probably understands his attraction to her, and even sympathizes with him. However, there is little to justify Alekhin's invoking of the pronoun "we" to relate what he perceives to be a shared experience of tragic sorrow. The small degree of affection that Anna does express may be a magnanimous, even frustrated, expression of sympathy rather than love. Even more convincing is the finale of the incident: Anna attempts neither to stop him when he goes, nor to follow him into the neighboring car where he sits alone and weeps. It would appear that Alekhin has "poeticized" and "embellished with roses" this instance just as he has the entire "affair."

In effect, Alekhin's outburst on the nature of loving is a reprise of Ivan Ivanych's similar outburst on the nature of happiness and strikes a similar discordant note. Here is what Alekhin has to say: " 'I understood that with love, one's thoughts must begin with something exalted, something more important than happiness or unhappiness, sin or virtue in their common sense, or one must not think about it at all' " (74). Whatever truth there may be in this utterance, it is entirely out of place in the context of the story that has just been told. Even if Alekhin had acted in accordance with this reasoning, there is no real indication that anything would have come of it. The pathos of the situation arises not from the tragedy of unrequited love — as Alekhin sees it — but from the tragedy of Alekhin's misguided life: He has become obsessed by a dubious love while failing to notice that his life was wasting away in the depths of the country. The disparity between these two views is created by a gap that exists between the point of view of Chekhov's narrator and the point of view of his created character, Alekhin.

Following Alekhin's retelling of the train scene, the narrator once again steps in and describes the effect that the story has had on Burkin and Ivan Ivanych. The two of them "regretted that this man with good, intelligent eyes who had told his story with such sincerity truly was spinning 'round here like a squirrel in a cage on his enormous estate instead of busying himself with science or something else . . ." (74). The narrator deflects our attention from the story of unrequited love, indicating that Alekhin's real tragedy is his inability to comprehend the more probable source of his unhappiness and dissatisfaction. Our final meeting with Anna — the first and only one that is not portrayed through Alekhin's consciousness — occurs in the story's final sentence when the narrator laconically tells us that Burkin and Ivan Ivanych both occasionally met her in town and that "Burkin was even acquainted with her and found her to be pretty" (74). This almost flippant observation about Anna stands in stark contrast to the more intense portrayal we have received of her throughout the story. What a difference from the string of adjectives Alekhin used to describe her at their first meeting! Once again, the narrator redirects the reader's attention away from the atmosphere of the story Alekhin has told.

If Chekhov was not interested in providing his readers with instructive social or moral tales through the narratives of Burkin, Ivan Ivanych, and Alekhin, what did he intend by imparting authorial bias to the characters and situations of his trilogy? Somerset Maugham offers a fitting insight: "It is natural for men to tell tales, and I suppose the short story was created in the night of time when the hunter, to beguile the leisure of his fellows when they had eaten and drunk their fill, narrated by the cavern fire some fantastic incident he had heard of" (47). Each story in the trilogy contains numerous references to the theme of story-telling, and in almost all cases the message is borne by Chekhov's narrator, either by direct narrative statement or by the manipulation of dialog, setting, and mood. It is in this manner that the characters all serve their primary function. Burkin, Ivan Ivanych, and Alekhin are, above all, story-tellers. Within the world of the work Burkin may have been a teacher of Greek, Ivan Ivanych a veterinarian, and Alekhin a petty land-owner, but for Chekhov's narrator they are hunters after stories; *raconteurs*, not *raisonneurs*.

Burkin, whose tale most resembles a traditional "story," seems to be the most conscious story-teller of the three. His tale is not a personal confession as are the tales of Ivan Ivanych and Alekhin, and he narrates it with "presumptuous" omniscience. He selects for his subject the eccentric Belikov and employs innuendo, prejudice, elaboration, and exaggeration for the sake of a good story. Burkin foils Ivan Ivanych whenever the latter wants to intrude on the flow of Burkin's story, and he plays the role of Ivan Ivanych's "editor" in "Gooseberries" by invariably cutting him short whenever he begins to digress.

Chekhov's narrator frequently tells us that both Ivan Ivanych and Alekhin want to say or tell something. Each of the three frame stories begins with similar overt statements (my italics): "They were *telling various stories*" ("The Man in a Shell" [42]); "Ivan Ivanych sighed heavily and lit his pipe so he could begin to *tell a story*" ("Gooseberries" [55]); Alekhin *told* about how beautiful Pelageia was in love with the cook" ("About Love" [66]). In "Gooseberries" Ivan Ivanych's initial attempt to tell his story is frustrated by a sudden downpour, but when he does begin his tale the narrator points out that "Ivan Ivanych *launched into his story*" (57). In "About Love" Chekhov's narrator elaborates on the theme of story-telling:

> It appeared that he [Alekhin] wanted to tell something. People who live alone always have something they would willingly tell about. In the city bachelors purposefully go to the baths and restaurants for no other reason than to talk and sometimes they tell the bath attendants or waiters very interesting stories. In the country on the other hand, they usually pour out their soul to their guests. In the window the gray sky and trees, wet from the rain, were visible. There was nowhere to go in such weather and there was nothing left to do but tell stories and listen.
>
> (67)

Story-telling, then, in addition to being a form of entertainment, is a way for people to share and participate in their lives. For Chekhov, whose appetite for religion had long ago been squelched, and for whom tendentiousness was synonymous with narrow-mindedness, honesty and art stood on the highest pedestal. There can be little doubt he would have heartily agreed with John Updike's assertion that, "Being ourselves is the one religious experience we all have, an experience shareable only partially, through the exertions of talk and art" (xix). Ultimately, it is not the "truth" of the tale that matters but the telling of it.

Even Chekhov's narrator cannot help but have a word to say in the final story of the trilogy. He too is struck by the beautiful Pelageia, who so astounds Burkin and Ivan Ivanych, and he too cannot refrain from admiring her beauty. While Alekhin may occasionally refer to her merely as Pelageia, Chekhov will not let his narrator be so indifferent. For him she is invariably the *beautiful* Pelageia, as she might be characterized in a folk tale. It is as though the cathartic act of story-telling has had its effect even on him. For those readers who have sought to find Chekhov in his stories, here he is: the craftily "absent author" who commands, as Virginia Woolf wrote, "exquisitely original and fastidious taste" (177), whose "melancholy" is distortion, whose "cruelty" is misinterpretation, and whose honesty, appreciation of beauty, and ability to spin an intriguing yarn are always the hallmark of his best stories.

Notes

1. Simon Karlinsky's reevaluation of the "dour, sickly" Chekhov in his introduction to *Anton Chekhov's Life and Thought* is the best and most balanced portrayal we have to date.

2. See, for instance, Brustein and Wilks.

3. Nivat relies heavily on Chekhov's notebooks and correspondence to support his reading of Chekhov as a "cruel" writer. This causes him to confuse ideas intended for independent works of literature with Chekhov's own.

4. Whether we call this narrator Chekhov himself or Chekhov's narrator is probably a moot point since he (the narrator) passes no judgment on his characters, serving merely to introduce them, place them in their necessary positions, and report the state of nature and the weather. However, for safety's sake, I will maintain a distance between Chekhov and the narrator of his stories by referring to Chekhov's narrator as "narrator" and to Burkin, Ivan Ivanych, and Alekhin as "story-teller" or "teller."

5. My translation. Page references refer to Anton Chekhov, *Polnoe Sobranie*, vol 10. I would have preferred to use an existing English text for reference, but I found such numerous crucial errors that this proved impossible. The versions by Ronald Wilks, Ronald Hingley, Avrahm Yarmolinsky, Adeline Daye, S. S. Koteliansky and Gilbert Cannan, Marian Fell, and Constance Garnett all betray the translators' occasional ignorance of certain of the stories' key subtleties (see note 9 for one such instance). Of these the best is Hingley. Since a good discussion of the pitfalls encountered in translating Chekhov would require far more space than is available here, suffice it to say that D. S. Mirsky was dead wrong when he claimed Chekhov has less to fear from the "treachery of translators" than any other writer (382). Translating Chekhov requires the same subtlety that reading him does. Few have succeeded.

6. "Shchedrin's Judas" refers to the degenerate protagonist of Mikhail Saltykov-Shchedrin's novel from the 1870s, *The Golovlyov Family*.

7. Winner (197–201) mentions in passing that the effect of Ivan Ivanych's narration is ironic, but he does not elaborate this point. Mays was one of the first to fully bring the error to light. Kataev (238–250) and Berthoff also clarify the problem. However, Nivat still assumes that Ivan Ivanych is Chekhov's unmediated mouthpiece and so judges "Gooseberries" to be "un des récits les plus mélancoliques de Tchekhov" (103).

8. See "The Lady with the Pet Dog" and especially "A Calamity" (also translated as "A Misfortune") for stories in which Chekhov indicates romantic involvement primarily through his characters' behaviour rather than through their words.

9. This key moment was mishandled by five of the story's seven translators. All but Ronald Wilks and Ronald Hingley arbitrarily and erroneously indicate that it is Anna's tears that flow. Both these translators, however, commit similar errors elsewhere.

Works Cited

Berthoff, Ann E. "Marvell's Stars, Schubert's Suns, Chekhov's Pipe: Recognizing and Interpreting Metaphor." *Sewannee Review* 89 (Winter 1981): 55–82.

Brustein, Robert. "Anton Chekhov." *The Theatre of Revolt*. Boston: Little Brown, 1964. 135–180.

Chekhov, Anton. *Polnoe sobranie sochinenii i pisem*. 30 vols. Moscow: Nauka, 1974–82. Vol. 10.

Daye, Adeline Lister, trans. *The Steppe and Other Stories*. By Anton Chekhov. New York: Stokes, 1915.

Fell, Marian, trans. *Stories of Russian Life*. By Anton Chekhov. New York: Scribner, 1915.

Hingley, Ronald, trans. *Eleven Stories*. By Anton Chekhov. London: Oxford, 1975.

Garnett, Constance, trans. *The Wife and Other Stories*. By Anton Chekhov. New York: MacMillan, 1918.

Karlinsky, Simon. "The Gentle Subversive." *Anton Chekhov's Life and Thought*. Trans. Michael Henry Heim and Simon Karlinsky. Berkeley: U of California P, 1973. 1–32.

Kataev, Vladimir B. *Proza Chekhova: problemy interpretatsii*. Moscow: Moskovskii U. 1979.

Koteliansky, S. S. and Gilbert Cannan, trans. *The House with the Mezzanine and Other Stories*. By Anton Chekhov. New York: Scribner, 1917.

Lavrin, Janko. "Chekhov and Maupassant." *Slavonic Review* 13 (June, 1926): 1–24.

Liatsky, Evgeni. "A. P. Chekhov i ego rasskazy." *Vestnik Evropy* 1 (1904): 104–162.

Maiakovsky, Vladimir. *Polnoe sobranie sochinenii*. 12 vols. Moscow: Khudozhestvennaia literatura, 1939–1947. Vol. 1.

Maugham, W. Somerset. "The Short Story." *Points of View*. London: Heinemann, 1958. 142–188.

Maxwell, David E. "The Unity of Chekhov's 'Little Trilogy.' " *Chekhov's Art of Writing: A Collection of Critical Essays*. Ed. Paul Debreczeny and Thomas Eekman. Columbus, OH: Slavica, 1977. 35–53.

Mays, Milton A. " 'Gooseberries' and Chekhov's Concreteness." *Southern Humanities Review* 6 (Winter 1972): 63–67.

Mirsky, D. S. *A History of Russian Literature*. New York: Vintage, 1958.

Nivat, Georges. *Vers la fin du mythe russe*. Paris: L'Age d'Homme, 1982.

Pushkin, Aleksandr. *Polnoe sobranie sochinenii*. 10 vols. Leningrad: Nauka, 1977–1979. Vol. 3.

Saltykov, Mikhail. *The Golovlyov Family*. Ann Arbor: Ardis, 1977.

Shestov, Leon. "Creation From the Void." *Chekhov and Other Essays*. Ann Arbor: U of Michigan P, 1966. 3–62.

Updike, John. Introduction. *Sanatorium Under the Sign of the Hourglass*. By Bruno Schulz. New York: Penguin, 1979. xiii–xix.

Wilks, Ronald, trans. and Introduction. *The Kiss and Other Stories*. By Anton Chekhov. New York: Penguin, 1982.

Winner, Thomas. *Chekhov and his Prose*. New York: Holt, 1966.

Woolf, Virginia. "The Russian Point of View." *The Common Reader: First Series*. Ed. and introduced by Andrew McNeillie. San Diego: Harcourt, 1984. 173–182.

Yarmolinsky, Avrahm, trans. *The Portable Chekhov*. New York: Penguin, 1977.

"The Lady with the Dog"   Virginia Llewellyn Smith*

It will by now be apparent that Anna Sergeevna, the lady with the dog, can be considered symbolic of the ideal love that Chekhov could envisage but not embrace—that remained, so to speak, behind a pane of glass, as in Heifitz's film. But the significance of the whole story is much greater than that comprised in Anna Sergeevna alone.

No other single work of Chekhov's fiction constitutes a more meaningful comment on Chekhov's attitude to women and to love than does "The Lady with the Dog." So many threads of Chekhov's thought and experience appear to have been woven together into this succinct story that it may be regarded as something in the nature of a summary of the entire topic.

Gurov, the hero of the story, may at first appear no more closely identifiable with Chekhov himself than are many other sympathetic male characters in Chekhov's fiction: he has a post in a bank and is a married man with three children. It is because he has this wife and family that his love-affair with Anna Sergeevna leads him into an *impasse*. And the affair itself, involving Gurov's desperate trip to Anna's home town, has no obvious feature in common with anything we know of Chekhov's amorous liaisons.

And yet Chekhov's own attitudes and experience have clearly shaped Gurov's character and fate. The reader is told that Gurov "was not yet forty": Chekhov was thirty-nine when he wrote "The Lady with the Dog." Gurov "was married young" (*ego zhenili rano*): there is a faint implication in the phrase that an element of coercion played some part in his taking this step—a step which Chekhov, when he was young, managed to avoid. As in general with early marriages in Chekhov's fiction, Gurov's has not proved a success. His wife seems "much older than he" and imagines herself to be an intellectual: familiar danger-signals. She is summed-up in three words: "stiff, pompous, dignified" (*pryamaya, vazhnaya, solidnaya*) which epitomize a type of woman (and man) that Chekhov heartily disliked.

Gurov's wife treats sex as something more complicated than it is, and spoils it for him; and it is also spoilt for him by those mistresses of whom he soon tires: beautiful, cold women with a "predatory" expression who are determined to snatch what they can from life. "When Gurov grew cold to them, their beauty aroused hatred in him and the lace on their linen reminded him of scales." It would seem that exactly some such sentiment inspired Chekhov when he depicted Ariadna, Nyuta, and the other anti-heroines.

*From chapter 8 of *Anton Chekhov and The Lady with the Dog* by Virginia Llewellyn Smith (London: Oxford University Press, 1973). Reprinted by permission of the publisher. ©Oxford University Press.

Gurov has had, however, liaisons that were, for him, enjoyable — and these we note, were brief: as was Chekhov's liaison with Yavorskaya and indeed, so far as we know, all the sexual relationships that he had before he met Olga Knipper.

"Frequent experience and indeed bitter experience had long since taught [Gurov] that every liaison which to begin with makes such a pleasant change . . . inevitiably evolves into a real and extremely complex problem, and the situation eventually becomes a burden." That his friendships with, for instance, Lika and Avilova should evolve into a situation of this kind seems to have been exactly what Chekhov himself feared: he backed out of these friendships as soon as there appeared to be a danger of close involvement.

Gurov cannot do without the company of women, and yet he describes them as "inferior breed": his experience of intimacy with women is limited to casual affairs and an unsatisfactory marriage. Chekhov also enjoyed the company of women and had many female friends and admirers; but he failed, or was unwilling, to involve himself deeply or lastingly with them. That in his work he should suggest that women are an inferior breed can be to some extent explained by the limited knowledge of women his self-contained attitude brought him — and perhaps, to some extent, by a sense of guilt concerning his inability to feel involved.

Gurov's behavior to Anna Sergeevna at the beginning of their love-affair is characterized by an absence of emotional involvement, just such as appears in Chekhov's attitude towards certain women. There is a scene in "The Lady with the Dog" where, after they have been to bed together, Gurov eats a watermelon while Anna Sergeevna weeps over her corruption. It is not difficult to imagine Chekhov doing something similarly prosaic — weeding his garden, perhaps — while Lika poured out her emotional troubles to him.

Gurov's egocentricity is dispelled, however, by the potent influence of love, because Anna Sergeevna turns out to be the ideal type of woman: pitiable, defenceless, childlike, capable of offering Gurov an unquestioning love. Love is seen to operate as a force for good: under its influence Gurov feels revulsion for the philistinism of his normal life and associates. Soviet interpreters have made much of the theme of regeneration, of the idea implicit in the story that "a profound love experienced by ordinary people has become an enormous moral force."[1] In fact, although some idea of this sort is certainly implicit in the story, Chekhov is surely attempting above all to evoke what love meant to his protagonists as they themselves saw their situation. Chekhov originally wrote in the conclusion of "The Lady with the Dog" that the love of Gurov and Anna Sergeevna had "made them both better." He altered this subsequently to "changed them both for the better"; but still dissatisfied, finally he altered this once more to "had changed them both," and thus avoided any overt suggestion of pointing a moral.[2]

The point is that we are not seeing the lovers changed in relation to society, but in relation to their own inner lives. Gurov is shaken out of his romantic dreaming by a sudden recognition of the grossness of others in his stratum of society: but he does not give up his job or abandon his social life. Instead, he leads a double existence, and imagines that every man's "real, most interesting life" goes on in secret. It is this life that Chekhov is interested in, not in Gurov as a representative of his class or his time.

That Gurov and Anna Sergeevna are alone amongst their fellow-men does not point a moral, but it is where the pathos of their initial situation lies. We are not impressed by their moral superiority, but moved by their loneliness. Love is the answer to this loneliness, and there is no need to bring morality into it. Chekhov, where love was concerned, wrote from the heart, not the head.

Chekhov wrote "The Lady with the Dog" in Yalta in the autumn of 1899, not long after he and Olga were there together (although they were not, as yet, lovers) and had made the trip back to Moscow together. In the Kokkoz valley, it will be remembered, they apparently agreed to marry; and so by then, we may presume, Chekhov knew what it was to love.

How do Gurov and Anna Sergeevna love one another? Not unnaturally, Chekhov describes the affair from the man's point of view. As one might expect, Gurov's love for Anna Sergeevna has its romantic side. It is associated with the beauty of nature, for it is helped into existence by the view of the sea at Oreanda. When, back in Moscow, Gurov thinks of Anna, he poeticizes her: the whole affair becomes the subject of a daydream, and ultimately an obsession. So, perhaps, did Chekhov's thoughts dwell on Olga Knipper when she was in Moscow and he recalled their time in Yalta and journey through an area of great natural beauty.

Olga Knipper, however, was no dream. And Anna Sergeevna is not seen solely in terms of "poetry," even by Gurov. Forced to seek Anna out in her home town, from this point Gurov is back in reality. At the theatre he — and the reader — see her as a "small woman who was in no way remarkable, with a cheap-looking lorgnette in her hand." But this does not detract from her appeal for him (and it enhances her appeal for the reader). The romantic heroine has become a creature of flesh and blood, and Gurov still loves her: "she . . . now filled his whole life, she was his joy and his grief, the sole happiness that he now desired; and to the sound of the bad orchestra, the wretched philistine violins, he mused on how fine she was. He mused and dreamed dreams."

Gurov dreams — but dreaming is not enough for him. He has tasted happiness: the affair in Yalta was happy, in spite of Anna's sense of guilt. His love there developed from when, after Anna's self-recrimination and his irritation, they suddenly laughed together. This laugh denotes the beginning of communication: the tension relaxes and they behave normally, and find enjoyment in each other's company as well as in "love." Love, in fact, has come down to earth. Sex, communication, and simple companionship all play their part in it, in addition to "poetry."

And there the problem lies: the love-affair being rooted in reality, Anna and Gurov have to face the world's problems. Gurov, unlike Laevsky and Laptev, has found romantic love: but he also wants the companionship that Laevsky and Laptev had, and because he and Anna Sergeevna are already married, he cannot have it.

The situation, indeed the entire plot of "The Lady with the Dog," is obvious, even banal, and its merit as a work of art lies in the artistry with which Chekhov has preserved in the story a balance between the poetic and the prosaic, and in the careful characterization, dependent upon the use of half-tones. Soviet critics have a valid point when they regard Gurov as a sort of Everyman; "The Lady with the Dog" is an essentially simple exposition of a commonplace theme. Unlike in "The Duel" and "Three Years," in "The Lady with the Dog" Chekhov has made no attempt to investigate the problems of love: the conclusion of "The Lady with the Dog" is left really and truly open: there is no suggestion, nor have we any inkling, of what the future may bring: "And it seemed that in a very little while an answer would be found, and a new and beautiful life would begin. And to both it was evident that the end was far, far away, and that the hardest, most complicated part was only just beginning."

There can be no doubt but that the policy of expounding questions without presuming to answer them—that policy which Chekhov had declared to be the writer's task[3]—suited his style best. A full appreciation of Chekhov's work requires of the reader a certain degree of involvement, a response intellectual, or, as in the case of his love-stories, emotional, that Chekhov invites rather than commandeers. Ultimately, all depends on how Chekhov is read; but much depends on his striking the delicate balance between sentimentality and flatness.

All must surely agree that the right balance has been achieved in the final scene of "The Lady with the Dog," which is as direct an appeal to the heart as can be found in Chekhov's fiction:

> His hair was already beginning to turn grey. And it struck him as strange that he had aged so in the last few years, and lost his good looks. Her shoulders, on which he had lain his hands, were warm and shook slightly. He felt a pang of compassion for this life that was still warm and beautiful, but which would probably soon begin to fade and wither, like his own life. Why did she love him so? He had always appeared to women as something which he was not, and they had loved in him not him himself, but a creature of their own imagination, which they had sought again and again in their own lives; and then, when they perceived their mistake, they loved him all the same. And not one of them had been happy with him. Time passed, he would strike up an acquaintance, have an affair, and part, but never once had he loved; he had had everything he might wish for, only not love.
>
> And only now, when his hair had gone grey, he had fallen in love properly, genuinely—for the first time in his life.

This passage, read in the light of what we know of the author, gains a new dimension of pathos. The history of Gurov's relationships with women is a transmutation of Chekhov's history, and the essential point of the fiction was reality for him: true love had come too late, and complete happiness — poetry and communication and companionship — was impossible.

Chekhov wrote that Gurov and Anna Sergeevna "loved one another . . . as husband and wife." But how are we to explain the incongruity of this bland phrase "as husband and wife" in the context of Chekhov's entire oeuvre, in which the love of husband and wife is thwarted and cheapened — virtually never, in fact, seen to exist? Gurov and Anna are, after all, husband and wife, and he does not love his wife, nor she her husband. The irony here, whether conscious or unconscious, finds its origin in Chekhov's apparently unshakeable belief that an ideal love somewhere, somehow could exist.

2

It seems then cruel indeed that he should see fate cheat him of the chance of such love. His happiness was incomplete; and it is difficult not to regard Chekhov's situation as tragic. And yet one question remains. Could Chekhov, so happy as he stood on the threshold of love, ever have crossed that threshold, even in more fortunate circumstances? Could he have lived with love instead of dreaming about it? There is of course no evidence to suggest that his feelings for Olga Knipper would have altered with the passage of time, had she stayed constantly by his side. But evidence there is that, to the last, love as Chekhov conceived it retained its distant, intangible quality.

Konstantin Stanislavsky wrote of Chekhov's last years: "He dreamed of a new play . . . two friends, both young men, love one and the same woman. Their relationship with one another is complicated by their common love and jealousy. It ends with both of them setting off on a trip to the North Pole. The set for the last act consists of a huge ship wedged in the ice-floes. In the final scene of the play the two friends see a white phantom gliding across the ice. It is clear this is the shade of the soul of the beloved who has died far away in their country."

Despite the original visual effects this would have entailed — reminiscent of similarly unusual sound-effects in the plays that were realized — the ostensibly prosaic provincial world of those plays seems a far cry from this fantasy, and it is easy to comprehend Stanislavsky's comment that the plot was "somehow un-Chekhovian."

And yet it is truly, deeply, Chekhovian. This sketch of a plot shows clearly that, where love was the issue, a dissociation from facts and retreat into a dream world was for Chekhov a continuing process: that the romantic heroine could only be such in apotheosis. In the real world she provokes complications—but her shade is mysterious, beautiful, and fascinating.

And thus before we regard Chekhov's life as tragic, there is an important factor to bear in mind: the possibility that Chekhov, never to experience the reality of a normal marriage, was perhaps by this very misfortune preserved from a disillusionment in his ideal of love which might have proved more bitter than any irony of destiny. Thus the very significance—the supreme significance—which love as an ideal had for Chekhov provides us with an alternative view of his fate. It is not a tragedy: there is no victim. And Chekhov, whose dislike of self-dramatization was one of his most attractive qualities, would surely have preferred this latter view.

Notes

1. B. S. Meilakh in his article "Dva resheniya odnoi temy" states that in "The Lady with the Dog" Chekhov was seeking to present in terms of everyday people (i.e. not the nobility) the problem Tolstoy had posed in *Anna Karenina*: how can there be happiness in the false society that has made it possible for two such dissimilar people as Anna and Karenin to be united? Meilakh writes: Anna Karenina "perishes as the victim of the cruel mores which constituted the norm of existence for a person of her milieu." Chekhov, he holds, was showing his lovers to be in virtually the same predicament; but by not resolving the problem in death, Chekhov was suggesting that the more the situation seems impossible, the more one should intensify the search for an exit. In fact, Tolstoy was if anything more concerned with doing away with the evils of the old order than Chekhov: in "The Lady with the Dog" the lovers blame fate, not society, for their predicament, and the way in which they confront their situation probably only means that Chekhov preferred less dramatic effects and positive statements than Tolstoy, and did not wish to copy the latter too closely. For a discussion of the similarities between *Anna Karenina* and "The Lady with the Dog," and an interesting analysis of the artistic methods used in "The Lady with the Dog," see Winner, pp. 216–25.

2. K. M. Vinogradova, "Stranitsa iz chernovoi rukopisi rasskaza 'Dama s sobachkoi'." Vinogradova maintains that Chekhov's alterations to the first-published text of "The Lady with the Dog" were made to underline the theme of Gurov's regeneration. However, the changes she adduces seem rather to have been dictated by artistic considerations, and with the aim of making both lovers appear more ordinary, less wholly good, less wholly bad. Chekhov cuts out, for example, a series of coarse rejoinders that Gurov makes to Anna Sergeevna in the bedroom scene: which would have been better left in, had Chekhov wished to point up the change in Gurov's character to the utmost.

3. See letter to A. S. Suvorin, 27 October 1888, where Chekhov wrote: ". . . you are confusing two things: solving the problem and the correct exposition of the problem. In *Anna Karenina* and [*Evgeni*] *Onegin* not a single problem is solved, but they are wholly satisfying, just because all the problems in them are correctly set out."

On The Plays

[An Introduction to Chekhov's Plays]

Richard Peace*

Chekhov, as a playwright, is the inheritor of a Russian tradition which, deeply indebted to Western models, nevertheless has its own recognizable idiom; in the words of one critic it exhibits "a magnificent picture gallery, but no great narrative ingenuity."[1] Although this characterization specifically refers to the "comedic tradition that leads from Griboedov to Chekhov," the observation is broadly true for Russian literature as a whole, with its emphasis on character (i.e. psychology) at the expense of the neatly tailored plot.

Chekhov is also the inheritor of another Russian tradition, according to which seminal plays were written by authors excelling in other genres (Pushkin, Gogol, Lermontov, Turgenev, Tolstoy). Chekhov only achieved success in the theater towards the end of his life, when he already enjoyed an established reputation as a writer of short stories. This fact undoubtedly conditioned his approach to dramatic art; his stage settings at times contain evidence of a striving for total authorial control more appropriate to description in the short story than to the business-like deployment of properties and scenery for a producer and actors. Thus in Act IV of *Uncle Vanya* the stage directions describe the map of Africa as: [*obviously useless to anyone here*]; the setting for the first act of *The Three Sisters* has the direction: [*outside it is sunny, gay*]; and Chekhov's prescriptions for the set of Act II of *The Cherry Orchard* (with its town *"which can be seen only in very good, clear weather"*) push the technology of scenic illusion to its limits.[2] Such directions are at once specific and yet intangible. They recall the descriptive devices of Chekhov's short stories; for they are in essence indicators of mood.

"Mood" may seem a term over-used in Chekhovian criticism, but it is an indispensable concept. The very essence of mood is its lack of precision: it is a complex, emotional, only just sub-rational reaction to meaning and significance not clearly apprehended: a response to elusive suggestion

---

*From *Chekhov: A Study of the Four Major Plays* by Richard Peace (New Haven, Conn.: Yale University Press, 1983), 1–15. Reprinted by permission of the publisher.

rather than precise statement. Unfortunately its very vagueness has often led to its being used in criticism as a woolly dampener to further analysis and discussion.

Chekhov's preoccupation with the elusive, less dynamic emotions of "mood" appears to cut across the traditional concept of drama as action. Thus Harvey Pitcher comments on the development implied in the reworking of the earlier *Wood Demon* into *Uncle Vanya*: "What Chekhov has done is to replace a play of action by a play of emotional content."[3] The observation is good as far as it goes, but Pitcher (who wishes "to bury alike both Chekhov the social partisan, and Chekhov the ironist") reduces everything to "emotion" and is against "vast coded documents which can only be deciphered with the utmost patience."[4] The truth lies somewhere in between: literature is not an abstract art — it cannot abrogate meaning. Chekhov's world is poised between emotion and reason, and his drama combines mood with action, much as his comedy mixes laughter with pathos.

The emotional atmosphere (mood) of a Chekhov play is achieved through numerous devices. His titles may call obvious attention to symbol (*The Seagull, The Cherry Orchard*) but for the creation of mood such symbolism must retain a degree of ambiguity throughout. The sets, in their evocation of significant place, are also redolent of symbolism (the nursery in *The Cherry Orchard*; the study-cum-estate office in *Uncle Vanya*; the garden and the trees in the final act of *The Three Sisters*). A natural setting may be conducive to a lyrical mood, and atmosphere can be evoked through sounds — some musical: piano, guitar, concertina, snatches of song; some ominous: a distant shot, a breaking string, the thud of axes. Omen itself has a distinct role to play in the building up of vague feelings of presentiment. Akin to this is the extensive use of literary quotation, which surrounds each play with a penumbra of partially stated meaning. This shadowy periphery is also the abode of non-appearing characters, whose influence upon those on stage may often be considerable, and from this realm beyond the wings there stray from time to time odd episodic characters, vatic vagrants whose presence is inexplicably disturbing. Conversations, which seem disconnected and are interrupted by random remarks, contrive, nevertheless, to suggest some interrelated significance.[5] The device is most obvious at the beginning of *The Three Sisters*, where two apparently unrelated conversations form a dramatically meaningful whole. Nonsense words (*tram, tam, tam* or *ta-ra-ra bumbiya*) can also be imbued with significance, and gestures and small actions communicate meaning symbolically and visually (Gaev's imaginary billiard game, and the constant looking at watches). Above all there is the adroit use of pauses, where silence takes on an eloquence denied to mere words.[6]

All these devices have a common factor: they are referential and allusive — they suggest rather than state. As such they invite interpretation, and must have seemed to Nemirovich-Danchenko and Stanislavsky ready-made material for the new director-dominated productions of the Moscow Arts Theater. The interpretation of mood was one of the chief sources of disagreement between author and producer, but although Chekhov on occasion seemed to be in despair at the way his plays were being staged, the only advice he seemed capable of giving was to hint in the enigmatic, elusive spirit of the plays themselves. To Stanislavsky's appeals for elucidation Chekhov replied: "But I have written it all. I am not a producer. I am a doctor." Such observations as he did vouchsafe were felt by Stanislavsky to be "puzzles" (rebuses).[7] In this respect Chekhov's attitude to his later plays appears to differ markedly from his earlier urge to analyse and interpret *Ivanov*.[8]

Chekhov did not invent "mood" in the theater, but he brought its techniques to perfection. A. N. Ostrovsky's play *The Thunderstorm* (1859) has many of the lyrical, poetic qualities often associated with Chekhovian theater. The symbolism of the title and the motif of birds are developed in the play itself. Ostrovsky's outdoor sets breathe an almost Chekhovian magic, and atmosphere is created through omens (the mural depicting Gehenna) as well as by episodic vatic characters (the mad noblewoman). Particularly Chekhovian are the sounds of the guitar, the snatches of song and the literary quotations: Ostrovsky's autodidact Kuligan seems to find at least a nominal echo in Chekhov's representative of provincial intelligentsia in *The Three Sisters* — Kulygin. Moreover, like Chekhov, Ostrovsky is interested in the psychology of his characters (particularly his heroine) rather than in dramatic action as such.

Turgenev's play *A Month in the Country* has also been seen as a forerunner of Chekhovian theater. Here too action is subordinated to psychological portraiture. Valency, in comparing Chekhov's methods with those of Turgenev, has made a strong case for the innovatory nature of Turgenev's characterization, which he claims is the technique of impressionism: the characters "discover themselves little by little, and are constantly surprised at the things they feel and do."[9] Nevertheless for the purposes of his plot Turgenev relies on the well-worn device of eavesdropping—a stock situation also found in his novels. It is significant that Chekhov uses this theatrical cliché in his early plays *Platonov* and *Ivanov*, but in his later plays it is used only once (*Uncle Vanya*) and there its psychological role transcends any suggestion of a mere hackneyed mechanism of plot.[10] Indeed the recurrent situation of the true Chekhovian play is not overhearing but "underhearing"—the inability, even refusal, of one character to listen to another. Such psychological "deafness" had already been developed as a social theme in Griboedov's *Woe from Wit* (1825), indeed Chekhov's comic characters Ferapont (*The Three Sisters*) and Firs (*The Cherry Orchard*) may owe something to Griboedov's Tugoukhovsky, but, more importantly, in *The Cherry Orchard*, as in *Woe from Wit*, the younger generation is the bearer of truths which an older generation does not wish to know; Lyubov Andreevna, like Famusov before her, covers up her ears in a symbolic act of non-hearing.[11]

Nevertheless, *A Month in the Country* is obviously far closer than *Woe from Wit* to the later plays of Chekhov. It is closer in its naturalism as well as in its poetic symbolism. Turgenev, as he does elsewhere, uses trees symbolically. Thus Rakitin, whose very name is derived from a tree (*rakita* = "willow") attempts to evoke a romantic mood in his wayward mistress by poetic words on nature, but his contrast of the strong oak to the radiant birch is obviously to be taken as a symbolic statement about himself and Islayeva. Like Gaev in *The Cherry Orchard* he is rebuked for such elevated thoughts on nature. The motif of trees recurs frequently in Chekhov's plays, but his symbolic use of the theme is at once more subtle and more generalized. This scene between Rakitin and Islaeva strikes yet another Chekhovian note in the "silences" which Turgenev calls for in his stage directions.[12]

The allusive quality of Turgenev's writing is important. In Act IV of *A Month in the Country* Shpigel'sky seeks to explain himself through a song, but more significant is the use of literary quotation. Rakitin is the friend of Islayeva's husband, and when in Act I Islaeva tells Rakitin: "You see, I, like Tatyana, can also say: 'What's the point of dissembling?' " her fragment of quotation alludes to far more than it actually states: it indicates her love for Rakitin, whilst at the same time asserting her faithfulness to her husband. Every Russian audience would catch the reference to Chapter Eight, stanza XLVIII of Pushkin's *Eugene Onegin*, would know what precedes these brief words and what comes after: "I love you (what's the point of dissembling) / But I have been given to another. / I shall be eternally faithful to him."[13] The impact of any play depends as much on its audience as it does upon its performers, and the special susceptibilities of a Russian audience are often overlooked by Western critics. Education in Russia has traditionally been based on oral skills to a greater extent than in most English-speaking countries. Every educated Russian has a rich fund of poetry which he knows by heart, and public recitations of poetry, both classical and contemporary, are a prominent feature of Russian cultural life. Anyone who has attended such a recital, given perhaps by a well-known actor, will know that the performer has only to falter a moment for there to be innumerable voices from the audience prompting him with the correct lines, so that the impression may be gained that the audience knows the poem better than the reciter himself.

Far more, perhaps, than in any other culture, a writer in Russia can play upon the literary memory of his audience or of his readers. It is important to bear in mind this ability of a Russian audience to participate in the creative act through its literary memory, when we come to look at the use Chekhov makes of literary quotation in his own plays (such as the repeated quotation in *The Three Sisters* of lines from Pushkin's *Ruslan and Lyudmila*).

The tradition of censorship in Russia has been such that readers and audiences alike have long been attuned to the finer points of oblique statement and innuendo. Theater in Russia can be particularly vibrant; producers and actors have a way of bringing pointed meaning to words which look innocuous on the printed page. Thus classics of the nineteenth-century repertoire, such as *Woe from Wit*, or the stage adaptation of Dostoevsky's story *The Village of Stepanchikovo and Its Inhabitants* can be played in such a way that without any deviation from the text a Soviet audience is aware of its relevance for contemporary life.[14]

Having said this, it must also be conceded that Chekhov could not always count on his audiences. The dispiriting failure of the opening night of *The Seagull* was as much due to the audience's expectations (see p. 17), as was its spectacular success when it was later produced by the Moscow Arts Theater. Chekhov's plays were unfamiliarly new; but for all that, they built on the work of previous dramatists. When Styan lists among Chekhov's new techniques: "experiments with the empty stage, his use of sounds to enlarge the area of our perception or to illuminate the condition of a character," we must not forget that, almost seventy years before, Gogol had shown him the way.[15] At the end of Act IV of *The Government Inspector* the stage is left empty for the departure of Khlestakov, which is impressionistically conveyed through off-stage conversations, cries and the sound of troyka bells. Chekhov, like Gogol, shuns the sub-plot, but suggests intrigue beyond the confines of the stage through his use of non-appearing characters — a device which goes back, in fact, to Griboyedov.[16]

Elements of the Chekhovian play may even be seen in eighteenth-century comedy. Thus in *Uncle Vanya* Marina's "comic" prop of the knitted sock, has its precursor in D. I. Fonvizin's *Brigadier* (1769) which opens, like the Chekhov play, with one of its characters (the brigadier's wife) knitting a sock on stage.[17] V. V. Kapnist had also experimented with the ironical effects of the interdependence of apparently unrelated conversations in his comedy *Malicious Litigation (Yabeda)* of 1798. In Act I scene viii of Kapnist's play an attorney conducts one conversation with the chairman of a civil court about his employer's litigation, whilst at the same time he carries on another with the chairman's wife concerning goods which he has brought with him as bribes.[18]

One can sense Chekhov himself experimenting with his techniques in the earlier playlets. Thus *Swan Song* (1887) which is the dramatic reworking of the short story *Kalkhas*, can be seen as an exercise in the extended use of literary quotations, and *Tatiana Repina* (1889), which is Chekhov's theatrical reply to Suvorin the dramatist, has been seen by at least one scholar as: "the first glimmerings of the drama of mood."[19] The playlet is remarkable in that it is constructed entirely of parallel and apparently unrelated areas of speech, through which Chekhov suggests ironical commentary (scandalous gossip conducted against the background of the wedding service). A second Chekhovian feature is the centering of *Tatiana Repina* not on dramatic action but on a ritualized event, capable of charging the playlet with its own "ready made" atmosphere and drama.

Success in the theater for Chekhov was by no means immediate, yet he wished to write plays almost from the start of his literary career. His first attempt dates from 1878 — a play without an authenticated title, which is usually referred to as *Platonov* in English (after its chief protagonist) but should perhaps be called *Fatherlessness (Bezotsovshchina)*. It has a long rambling plot, but it is full of glimpses of the mature Chekhov, and Donald Rayfield is probably right to see it as the source of all his later plays.[20] *Ivanov*, Chekhov's next full-length play, certainly appears to be a reworking of *Platonov*. It exists in two versions (1887 and 1889) both of which, unlike the earlier play, were staged. In its revised version *Ivanov* enjoyed a measure of success, nevertheless it cannot be regarded as a truly Chekhovian play. Its hero, Ivanov, is married to a young Jewish heiress, who has not brought him a dowry because she has been disowned by her staunchly religious parents. Heavily in debt, Ivanov becomes involved in a liaison with another heiress, Sasha, the daughter of a friend and neighbour. Ivanov's behavior drives his consumptive wife to an early death, but when he is free to marry Sasha he is denounced by his wife's doctor, and because of this, and the malicious gossip which surrounds him, he commits suicide (in the first version he succumbs to the pressure and dies a rather improbable natural death). Ivanov is hardly an edifying character, yet it is obvious that Chekhov is presenting him as a candidate for his audience's sympathy.

John Tulloch has persuasively argued that Chekhov based his portrait of Ivanov on the scientific theories of the time, and that the play has to be seen more as a socio-medical case study of neurasthenia. He stresses that Chekhov had the professional outlook of a doctor, which in the Russian tradition implied medicine with a sociological bias.[21] Yet one might also quote the words of Ivanov himself: "It is possible to be an excellent physician and at the same time not know anything about people."[22] If *Ivanov* shows evidence of Chekhov's professional outlook as a Russian doctor, it also bears the trademarks of his other, and more important, profession — the calling of a Russian writer. His hero fits into that tradition of Russian writing (Griboedov, Lermontov, Turgenev, Goncharov, Dostoevsky among others) which sought to create typical "heroes" of their time. Chekhov's very insistence on the name Ivanov seems designed to assert the typicality of his "Russianness."[23]

The decade of the 1880s, after the assassination of Tsar Alexander II in 1881, was a period of political repression and stagnation in Russian intellectual life. It was a time when heroism seemed impossible; a period of so-called "little deeds" (*malye dela*). It is in these terms that Sasha angrily taunts local society, in her defence of Ivanov: "Or if you could all *do* something, something quite small, hardly noticeable, but something a bit original and daring, so that we young ladies could look at you and say 'Oh,' admiringly, for once in our lives!"[24] Ivanov, himself, is a typical intellectual figure of his period, but as such he is aware of literary echoes from a previous age: "I'm dying of shame at the thought that I, a healthy, strong man, have somehow got transformed into a sort of Hamlet, or Manfred, or one of those 'superfluous' people, the devil knows which! There are some pitiable people who are flattered when you call them Hamlets or 'superfluous,' but to me it's a disgrace! It stirs up my pride, a feeling of shame oppresses me, and I suffer."[25] The term "Hamlet" was almost synonymous with "superfluous man" (cf. Turgenev's story *The Hamlet of the Shchigrovski Region*). References to Hamlet are particularly pronounced in *Platonov* (as well, of course, as in the later play *The Seagull*). Nevertheless the true era of the so-called "superfluous man" had been the three decades between 1825 and 1855 which corresponded to the reign of Tsar Nicholas I. Like the period of the 1880s this was a time of repression, which had also been occasioned by a political event—the suppression of the Decembrist uprising in 1825. Ivanov exhibits the characteristics of key figures in the literature of this earlier period. Like Griboedov's Chatsky he is at odds with local society.[26] Like Turgenev's Rudin he is a man full of great potential, which he seems incapable of realising; and again like Rudin, he demurs when his "heroine" suggests that they should abscond. Nevertheless the terms of his reply suggest yet another of these "superfluous" heroes: "I feel too lazy to walk to that door, and you talk of America . . ."[27]

The laziest man in Russian literature is the hero of I. A. Goncharov's novel *Oblomov* (1859). Like the other figures discussed above, Oblomov is incapable of forming a serious relationship with a strong heroine, yet she, Olga Ilinskaya, wishes to "resurrect" him. In a similar way Sasha is accused by Ivanov of having set herself the goal of resurrecting the human being in him and he characterizes their love affair as a literary stereotype:[28] "And this love affair of ours is all just something commonplace and trite: 'He lost heart and lost his grip on things. She appeared, cheerful and strong in spirit, and held out a helping hand.' It's beautiful, but it's only like what happens in novels. In real life you don't. . . ."[29] In Goncharov's novel the psychological motivation of Olga Ilinskaya is equally as fascinating as that of Oblomov himself. Sasha provides us with an insight which could be just as valid for Olga: "There are a lot of things men don't understand. Every girl is more attracted by a man who's a failure than by one who's a success, because what she wants is active love. . . . Do you understand that? Active love. Men are taken up with their work and so love has to take a back seat with them. To have a talk with his wife, to take a stroll with her in the garden, to pass time pleasantly with her, to weep a little on her grave—that's all. But for us—love is life."[30] In a variant of this scene Sasha actually calls Ivanov "Oblomov," but Chekhov discarded such open identification.[31] In reinterpreting Goncharov he undoubtedly wished to avoid the ready-made stereotype, and a polemical point is the disowning of positive features which certain critics had attributed to Oblomovism itself:

> IVANOV. I can't enjoy spiritual idleness and see it as something noble and lofty. Idleness is idleness, weakness is weakness—I don't know any other names for them.[32]

Central to the play is the assertion that man is psychologically far more complex than the gossip-mongers of local society and the self-appointed moralist, Dr Lvov, can ever imagine. In an important speech in Act III, scene vi, Ivanov not only rebukes Lvov for his simplistic view of human motivation, but at the same time appears to take up Lebedev's observation in the preceding scene, that man is a mere samovar.[33] This polemical point about the complexity of human psychology will be illustrated more impressively in the later plays: in *Ivanov* itself it has more the role of a programmatic statement.

Nevertheless it is national psychology and sociological interpretation which are uppermost in the detailed explanation of his play communicated to Suvorin in a letter of 30 December 1888. It appears from this that *Ivanov* is about the Russian temperament itself, which Chekhov sees as conditioned by periods of excitability followed by troughs of depression. He even draws a graph to illustrate his argument showing that with each successive phase the troughs of depression get lower: "Disillusionment, apathy, nervous instability, being easily tired are the invariable results of excessive excitability and such excitability is characteristic of our young people in the highest degree. Take literature. Take the present. . . ."[34] Although Chekhov here seems to be offering a national and social account of the medical condition known as manic depression, his view of the polarisation of the Russian temperament between excitability and depression, bouts of activity and periods of lethargy, is not new. The critic N. A. Dobrolyubov, pointing to a similar pattern in Russian history, had likened the intelligentsia of his day to the legendary folk hero Ilya Muromets who slept for thirty years then awoke to perform doughty deeds.[35]

Chekhov's argument in his letter to Suvorin, as we have seen, is partly based on literature, and here he may have had *Oblomov* in mind; for there had also been "high-points" of activity in Oblomov's life (initially, as a young man, under the influence of Shtolts and later in response to Olga). Indeed, in giving his hero both the name and the patronymic of Ilya (Ilya Ilyich) Goncharov may have been seeking to link him with the symbolic figure of Ilya Muromets.

In *Ivanov*, the aristocratic Shabelsky says of Ivanov's self-appointed critic Dr Lvov, that he thinks of himself as a second Dobrolyubov, and regards him (Shabelsky) as a rogue and a serf-owner, because he wears a velvet jacket and is dressed by a manservant.[16] There are clear references in this to Dobrolyubov as the critic of "Oblomovism." In 1859 Dobrolyubov had written an extremely influential article on Goncharov's novel (*What Is Oblomovism?*) in which he had argued that Oblomov was the summation of all the gentleman heroes in literature up to that point: that he was the quintessential "superfluous man." A similar objective seems to have been in Chekhov's mind when writing *Ivanov:*

> I cherished the daring dream of summing up all that has been written up to now about whining and melancholy people, and to put an end to these writings with my *Ivanov*. It seemed to me that all Russian men of letters and playwrights had felt the need to depict the depressed man, and that they had all written instinctively without having definite images and a view on the matter. In conception I more or less got it right, but the execution is worthless, I should have waited.[37]

It is interesting that this same letter contains the often quoted statement about himself as a writer of lowly origin who had to squeeze the slave out of himself drop by drop and who one day woke up to find real human blood in his veins. His injunction to write a story about such a figure was never fulfilled. The nearest he came to depicting such a social parvenu in positive terms was in his play *The Cherry Orchard*. Lopakhin has certain autobiographical features and is a more credible version of Goncharov's Shtolts – the practical man of affairs of mixed social origin.

In 1886 Chekhov published a "Literary Table of Ranks" in the humorous publication *Splinters (Oskolki)* (No. 19, 10 May).[38] This parody of the hierarchy of ranks in the civil service left the top grade as yet unoccupied, but placed Tolstoy and Goncharov together in the second grade. Nevertheless in 1889, after the production of the second version of *Ivanov*, Chekhov reread *Oblomov* and, in a letter to Suvorin at the beginning of May, wrote of his disillusionment with the novel and its author: he had completely revised his views of its artistic merits. In his next letter to Suvorin (4 May 1889) Chekhov defends himself against the charge of laziness, but fears that he is like Goncharov: "whom I do not like and who is ten times head and shoulders above me in talent."[39]

In *The Wood Demon* (1889) Hélène is seen as the embodiment of laziness, and she is characterized by Voynitsky as an "Oblomov."[40] This reference was removed when the play was rewritten as *Uncle Vanya*, and Chekhov strongly objected to critics who attempted to interpret the play in terms of Goncharov's novel:

> I have read reviews of *Uncle Vanya* in the *Courier* and *News of the Day*. I saw an article about "Oblomov" in the *Russian Record*, but I didn't read it. I can't stand this making something out of nothing, this forced linking with *Oblomov*, with *Fathers and Sons* etc. You can forcibly compare any play with what you want, and if Sanin and Ignatov had

taken Nozdrev and King Lear instead of Oblomov, it would have turned out equally profound and readable. I do not read such articles, so as not to foul up my temper.[41]

Given such a categorical authorial pronouncement, it might seem that any critic would be foolish to draw further parallels between Oblomov and Chekhov's heroes, yet the echoes are there in the later plays; indeed in the recurrent theme of ineffectuality confronted by the exhortation to work we have something of the dilemma which lies at the heart of Goncharov's novel.

Chekhov felt the parallel with Oblomov even in his own life. We have already seen that in reply to Suvorin's charge of laziness, he conceded that he felt like Goncharov, and he made a similar excuse to Stanislavsky towards the end of his life as he was working on *The Cherry Orchard:* "I was ill, but am recovered now, my health has improved, and if I do not work as I ought, it is because of the cold (it is only eleven degrees in my study), lack of company and, probably, laziness, which was born in 1859, that is one year before me."[42] The reference to the publication date of *Oblomov* is unmistakable, yet Chekhov was anything but a lazy man; he did, however, suffer from a debilitating disease, and did not wish to face up to it. A jocular condemnation of the "Oblomov" within himself was one way of minimizing his symptoms and coping with a problem he knew to be incurable. The charge of "Oblomovism" from others was another matter—it touched on a sensitive area of his own life, even though the term was applied solely to his heroes. It is undeniable, nevertheless, that the protagonists of his plays lack drive: "The usual Chekhovian character is a half-hearted participant in an action that barely excites his interest."[43] Through such heroes Chekhov was not merely purging an element which he most dreaded in himself, he was also portraying a state of mind endemic in Russian society at the end of the nineteenth century. In the political reaction which followed the assassination of Tsar Alexander II even the most energetic leaders of the intelligentsia suddenly felt themselves superfluous. M. Ye. Saltykov-Shchedrin (of whose great output Chekhov felt envious)[44] expressed this mood most strikingly in his Gogolian "Fairy Tale" *The Adventures of Kramolnikov* (1886) — Kramolnikov wakes up one morning and suddenly realizes that he doesn't exist.[45] Such new "non-people" could obviously be related to the former "superfluous men," of whom Oblomov had been seen as the epitome. But *Oblomov* is also a novel about social change (it purports to have been written in answer to the question: "where do beggars come from?").[46] The reforms of the 1860s, anticipated in Goncharov's novel, had resulted by the turn of the century in a rapidly changing society. The old landowning gentry were a waning social force, losing ground to the new and energetic entrepreneur, whom Goncharov had not so much depicted, as prophesied, in the figure of Shtolts. The social theme is important for all Chekhov's plays and it is significant that its dominant motif is dispossession.

It has often been observed that Chekhov's theatrical technique combines a subtle blend of naturalism and symbolism.[47] He wrote at a time when the Russian theater had found, in Stanislavsky, its great exponent of showing life as it is. The Moscow Arts Theater productions stressed the naturalism of the plays to the point where, Chekhov felt, it became absurd. The naturalism of sets, acting and effects was boldly emphasized, and Stanislavsky was particularly fond of multiplying incidental, off-stage sounds far in excess of those called for by the author. Stanislavsky tells the following story against himself: " 'Listen!' Chekhov told someone, but so that I could hear, 'I shall write a new play and it will begin like this: "How marvellous, how silent! No birds can be heard, no dogs, no cuckoos, no owls, no nightingales, no clocks, no bells and not a single cricket." ' Of course he was getting at me."[48] Stanislavsky's philosophy of production, his famous "method," was constantly developing. Later he would take a different view of his earlier Chekhov productions.[49]

Nevertheless, naturalism as such was not the order of the day. Throughout Europe the 1890s marked an almost universal flight from the humdrum and everyday; symbolism, decadence, impressionism dominated the fin de siècle mood. Chekhov was aware of these currents, and in his new theater of the 1890s he contrived, whilst retaining the naturalistic surface, to incorporate an element of intangibility and mystery proclaimed in the new art forms—a dimension characterized by Valency as the "Chekhovian 'Beyond' ": "The strangely unreal atmosphere in which the realities of his later plays are suspended. It is an atmosphere less mysterious and less explicit than the Maeterlinckian *au-delà*, and certainly more intelligible."[50]

Chekhov's earlier heroes, Platonov, Ivanov and Voynitsky (in *The Wood Demon*) are romantic figures alienated from the prosaic world in which they live. Not only do they convey a sense of looking back to an earlier period of Russian literature, but such self-indulgent, self-destructive romanticism is artistically at odds with the naturalistic vehicle of the plays themselves. It is significant that *The Seagull*, the play which gave Chekhov his first major success, and marked the onset of the theater of mood, should project the romantic, alienated hero at odds not merely with the society around him, but more importantly with that society's concept of theater. Treplev, in calling for new forms, is Chekhov struggling to find a way out of his own artistic impasse. The rivalry between Trigorin and Treplev reflects a debate within the author himself. The first "Chekhovian" play is a play of re-evaluation and self-examination.[51]

Notes

References to Chekhov's works are to the Academy of Sciences edition: A. P. Chekhov, *Polnoe sobranie sochinenii i pisem v tridtsati tomakh*, Moscow, 1974 onwards. For convenience this edition will be recorded as: *PSSP*, followed by a volume number in Roman and a page reference in Arabic numerals, but as the volumes devoted to letters are numbered independently, reference to these volumes will have the indication "(Letters)" before the Roman numeral.

1. M. Valency, *The Breaking String: The Plays of Anton Chekhov*, New York, 1966, p. 17 (cf. also *ibid*. p. 222).

2. Cf. Francis Fergusson, "*The Cherry Orchard*: A Theatre-Poem of the Suffering of Change," in *Chekhov, A Collection of Critical Essays*, ed. R. L. Jackson, Englewood Cliffs, New Jersey, 1967, p. 152.

3. Harvey Pitcher, *The Chekhov Play*, London, 1973, p. 78.

4. *Ibid*. pp. 4, 214.

5. Nils Åke Nilsson denies any significance other than compositional to such remarks. See his "Intonation and Rhythm in Chekhov's Plays," in Jackson, pp. 172–3. Valency, however, considers that "it is seldom that the associative links are entirely lacking," but adds: "It is entirely probable that the seemingly disjunctive nature of Chekhov's dialogue reflects his own habit of mind." See Valency, p. 237. Pitcher considers such speech habits a trait common to Russians. See Pitcher, p. 28.

6. "During the pauses it is as though inaudible words are carried across the stage on light wings," Yu. Aykhenval'd (quoted in *PSSP*, XIII, p. 510).

7. K. S. Stanislavsky, *Moya zhizn' v iskusstve*, Moscow, 1962, p. 328.

8. Cf. Chekhov's long letter to Suvorin on *Ivanov* (30 Dec. 1888) *PSSP* (Letters), III, pp. 108–16.

9. Valency, p. 45.

10. Styan, however, sees Voynitsky's surprising of the "amorous" scene between Astrov and Yelena as "a grotesque stage trick." See J. L. Styan, *Chekhov in Performance. A Commentary on the Major Plays*, Cambridge, London, New York, Melbourne, 1971, p. 126.

11. Harvey Pitcher denies "lack of communication" as a theme in Chekhov's plays. See Pitcher, p. 25.

12. Cf. I. S. Turgenev, *Polnoe sobranie sochinenii i pisem v dvadtsati vos'mi tomakh*, III, Moscow, 1962, pp. 75–6.

13.   *Ya vas lyublyu (k chemu lukavit'?)*
                   No ya drugomu otdana,
                   Ya budu vek yemu verna.

Cf. Turgenev, *Poln. sob. soch.*, III, p. 58. Pushkin's "Novel in Verse" is itself full of literary allusions. For Russians literary echoes not only permeate literature, they also permeate life. See Peace, *Russian Literature and the Fictionalisation of Life*, Hull, 1976.

14. In Ostrovsky's play *The Forest* an actor manages to pass an outspoken judgement on local society by reciting a speech from Schiller's *Die Räuber*, and cannot be brought to account because, as he says, it has been passed by the censor. See A. N. Ostrovsky, *Polnoe sobranie sochinenii v dvenadtsati tomakh*, Moscow, 1974, III, p. 337.

15. Styan, p. 339.

16. For the influence of Gogol on Chekhov see Peace, *The Enigma of Gogol, An Examination of the Writings of N. V. Gogol and Their Place in the Russian Literary Tradition*, Cambridge, 1981, pp. 52, 89, 150, 191, 204, 247, 299, 321 n. 31, 330 n. 38, 337 n. 16.

17. See *Russkaya literatura XVIII veka*, compiled by G. P. Makogonenko, Leningrad, 1970, p. 290. Rayfield compares *Platonov* with *The Brigadier*. See D. Rayfield, *Chekhov: The Evolution of His Art*, London, 1975, p. 98 (but cf. Platonov's own rejection of the "raisonneur" figures of Fonvizin, *PSSP*, XI, p. 38).

18. Makogonenko, pp. 495–6. The following part of this exchange seems particularly pointed semantically:

KRIVOSUDOV. But I fobbed him off. He would have gone on with a whole lot of improbable things about the case, but I shut him up.

NAUMYCH   [to FEKLA]. A pound of mustard.

KRIVOSUDOV. I got him off my hands.

NAUMYCH. How much, sir, my master to you is indebted [to FEKLA] a skirt length of silk.

19. A. S. Dolinin (quoted in *PSSP*, XII, p. 368; cf. also *ibid.* p. 316).

20. Rayfield, p. 94.

21. J. Tulloch, *Chekhov: A Structuralist Study*, London and Basingstoke, 1980, pp. 7, 90.

22. *PSSP*, XII, p. 56.

23. Cf. Rayfield, p. 101. Chekhov spoke to V. G. Korolenko of writing a drama to be called *Ivan Ivanovich Ivanov*—"you understand. There are thousands of Ivanovs, an ordinary man, absolutely not a hero . . . ," *PSSP*, XII, p. 412. Chekhov also commented: "The word Russian often crops up when I describe Ivanov." See *The Oxford Chekhov*, trans. and edit. Ronald Hingley, London, New York, Toronto, 1967, II, p. 295.

24. *PSSP*, XII, pp. 29–30.

25. *Ibid.* p. 37.

26. His uncle Shabel'sky says that he himself played at being Chatsky as a young man, *PSSP*, XII, p. 33. Rayfield notes the influence of *Woe from Wit* on both *Platonov* and *Ivanov*. See Rayfield, p. 98.

27. *PSSP*, XII, p. 38.

28. *Ibid.* p. 72.

29. *Ibid.* p. 57.

30. *Ibid.* p. 59.

31. *Ibid.* p. 250 (cf. Hingley on Chekhov's "endearing distrust of clichés and literary stereotypes," *The Oxford Chekhov*, II, p. 6).

32. *PSSP*, XII, p. 71.

33. Cf. *Ibid.* pp. 50, 54–6.

34. *PSSP* (Letters), III, p. 111 (a somewhat similar view on the Russian as a sieve was expressed to Gorky. See Jackson, p. 202).

35. N. A. Dobrolyubov, *Sobranie sochinenii*, Moscow 1935, I, pp. 183–4 (cf. also the use of Dobrolyubov's term "A Realm of Darkness"—*temnoe tsarstvo*—in *Ivanov*, *PSSP*, XII, p. 34).

36. *PSSP*, XII, p. 33.

37. *PSSP* (Letters), III, p. 132.

38. *Ibid.* p. 421.

39. *Ibid.* pp. 201–2, 203.

40. *PSSP*, XII, p. 165.

41. *PSSP* (Letters), VIII, pp. 319, 596 and *PSS*, XIII, pp. 419, 459.

42. *PSSP* (Letters), XI, p. 142.

43. Valency, p. 246.

44. *PSSP* (Letters), II, pp. 332, 512.

45. Ye. M. Saltykov-Shchedrin, *Sobranie sochinenii v dvadtsati tomakh*, Moscow, 1976, XVI(1), p. 197.

46. I. A. Goncharov, *Sobranie sochinenii v shesti tomakh*. Moscow, 1972, IV, p. 510.

47. Cf. Stanislavsky, *Moya Zhizn'*, p. 275 and Vs. Meyerhold, "Naturalistic Theater and Theater of Mood," Jackson, pp. 62–8.

48. Stanislavsky, *Moya Zhizn'*, p. 329.

49. Vl. Prokof'ev, *V sporakh o Stanislavskom*, Moscow, 1976, p. 86.

50. Valency, p. 298.

51. "Written after a vow not to work for the theater again, it is an act of vengeance," Rayfield, p. 202.

Anton Chekhov and His Play without a Title

Thomas A. Eekman[*]

Chekhov's first play, the longest he ever wrote and with the largest cast, was finished in 1881 but never performed during his lifetime. The manuscript was discovered and published twenty years after his death,[1] and a first adaptation was staged almost thirty years after that.[2] It is a play without a title, because the title page was torn off; but following the example of David Magarshack, I shall call it *Platonov*, after the main protagonist. It has been studied by a few investigators[3] but not in such detail as Chekhov's other dramatic works, in any case not in a way commensurate with its significance as an early stage in his development as a writer.

Platonov is in some respects a peculiar work: in the first place, as mentioned, by reason of its length (it is about three times as long as the average of his later dramas) and the number of dramatis personae (twenty, not including "guests and servants"; *Uncle Vanya* has only eight, not including the "workmen"). Adaptions for both stage and film have had to shorten and simplify the action considerably. As an early text of the young Chekhov it deserves our attention. Its publication has modified existing views of Chekhov as a prose writer and dramatist.

Chekhov wrote his play when he was twenty or twenty-one years old, and a student of medicine at Moscow University. He had just left the provincial town of Taganrog to join his family in their poor and cramped lodgings. At the advice of his brother Alexander, he began sending short humorous pieces to the editors of third-rate weekly magazines, and many of them were published. It has often been pointed out that most of these early products did not have much literary value, as they were written hurriedly, without much inspiration or indeed, literary pretension, just to earn an extra ruble for the family. This judgment, if it is correct as far as

*From *Revue des études slaves* 31 (1954): 56–70, originally published as "Anton Tchékhoff et sa pièce sans titre." Translated for this volume by the author and reprinted by permission of the publisher, L'Institut d'études slaves, Paris.

his short stories are concerned, does not hold for his play. It may be long, even prolix, but it does not give the impression of having been written in haste. To the contrary, it seems that Chekhov devoted much time and effort to this work. The small copybooks in which he wrote it, and which he carefully preserved all his life, appear to have undergone at least three thorough revisions. His manuscript was copied by his younger brother Mikhail, and Chekhov showed it to Maria N. Ermolova, a celebrated actress of the period, hoping it would be accepted for production at the Moscow *Maly Teatr*. This proves the importance he attached to it; but unfortunately the result was a rejection, and the fair copy was torn to pieces.

After this first rebuff in his career as a playwright, Chekhov did not attempt to have his drama staged elsewhere or to have it published, and, as far as we know, he never returned to the text to adapt or revise it. Nonetheless, a whole series of elements from it (themes, characters, ideas) found a place in his later plays and even in some of his stories. It seems worth while to pay closer attention to these connections.

Numerous critics who have followed Chekhov's evolution as a writer point to the imperfections of his early production as evidence of a lack of personal and artistic maturity; whereas during the last ten or fifteen years of his life, notably in the dramatic works, he explored new directions and only then found his own road, his own themes and style. According to A. Derman, Chekhov is an artist who matured slowly and relatively late.[4] However, a close reading of *Platonov* shows that, notwithstanding its extravagance, the weakness of its construction, the long-winded dialogues, the excess of dramatic events and highly emotional words, this first more ambitious work by Chekhov displays an excellent mastery of stage technique, a remarkable understanding of theatrical potentialities, and skillful handling of dialogue, which is in many instances expressive and lively and at times creates a typically "Chekhovian" mood.

From childhood Chekhov had been a great theater lover and theatergoer. It seems certain that, even before writing *Platonov*, he had tried his hand at drama, although nothing is left of these early experiments.[5] We can therefore speak of *Platonov* as his first play. It is more than likely that he was influenced by certain second-rate Russian dramatists of the day.[6] But *Platonov* contains some features that are characteristic of his mature dramatic style: the incoherent conversations, the numerous pauses, the melancholy references to the good old days, to a desire to start life all over, or to escape this dull and dissatisfying existence.

It also turns out that the principal themes and even the main characters of his later writings are already recognizable in this early experiment. Chekhov has stated that in his literary work he dealt exclusively with what he knew from his own experience. Researchers have dug into his life in order to discover where and when he could have seen the character types that figure in his stories and plays, or at least the environment in which they occur. Thus it has been established that during his sojourn in Sumy in 1888, he must have first observed the types and the life-style of the landed gentry, gradually losing their wealth and energy — a preferred milieu of Chekhov's, especially in his dramas.[7] However, *Platonov* shows us that he had depicted this minor-gentry milieu in exactly the same way some eight years earlier, as a twenty-year-old student who never had any close relations with this class of Russian society. In general, his early writings do not directly reproduce his experience of his surroundings, contrary to his statement about creating exclusively from memory and experience. He rarely portrayed the people with whom he was most in contact — students, the university world, his family — and only somewhat more often, the world of lower journalism. He looked for his characters and themes primarily among the petite bourgeoisie, low officials, and similarly undistinguished, half-educated city dwellers, who were the most common and popular targets of the magazines in which Chekhov published his early short stories. And he also found them fairly often among the landed gentry, as was traditional for all Russian fiction, with the proviso, of course, that the censorship did not allow him to write too negatively, critically, or satirically about the highest echelons of society.

It seems reasonable to suppose that his preference for the portrayal of characters from the land-owning class can be at least partially explained by his attachment to certain literary traditions of his time. Thus Platonov and Ivanov, the protagonist of his next full-length play, can be regarded as the successors of types to be found in Griboedov, Pushkin, Lermontov, Turgenev, and others. One of the characters even compares Platonov to Chatsky. This is especially true of his theatrical works. Indeed, a play taking place entirely among peasants, lower-middle-class characters, clerks, etc., was most unusual throughout the entire nineteenth century. (For the peasant milieu, Pisemsky's *A Bitter Fate* and Tolstoy's *The Power of Darkness* were exceptions.) In Russian society — backward and predominantly agricultural — the *pomeshchiki* constituted a category that distinguished itself at least to some extent by a more colorful, varied, attractive way of life and a better education than the rest of the population. Chekhov wanted to portray the protagonist of his drama, Platonov, as he had observed the type in life around him, but he transposed him to the landed gentry, the normal and accepted milieu for any play. Chekhov was fascinated by this type; apparently he had known and observed it in his own surroundings, probably in the persons of his two older brothers.[8]

These brothers, Alexander and Nikolai, were rather well educated young men, and artistically gifted. However, they lacked the energy and perseverance to develop their talent, to be successful in their personal and professional lives, and were often lax and dissolute. Anton, younger but much more energetic and disciplined, constantly reproached his older brothers for their loose lives. Indolent types and misfits occur regularly in his works. Platonov is a young nobleman, initially a lad of great promise and an idealistic student. However, he will soon disappoint his friends, and he will not rise any higher than the post of village teacher. (Chekhov's choice of his hero's profession is a bit unusual for a Russian of Platonov's station in life and in those times; but after all, the movement of *khozhdenie v narod* had not taken place so long before.) Platonov possesses, or rather had possessed, high moral principles and is properly married, at least at the beginning of the play. He sometimes vehemently, and occasionally coarsely, protests against anything that seems vile to him. However, he is weak and lacks the force to assert his opinions. He gets carried away by his passions and fully recognizes that he is a failure — just like the "rascals" whose conduct he censures.

Ivanov, the hero of the 1887 drama that bears his name, resembles Platonov in more than one respect. In his letters Chekhov expressed his opinion on Ivanov, as he never did on Platonov, but we have to realize that in 1880–81 he had no correspondents with whom he could discuss literary matters. Most importantly, he had no Suvorin. It is precisely Suvorin to whom he confided later on, in connection with Ivanov, that he had wanted "to sum up everything that had been written until now about glum and whining people and to put an end to these writings."[9]. But far from putting an end to them, he returned repeatedly to this type of the educated but spineless Russian, promising and idealistic in his early years, but soon after his studies are concluded lapsing into an idle and vegetative life. Sometimes this type does not even finish his university studies, like Platonov and a whole series of similar figures after him. Some of them have occupations that have nothing whatsoever to do with their studies. They disavow their scholarly training and the ideals of their student years, they forget what they have learned, they often get absorbed in petit bourgeois and parochial worries and interests, and they take to drink and decline both morally and socially. There is no need here to enumerate the characters of this type in Chekhov's works: drawn from the intelligentsia of his times, they are very numerous.[10]

After the failure of his bold plan to write a serious drama, Chekhov renounced all dramatic creation for a number of years. But in September 1885 he adapted for the stage one of his short stories, "In the Autumn" (written in 1883), transforming it into "a dramatic study in one act" entitled "On the High Road." The main protagonist, the tramp and robber Merik, strikingly resembles Osip in *Platonov*. Osip is also a freebooter and a thief who seems to be not without noble feelings; nonetheless, he does not shrink from committing murder in order to reach his goal or to satisfy his passions. Both these characters attempt to take a person's life and almost succeed. Both distinguish themselves by their abuse of power and their inclination to humiliate distressed fellow human beings. Osip forces a domestic servant to kneel in front of him; Merik, in a tavern, forces a workman to yield his berth to him and the tavern keeper to take off his boots.

The second main character of "On the High road" is a *pomeshchik* who is totally down and out, addicted to alcohol (this time from unhappy love), and so deeply fallen compared even to other degraded members of the gentry—so numerous in Chekhov's work—that the censor prohibited the play for being "dirty and lugubrious."

Shortly thereafter, Chekhov wrote a humorous monologue, originally intended for the comic actor Leonid A. Gradov-Sokolov, entitled "On the Harmfulness of Tobacco." It was his first published dramatic work (February 1886), and it was followed in January 1887 by a "dramatic study," "Kalkhas," adapted from a story of the same title. These two short works are of no great significance for the understanding of Chekhov's drama and have only a few points of resemblance to *Platonov*.

However, in September and October of the same year, 1887, Chekhov wrote *Ivanov*, the first large-scale theatrical piece that he did not disavow; it was published and performed several times. I have already pointed to the striking similarity between the two protagonists; this has been noted by some earlier investigators as well. Entire monologues of Ivanov could have been put into Platonov's mouth and vice versa. Both characters are unhappy about the depravity and foulness of the world that surrounds them, and other human beings' lack of understanding for them. Both talk about their powerlessness, which they fully recognize and which they realize is in fact ridiculous: "Who is going to hold me up to ridicule one day?," Platonov exclaims. "I am a laughable rascal!"[11] And Ivanov says, "That psychosis of mine with all its accessories can only serve as material for a good laugh and nothing else!"[12] Owing to their education and to their posture as idealists (or at least former idealists), they are both regarded by those around them as more or less eccentric, so that some attack them vehemently and even libel them, whereas others view them with hope, respect, and confidence. But they themselves do not care: in their own eyes, they are guilty and abject and nothing more. Platonov deems himself "weak, infinitely weak!" And Ivanov says, "I have done less than a sparrow, and yet here I am, already spent, even at the end of my strength." They have lost all illusions to the extent that they infect those around them as well. Ivanov will end up a suicide; Platonov is at the point of doing the same.

It is true that Ivanov carries his self-criticism much further. Whereas Platonov insists more on the fact that all men are vile and corrupt, Ivanov is conscience-stricken and does not stop repeating that he considers himself profoundly guilty. "At age thirty-five," he says, "I am already broken by fatigue, disillusioned, crushed by futile exploits; I'm eaten up with shame. . . . When I was thirty, I already had a hangover; right now I'm old, I'm already wearing a dressing gown." Platonov is younger: "Evil rages all around me . . . but I am staying where I am, with crossed arms, as if after hard labor; I sit, I let things happen and I keep silent. . . . I am twenty-seven, but when I'm thirty, I'll be exactly the same, I don't foresee any change. I will continue living in this dressing-gown atmosphere. . . ."

Thus in his case the decline appears at an early age. But his moral bankruptcy is not yet as complete as Ivanov's: as we have seen, he sometimes still protests against the baseness he notices around him. He has not yet passed the age of which Ivanov speaks: "I was young, ardent, honest, intelligent, I loved, I hated and believed differently from everybody else, I worked and hoped like mad, I joined battle with windmills, I ran with my head against walls. . . ." Presumably, Platonov has chosen the teaching profession and assumed his role as helper of the peasants out of idealism. While the close kinship between Ivanov and Platonov is beyond any doubt, the latter also somewhat resembles Ivanov's antagonist, Doctor L'vov. Just as L'vov prides himself on being "an honest fellow" whose duty it is to tell everyone the truth to his face and who meddles unpleasantly in Ivanov's private life, so Platonov brings upon himself the reproach that for all his affectation of integrity and honesty, he only importunes other people and obtrudes himself upon them in a disagreeable way.[13]

There is another character in *Platonov* who reminds one of L'vov. He is Isak Abramovich Vengerovich, the student son of a rich Jewish businessman: "I am an upright man and no cad," he states when introducing himself. And he rails at Platonov, pretending to hate him "for his triviality, idleness and buffoonery." Platonov describes this Isak as depraved, and indeed he is a disagreeable type. His father is presented as a petty merchant, a huckster and schemer, a swindler. It is he who, behind the scenes, buys Voinitseva's house and so causes the misery of its inhabitants. But it would be a mistake to see in this detail signs of anti-Semitism. It is true that in his younger years Chekhov's tone toward Jews is occasionally mocking, as was more or less the norm in his environment. The producers of copy for the comic magazines eagerly sought nonprohibited targets for their humor, and the Jews were an attractive alternative. Let us remember that Ivanov's wife, Sarra, born in a rich Jewish merchant family, is presented as a tragic and likable character.

As in most of Chekhov's dramas, there is a medical doctor in *Platonov* — Dr. Triletsky, Platonov's brother-in-law. It is repeatedly said of him that he does not occupy himself with medical science, that he has forgotten his profession, that he does not know anything anymore. In his indifference he goes so far as refusing to visit his patients, even when they are gravely ill. In this respect he resembles various other physicians in Chekhov's work — Dr. Ragin in "Ward No. Six," for instance, and particularly Dr. Chebutykin in *The Three Sisters*. Chekhov the medical student apparently had come across such characters in his life.

Sasha, the young girl in *Ivanov*, who is in love with the hero and who claims that by her "active love" she will pull him out of his apathy and orient him toward a new life, resembles Sofia Egorovna of *Platonov*. The latter, too, although she is a married woman, talks about the "new life" she is going to embark upon with the flabby and wavering Platonov. Both women are idealists; they take offense at the banality of the world in which they move and energetically attempt to save the men they love. "Believe me, I am going to set you on your feet again, my darling," Sofia Egorovna says. "I shall lead you to where there is more light, where none of this filth exists, this dust, this laziness, this dirty shirt. . . . I'll make a man out of you. *Happiness*, that's what I'll give you! Listen to me! *(Pause)* I'll make a worker out of you! We shall be real human beings, Michel! We shall eat our own bread, we shall sweat and get calluses . . . *(She leans her head on his breast)* I shall work. . . ."[14]

How clearly we hear in these words the summons of so many of Chekhov's heroes! That of Laevsky and Nadezhda Fyodorovna in "The Duel," of Sonia in *Uncle Vanya*, of Tusenbach and Irina in *The Three Sisters*, of Sasha in "The Betrothed," of Trofimov and Anya in *The Cherry Orchard*. A cry urging: "Let's go far away, far from this world in which we suffocate towards a future of light and beauty." A voice that proclaims: "We shall work and build a new, better existence!" It is an appeal in which the heroes and heroines believe at the time they pronounce these words, but which they usually forget soon after, and which in any case they never put into practice. It seems obvious that Chekhov himself did not believe in the depth and force of this unstable idealism. Elsewhere the same Sofia Egorovna is thus characterized by Dr. Triletsky: "She imagines that she just has to move her little finger and the whole universe will go into ecstasies before her. . . . There is no clever novel in which you'll find as much foolishness as in her. . . . But in fact she isn't worth a dime. She is ice! A rock! A statue! . . . Not a grain of force!"[15]

In Sofia Egorovna we find another motif that comes back time and again in Chekhov's work: that of love grown cold. She is married (unlike Sasha in *Ivanov*), but although it has not been for long, she has to admit: "I am already capable of not thinking of my husband for days at a time, of forgetting he is present and not paying attention to what he is saying. . . . What can I do? It's terrible! The wedding . . . it was such a short time ago, and already. . . . And everything is Platonov's fault!" She begins to realize that her husband is a dull good-for-nothing. Of course, this reminds us of Masha in *The Seagull* and the other Masha in *The Three Sisters*, as well as of a good number of women in the stories. And it reminds us of some men, too, once more particularly of Ivanov. Frustration and human failure are themes that Chekhov preferred to treat in the sphere of conjugal love, where they could be relied on to find an easy echo in readers and spectators.

Three women in addition to Sofia aspire to Platonov's love. The landed proprietress Anna Petrovna Voinitseva goes about it in a different way from her rival, by appealing not to the ideal of a new life, more beautiful and more active, but to a better organized material existence. "What you absolutely need is a change of air! Go take horseback trips, see people, go to the theater, breathe fresh air! . . . You want me to accompany you? . . . We'll make a trip, the two of us, we shall have a marvelous time!" She is none too chaste and calls herself immoral, but she seems more human and more vividly characterized than Sofia. The role is a large one, full of potential for a good actress. Chekhov no doubt had Ermolova in mind for it when he tried to interest her in his drama.

Platonov's wife Sasha, who knows she is being deceived and twice attempts suicide, is a good-hearted and tragic character. Yet she is close to the type of the narrow woman, exclusively oriented toward earthly things, a type Chekhov disliked and represented negatively many times. (Natasha in *The Three Sisters* is the most striking example.) Sasha has a very limited mind, as Chekhov makes us understand. She only talks about household matters and her child. When she realizes her husband has deceived her she says: "I don't want to live with you anymore. . . . Everybody will find out what a scoundrel you are! How do you expect me to bear it?" Public opinion, decency, are what comes to her mind first.

The other characters of *Platonov* — Glagoliev, Petrin and Shcherbuk — are ignoble, drunken, penurious landowners, whose like Chekhov portrayed in large numbers. We find two of these types in *Ivanov:* Shabel'sky and Lebedev.

After *Ivanov*, Chekhov wrote the one-act comedies that brought him tremendous success. Two of them, *The Bear* and *The Proposal* (both 1888), once more evoke the milieu of the landed gentry from which he was unable to disengage himself. The same is true of the full-length play that followed, *The Wood Demon*, which he started in the fall of 1888 and finished only in 1890, and which in 1897, after a thorough revision, was renamed *Uncle Vanya*. New themes are introduced and new characters appear on the scene, like Uncle Vanya's mother, the intellectual pedant Maria Vasilievna, and the selfish professor Serebriakov, a type that Chekhov may have encountered during his years of study or soon thereafter and which he showed from a different side in his masterpiece of about the same time, "A Dreary Story."

And yet in this play, too, it is not hard to find parallels with *Platonov*. The fact that Chekhov borrowed a few characters' names from the first play may not be significant. Voinitsev from *Platonov* became Voinitsky in *The Wood Demon* and *Uncle Vanya* (just as the names of two main female roles in *Platonov*, Anna Petrovna and Sasha, are identical with those in *Ivanov*). More interesting is the affinity between Platonov and Voinitsky. Once again the protagonist has grown older: he is forty-seven. He, too, is dissatisfied with his life. He berates himself: "Me, a shining personality? No joke could be more venomous!" He, too, complains about growing old and having spoiled his life. And finally (at least in the first version) he does what Platonov attempts to do: in despair, he takes his own life. He regrets that he did not marry Elena, whom he has known for a long time and still loves, but who has since married Serebriakov. The situation is analogous to that of Platonov and Sofia Egorovna. These two women have much in common. They do not love their husbands but nevertheless reject their old lovers (although Sofia succumbs in the end). Both are reproached by their lovers for being lazy, for letting other people do the work, and for leading useless and frivolous lives.[16] (Laziness, mental as well as physical — *len'* — is a birth defect of many of Chekhov's characters.)

Chekhov bestowed certain of Platonov's features on two characters in *The Wood Demon*, just as he had done in the case of *Ivanov*. Dr. Khrushchov (Astrov in *Uncle Vanya*) has traits in common with the hero of the "Play without a Title." Both are named Mikhail. The doctor is generally considered an idealist, but he accuses himself of moral decadence ("I feel I am growing more and more stupid every day, more narrow-minded and less able"; "I am petty, without talents, blind, and at the same time the whole district and all women look at me as a hero, an eminent man.") Khrushchov–Astrov is also loved by two women, one of whom is married. There are certainly numerous differences, but they do not diminish the fact of these rather striking similarities. The "wood demon" reminds us also of Dr. Triletsky in *Platonov*: he, too, is a landowner who has studied medicine but who practices only rarely and reluctantly.

The original version of *The Wood Demon* contained a few more characters who have been eliminated from *Uncle Vanya*: friends, landowners distinguished by their gratuitous chatter and gossip and by a coarse simplemindedness and drunkenness, just as we find them in *Platonov*. Among them, Orlovsky and his son remind one of Glagoliev and his son in *Platonov*. The comic personage of Diadin (Telegin), an insolvent ex-landowner who is given to quasi-sublime, ludicrously elegant turns of phrase, seems to be an amplification of Shcherbuk in the first play.

After *The Wood Demon* Chekhov did not write any dramatic pieces for six years. Only toward the end of 1895 did he finish *The Seagull*. One would expect that this long interval would have caused reminiscences of *Platonov*, so vivid in his previous works, to pale somewhat. However, again, it is not difficult to find some analogies. Once more the scene is laid in a country house. The owner, Sorin, and the protagonist Trigorin are both the kind of irresolute persons we know so well by now. Prominent in their thinking are disappointment and despair regarding their own value, their position in life, and the aim of their existence. It is true that most characters of the play belong to a different psychosocial category from those of *Platonov*. Yet we notice the following. In *The Seagull* Trigorin receives from Nina a locket on which a page number and line number are engraved. Trigorin finds the book (his own book, of course) and reads at the indicated spot: "If you ever have need of my life, come and take it!"

Now, a friend of Chekhov's, Lidia Avilova, claims in her memoirs that Chekhov took this little episode from reality, as she once made him a present of a locket with a similar inscription, referring to a page and line in Chekhov's latest book. The provocative sentence does indeed occur in the story "Neighbors," written in 1892. But as early as 1880–81, in the "Play without a Title," Platonov is secretly given a note from Sofia Egorovna that reads "Come and take me. I am yours."[17]

In 1900 Chekhov wrote *The Three Sisters*. Exceptionally, the action is not laid in a country estate. However, the characters belong to the same social stratum as in all his other plays. Here, too, young noblemen do a great deal of philosophizing, complaining of the vile and absurd character of their existence and the life that surrounds them. They talk incessantly about their laziness and the necessity of working, without ever doing anything. It is true, two of the sisters, Ol'ga and Irina, do work, but their jobs only exhaust them without providing any satisfaction. The principal theme of the play is the frustration of the sisters, who in the beginning still hope for much from life, but who are gradually driven away from their house by their implacable sister-in-law, Natasha, then ruined by their brother Andrei, and disillusioned in their work and in their loves. At the end, when the garrison is leaving their provincial town, they remain behind, abandoned, dissatisfied, and languishing.

Among the characters there is again a medical doctor and no less than three teachers, like Platonov and also like Medvedenko in *The Seagull*. Even more than Triletsky, Dr. Chebutykin is a caricature of a physician. He does not practice and admits he has forgotten everything. Andrei reminds us of Sergei Voinitsev in *Platonov*: he has studied at the university, he is the great hope of his family, but he is weak-willed. Voinitsev is thus addressed by his mother-in-law: "You are a philologist, a decent man, you don't occupy yourself with questionable affairs, you have your convictions, you are a quiet, married man. . . . If you only want to, you will go far!"[18] However, both characters are unhappily married, even though the circumstances are different. Both manage their house and property badly and lose their money. The well-known monologue by Andrei in the fourth act could have been pronounced by Sergei in *Platonov*, as well as by Ivanov: "Oh, where is it, my past, where did it go? The time when I was young and happy, clever, when I had beautiful ideas and noble dreams, and the present as well as the future were illuminated by hope. . . . Why is it that we have just started living and we're already becoming dull, grey, uninteresting, lazy, indifferent, useless, unhappy. . . ."[19]

Just like Sofia Egorovna in *Platonov*, Masha, the third sister, is unhappy, disappointed in her nonentity of a husband. When speaking of love, Sofia Egorovna recites bitterly "Amo, amas, amat . . . ," and Masha does the same thing.[20] The lieutenant Solyony represents the type that bullies women, a type encountered in *Platonov* (Triletsky and others), *Ivanov* (Kosykh), and *The Wood Demon* (Fedor Ivanovich). Chebutykin's habit of perpetually reading newspapers has been borrowed by Chekhov from his first play, in which Petrin had the same idiosyncrasy.

While *The Three Sisters* contains a number of reminiscences of

Platonov, many more can be found in *The Cherry Orchard.* Of all Chekhov's stage works, it is the richest in references to his first play. The situation is analogous to that in *Platonov.* Both plays start with the return to her estate, after a long journey, of a still rather young widow. The two women resemble each other: they both represent a lazy, indolent, and somewhat frivolous type. To a certain degree they are also comparable to that other widow, Arkadina, in *The Seagull* and in some respects to Elena in *Uncle Vanya.*

In *The Cherry Orchard* relatives and neighbors meet at the young widow's estate and talk. Their "philosophy" contains the elements we are familiar with from the other plays. Just like the couples Tusenbach–Irina in *The Three Sisters* and Platonov–Sofia Egorovna, here Trofimov and Anya speak of a radiant future and the new life they are going to build. Among the people present on the estate are two representatives of the well-known type of the impoverished, irresolute, unenterprising landowner: Gaev and Simeonov-Pishchik. The latter constantly wants to borrow money, like Triletsky; and from Ivan Ivanovich (another character in *Platonov*) he has inherited the habit of falling asleep during conversations. The type of the practical, calculating, somewhat narrow-minded house-wife (Sasha in *Platonov,* Yulia in *The Wood Demon,* Natasha in *The Three Sisters*) is represented in *The Cherry Orchard* by Varia. Among the other characters is a student, Trofimov, as there was Isak Abramovich in *Platonov* (though their characters are otherwise quite different). The servant Yasha, with his pedantic gallomania and russophobia, reminds us of the young Glagoliev in the first play, as has been noted by David Magarshack.[21] And finally there is Lopakhin, a peasant's son who got rich and who displays many characteristics of Bugrov in *Platonov.* Both of them are upbraided as rascals by the characters who are members of the nobility, while these same characters receive them, albeit reluctantly, because they are able to lend some money. Each of them complains that he is just an illiterate ignoramus, a peasant's son. Meanwhile the denouement is approaching: while in the first play a neighbor, and in the second a brother of the lady who owns the estate, intend to buy the properties at auction in order to somehow save the situation, they are actually acquired by the two upstarts, Bugrov and Lopakhin, who enter to announce the news, more or less apologetically. (In *Platonov* it is Vengerovich who buys the property, but in Bugrov's name.)

Thus we have seen how the "Play without a Title" served as point of departure and multifarious source for Chekhov's subsequent dramatic works, and how it forecast their tone, atmosphere, characters, situations, and partly their action. I have not paid attention here to the impact on his prose work, but it can be easily demonstrated that this youthful effort was highly significant for the content of a large number of short stories and novellas.[22] Obviously, it was not a superficial experiment, but the reflection of deep-seated ideas and feelings on the part of the young Chekhov. To be sure, the serious beginnings of an artist are almost always crucial for his further development. Thus it is perhaps curious, but not implausible, that *Ivanov*, which followed *Platonov* after a hiatus of six years, should be built on the same foundation as the first and present numerous analogies to it. However, it is quite surprising that during the last year of his life, almost a quarter of a century after the creation of his first play, after repeated statements that "something new is necessary" on the Russian stage, and after announcing that he was going to write a "merry, joyous play" that would reflect the new climate he preceived in Russian society, Chekhov returned once more to *Platonov* and borrowed from it the basic elements of *The Cherry Orchard* — its content, mood, characters, and even certain details.

A number of literary historians, especially but not exclusively in the Soviet Union, have insisted that particularly in his dramatic work, Chekhov intended to present a panorama of the social conditions of his epoch and so was led to paint a picture of the leading class in decline and the bourgeoisie on the rise. It is true that *The Cherry Orchard* in particular was created at a time when Chekhov showed an increasing interest in social and political problems and was considered a "progressive intellectual" who expressed himself with more optimism than before on signs of improvement and progress in Russian society; and that play does seem to symbolize the decay of the gentry, the agony of the old feudal Russia, and the birth of a new generation and a new social order. Yet there is no convincing evidence for this view, widespread though it may be. From Chekhov's correspondence and his comments on his writings, it does not follow that he always and everywhere strove to depict the nobility as a class, even less that he hated this class and applauded its decline. By the same token, nowhere does he deride or show his dislike for those demoralized and bankrupt intellectuals from the noble class whom he portrayed time and again on stage and in his stories. Chekhov was by no means a "social" thinker, in that questions of social structure did not much occupy his mind and he did not care about predictions of social transformation. Even if it is true that in *The Cherry Orchard* he wanted to show the decline of feudalism in Russia and the birth of a democratic and capitalist society, how would he have been able to do that as he worked on *Platonov* in 1880, when the economic decline of the land-owning class was not yet as clearly evident? Moreover, as a twenty-year-old medical student, a grocer's son freshly arrived from a distant province, he knew only a small segment of Russian society and had virtually no firsthand knowledge of the way of life, mentality, and socioeconomic position of the gentry. That does not prevent David Magarshack, for example, from writing about the representation by Chekhov of the old aristocracy and the new class of Bugrovs and Vengeroviches, both, according to him, doomed to ruin — a ruin Chekhov is supposed to have prophesied unceasingly.[23]

Chekhov himself, however, was of a different opinion. His comments on *Ivanov* show that in his eyes, the spiritual prostration of his heroes, who so easily "strain themselves," is an individual and at the same time a universal affair, and one that seemed to be particularly prevalent among Russians. He stresses continually that Ivanov (and, of course, his proto-type, Platonov) are not abnormal phenomena, figments of his imagination brought on the stage, but representatives of a common, even banal type that he had frequently encountered. He intentionally called his hero "Ivanov" (and even considered "Ivan Ivanovich Ivanov"), the commonest name imaginable in Russia, to make his hero a sort of Russian Everyman. "The play is bad," he admits, "but the characters are alive and not invented."[24] So he had definite models in mind (possibly his brothers, as I have mentioned), and he endeavored to present a general psychological type, not typical representatives of one particular social class. Ivan Bunin held that as Chekhov did not know the life of the landowners, he depicted it badly and would be well advised to abandon the attempt.[25] But Chekhov never pretended to present a realistic picture of that life!

The common opinion that in his works he expressed a hatred of the propertied class seems to proceed from false premises. If it were correct, then why, from the very first to the very last of his works, would he so consciously and tirelessly reproduce these types of eternally discontented, impotent, and inactive heroes, without ever confronting them with energetic and positive characters for contrast? Nor did he make them totally negative, unpleasant, uncongenial, as he might have. To the contrary, we accept them with sympathy, or at least without aversion, because they are not simply dull or morally deficient, but are *aware* of the shortcomings and weaknesses of their characters. They grieve and suffer because of it. Had the author hated them, he would have expressed admiration for the persevering, energetic, honest working type, faithful to his principles, and of a superior character that does not degenerate at the end of adolescence. And perhaps he did admire people of that sort, as witness the eulogies he wrote (in letters, not in his fiction or drama) to such energetic and noble personalities as Timiriazev, Przewalski, Tolstoy. But such personalities do not occur in his literary work. He was not inclined to portray them, and felt he would not succeed if he tried.

This may simply represent the limited range of Chekhov's social observation, but it may also reflect a certain affinity on his part for these weak-willed types. Was there in fact some sort of natural inclination or attachment to his indolent heroes? Such a surmise may not be untrue. From his early years, was he not always a bit suspicious of anything flowering and prosperous, anything happy and harmonious, especially in human relations?[26]

Like a dream that, against the dreamer's will, returns repeatedly and presents the same matter in different forms, in five out of his seven plays an important motif is the sale and loss of a house or landed estate. We are reminded of the oppressive scene in which Bugrov announces that he has become the new owner of the estate, which means the Voinitsevs will be driven from their home; however, they are absorbed by personal, amorous affairs and hardly understand the seriousness of what is happening to them. In *The Cherry Orchard* a similar situation occurs and the actions and reactions of the characters are comparable to those in *Platonov*. In *The Wood Demon, Uncle Vanya,* and *The Three Sisters,* the loss of either a property or a house lends these plays the same oppressive atmosphere.

It is conceivable that by means of this motif and this concrete, tangible situation, Chekhov wanted to symbolize and make explicit the climate of decadence prevailing in the Russia of his day. We may speculate that these homes or estates and these families stand for the decaying Russian aristocracy, for the old social order on the brink of ruin, and many have done so. To be sure, nothing about such an emblematic conception of his work can be deduced from what Chekhov stated in his correspondence or conversations. Rather, the motif signalized here reminds us of a concrete event in Anton Pavlovich's childhood. In 1876 his father, harassed by his creditors, sought refuge in Moscow. His mother, left behind in Taganrog, still deeply in debt, found herself obliged to sell their house. This she did with the assistance of a boarder, a rather young bachelor, who promised to help her, but who came home with the announcement that the house had been sold — and that he was the buyer. She was forced to leave her home, leaving behind nothing but an old armoire.[27] It is perfectly conceivable that this event impressed the high school student Anton so deeply that the bankruptcy of his parents, consciously or unconsciously, turned up as a strong recurrent motif and moving force in his dramas (as well as in his prose, as I have shown elsewhere).[28] The old armoire even figures in *The Cherry Orchard.*

The parents left Anton in Taganrog while the rest of the family moved to Moscow. He remained behind in the old house that had changed owners no doubt feeling humiliated, bitter, and sad. It should be remembered that in all the plays (except *Ivanov*) the departure of the characters, or of one of them, is central. And often there is someone — or more than one person — who is left behind, pathetic and more or less in distress. And let us finally remember the call "To Moscow, to Moscow!," not only of the three sisters, but of several other heroes.

One might draw the conclusion from all this that Chekhov in his power of invention, his choice of themes, and the range of his preoccupations appears to be somewhat simplistic and limited. However, within these limitations he has proved himself such a master that we can be only grateful for the way he sublimated a youthful trauma in his writings. Is his current worldwide reputation, so many decades after his death, not due at least in part to his reluctance to address himself to a description of contemporary social conditions in his country, in favor of expressing his most private and intimate thoughts and sentiments, that is, profoundly human thoughts and sentiments that can evoke an understanding response in readers everywhere and at all times?

Notes

1. By N. F. Bel'chikov (Moscow, 1923).

2. Basil Ashmore's abridged adaptation, *Don Juan in the Russian Manner*, performed in 1952 in England.

3. Cf. passages in Iurii Sobolev, *Chekhov* (Moscow, 1934), and Avram Derman, *A. P. Chekhov* (Moscow, 1939). See further E. Lo Gatto, "Neskol 'ko zametok o neizdannoi p'ese Chekhova," *Slavia* (Prague) 19, no. 3 (1950):363 ff.; David Magarshack, *Chekhov the Dramatist* (London, 1952), 66; E. Kannak (Cannac), "Neizvestnaja p'esa Chekhova," *Novyi Zhurnal* (Paris), no. 44 (1956):114–23; David Magarshack, introduction to *Platonov, A Play in Four Acts and Five Scenes*, by Anton Chekhov (London: Faber & Faber, 1964), 9–13; N. Ia. Berkovsky, "Chekhov: ot rasskazov i povestei k dramaturgii," *Russkaja Literatura* (Moscow), no. 1 (1966):15–42.

4. Avram Derman, *Tvorcheskii Portret Chekhova* (Moscow, 1929), chap. 1.

5. Whether *Platonov* is the same play as *Bezottsovshchina* (Fatherlessness), written in the late 1870s in Taganrog according to Chekhov's brother Mikhail, is still a moot question (cf. Mikhail Chekhov, *Vokrug Chekhova, Vstrechi i Vpechatleniia* [Moscow: Khud. Lit., 1981], 43). In the twenty-volume edition of Chekhov's *Polnoe Sobranie Sochinenii i Pisem* (Moscow, 1944–51), the text bears the title "Play without a Title," but in the thirty-volume edition (1974-83) it received the title "Fatherlessness." The identification of the two manuscript plays seems rather dubious because of the difference in time and the fact that the idea of "fatherlessness" is absent from the play under consideration.

6. Cf. Lo Gatto, "Neskol 'ko zametok o neizdannoi p'ese Chekhova," 368, 370.

7. Irène Némirovsky, *La vie de Tchékhov* (Paris, 1946), 146.

8. Ibid., 136–38.

9. *Polnoe Sobranie Sochinenii i Pisem*, 14 (Moscow 1949):290.

10. I deal with these types in my published dissertation: *Anton Tsjechov en de Russische Intelligentsia* (Arnhem: Van Loghum Slaterus, 1951).

11. Chekhov, in *Polnoe Sobranie Sochinenii i Pisem*, 12:92.

12. Ibid., 11:61.

13. Ibid., 12:41, 105–6.

14. Ibid., 12:115–16.

15. Ibid., 12:70.

16. Ibid., 11:205, 213; 12:80.

17. Ibid., 11:175, 12:108. Cf. *A. P. Chekhov v vospominaniiakh sovremennikov* (Moscow, 1947), 361, and *Polnoe Sobranie*, 8:94.

18. *Polnoe Sobranie Sochinenii i Pisem*, 11:143.

19. Ibid., 11:297.

20. Ibid., 11:284, 12:120. This fact was also pointed out by Magarshack, *Chekhov the Dramatist*, 66.

21. Magarshack, *Chekhov the Dramatist*, 66.

22. See my article "A Recurrent Theme in Chekhov's Works," *Scandoslavica* (Copenhagen) 8 (1962):3–25.

23. Magarshack, *Chekhov the Dramatist*, 80.

24. *Polnoe Sobranie Sochinenii i Pisem*, 14:280.

25. Ivan Bunin, *Sobranie Sochinenii* (Berlin, 1935), 10:225.

26. This point was made by Leo Shestov in his essay "Nachala i kontsy" (Beginnings and endings) [which opens our volume under the title "Anton Chekhov, Creation from the Void"]. Shestov obviously exaggerates, but his argument is not without some validity.

27. Cf. Mikhail Chekhov, *Vokrug Chekhova, Vstrechi i Vpechatleniia*, 39–41; Alexander Roskin, *Chekhov* (Moscow–Leningrad, 1939), 218–20; Némirovsky, *La vie de Tchékhov*, 65–68; David Magarshack, *Chekhov, a Life* (London, 1952), 31–32.

28. See note 22.

A Russian Hamlet
(*Ivanov* and His Age)   Tatiana Shakh-Azizova*

"IVANOV: I am dying of shame at the thought that I, a strong, healthy man, have become something of a Hamlet, perhaps a Manfred, or one of the superfluous men . . . the devil knows what I am!"
— Anton Chekhov, *Ivanov*

A comparison with Hamlet was always a great honor for any literary hero. And suddenly here is a man who does not wish to be a Hamlet or to be called a Hamlet, a man for whom such a comparison is "shame."

Why is this? Who is to blame — Ivanov for not understanding Hamlet, or his author, or the age that casts its shadow on Shakespeare's hero?

Hamlet is inseparable from Russian culture. There is something in the personality and fate of the Danish prince that frequently found an echo in Russian 19th-century society with its abundance of philosophical natures, "superfluous people" and misanthropes. Several generations were stamped in the Hamlet mould in different degrees — a tendency to reflection, the divorcing of words from deeds. . . . There cannot be a Hamlet without these characteristics even though they are not his only attributes.

Chekhov's attitude to this sort of Hamletism grew out of his irritation and hostility towards "moaning and sorrowing"; his hostility increased by the nineties, and resulted in a satirical outburst in his article *In Moscow* (1891).

"I'm a Moscow Hamlet. Yes, I am. In Moscow I visit houses, theaters, restaurants and publishers, and everywhere I say one and the same thing:

" 'My God, how dull! How oppressively boring!' "

"A Moscow Hamlet" could have "learnt and known everything".

" 'Yes, I could have! Could have! But I'm a rotten rag, rubbish, a misery, I'm a Moscow Hamlet. Drag me off to the Vagankovo cemetery!' "

*From *Soviet Literature* (Moscow), no.1, (1980): 157–63. Reprinted by permission of the publisher.

The article twice repeated the advice given to the hero by an unknown, infuriated gentleman: " 'Oh yes, take a piece of telegraph wire and hang yourself on the first available telegraph pole! There is nothing else you can do!' " But a "Moscow Hamlet" is not the type to be activated by his reflections. . . .

Of course a true Hamlet in Chekhov's imagination was not to be confused with his comic double. Even at the beginning of the eighties, when reviewing a performance of *Hamlet* at the Pushkin Theater, Chekhov mentioned particularly those traits in the Danish prince that were not inherent in his double: "Hamlet could not whine. Hamlet was an indecisive person, but he was not a coward; moreover, he was prepared to meet a ghost."

The problem of "Chekhov and Hamlet" is too big to be contained in a short article: it has been referred to many times, although it has never been specially discussed within the range of Chekhov's creative work. A small, but important, part of it concerns the interrelationship of Ivanov and Hamlet. The reason why Ivanov does not wish to be considered a Hamlet is understandable if we bear in mind the comic version of Hamlet created by the age. Rejecting Hamlet, Manfred, and superfluous men, Ivanov blames the distorting mirror of the times, which has disfigured their features. It is more difficult, however, to understand the true, objective correlation between Ivanov and Hamlet — "is he not a parody"?

In order fully to understand how extraordinarily characteristic a figure Ivanov was for the eighties, it would be necessary to study a great number of plays, poems, stories and humorous pieces, some presaging Ivanov, others echoing him, some continuing his motifs: "All Russian prose-writers and dramatists felt the need to depict a melancholy person," wrote Chekhov.

It is only necessary to take one constant reason for the melancholy that consumed Ivanov ("As soon as the sun goes down, melancholy starts to prey on my soul. Such melancholy!") — and its echo resounds through the literature of those years.

> *Almost from cradle days our hearts are ageing*
> *Doubts torment us, melancholy gnaws. . . .*
> *Even desire lacks passion,*
> *Even hate dwindles in sly suppression!*

lamented the poet Semyon Nadson (1862–1887), who was popular in those years. In his diary he wrote down a sad formula: "There is no purpose, and no sense, neither is there any possibility of happiness or satisfaction, — there is melancholy and melancholy."

A pretentious and wide-ranging panorama of various types of "dejected people," both in life and literature, was spread out in front of Chekhov. This provoked an unexpected and healthy reaction: "I cherished the audacious dream that I might sum up all that had ever been written about moaning and melancholy people, and with my 'Ivanov' put an end to this sort of writing."

He did not put an "end" to it, but he expressed himself so sharply and audaciously that his play gave a real shock to the public and to the critics. In the chorus of malicious, laudatory or confused voices the opinion of the famous Russian critic, Nikolai Mikhailovsky, was particularly important.

Without accepting Ivanov, Mikhailovsky was nevertheless merciful towards him, and did not place him among "petty Hamlets," though, at the same time, he did not notice in Ivanov that "sharp and sincere self-judgement," which he so valued in Hamlet. With all his severity, Mikhailovsky categorically blamed Chekhov for his "propaganda of a dull, grey, regular and careful life," and for "idealizing an absence of ideals."

It would have been difficult to expect anything different from populist critics, who were accustomed to differentiate clearly and absolutely between black and white, good and evil, and instructed their readers to do so. The upheaval caused by Chekhov's unthinkable objectivity ("He accused no one, and he justified no one . . .") was too sweeping and too sudden.

Mikhailovsky's tirade against the "propaganda . . . of a grey life" was evoked by the advice which Ivanov gives to Dr. Lvov in the first act: "My dear man, do not fight alone against thousands, do not attack windmills, do not beat your forehead against a wall. . . . May God protect you from all possible rational households, unorthodox schools, passionate speeches. Lock yourself up in your shell, and carry out the small work that God sent you. . . ."

In his detailed analytical letter on *Ivanov*, Chekhov himself is indignant at this tone of a "man exhausted before his time." Moreover, we should not consider that Ivanov's advice is given sincerely and that it reflects the moral apostasy common at the time. Otherwise he could not have recalled with anxiety and melancholy the period of "the windmills" as the best years of his life: "Well, is it not funny, is it not humiliating? Less than a year ago I was strong and healthy . . ." and so on.

The reproach of "the idealization of the absence of ideals" can be explained by the fact that the actual ideal of Chekhov's play is not personified, or stated, and no one discusses it, or tells the public that life without an ideal is bad. It is probable that Mikhailovsky missed in the play exactly these words which Chekhov used in the letter: ". . . a conscious life lived without any definite world-outlook is not life, but a burden, a horror." When the old professor in *A Dreary Story* made a diagnosis of his psychological illness, Mikhailovsky could immediately understand the writer's idea, and therefore completely altered his attitude to the writer.

Chekhov was expected to give an explanation: what made Ivanov behave as he did?

Ivanov is not a "Moscow Hamlet" — this is a more serious case, and it is accompanied both by the self-analysis of the hero, and — in the letters — by the author's analysis.

Ivanov attributes the changes that take place in him, the diminution of "life force," to the fact that he strained himself by taking on at an early age a burden of work and worry beyond his strength. Chekhov does not argue with him, and does not widen the scope of the analysis — from the single fate of the hero to a national calamity, but makes use of his favorite term "exhaustion" — in a medical, "clinical" sense, while actually speaking of social and psychological processes. According to Chekhov, exhaustion alternates with periods of social excitement, which are short-lived among the Russian intelligentsia, and result in a loss of strength and in disillusionment with life and oneself.

The true explanation of Ivanov as a character emerges gradually, from the whole of Chekhov's creative work in the eighties and nineties. It is then that the drama of a generation that has been deprived of its former faith, and longs for a new faith, emerges in its entirety.

At the same time it should be remembered that the epoch of the eighties, in the words of Lenin, was the epoch of "thought and reason."

A Hamlet type of intellectual hero is brought into a Hamlet situation; he stops and reasons at the turning point of the epoch, tormenting himself with problems of existence (". . . Who am I? Why do I live? What do I want?"). He is indignant with himself for his inactivity, although historically this is understandable — to us but not to him. Neither Ivanov's rational household, nor Hamlet's well-timed vengeance, would have altered the general order of things, or strengthened the "shattered age." Let Hamlet envy the energy of Fortinbras, who goes off to fight for a pathetic bit of land, an alternative not open to Hamlet. Let people close to Ivanov advise him to struggle against depression — this advice is in vain, as it refers to the effect and not the cause.

It is interesting that Ivanov, objectively close to Hamlet, does not wish to admit this, while others, whose pretensions are groundless, firmly proclaim themselves as Hamlets. Laevsky, in Chekhov's *The Duel*, thinks of himself tenderly after a regular bout of empty introspection: "I am like Hamlet in my lack of decision. . . . How right Shakespeare was! How true!" At the same time there is no real dramatic quality or depth in Laevsky's personality and psychological make-up, and he is not given a single action that would raise him to the Hamlet level or anywhere near it.

When, next to Laevsky, Ivanov arises — with his spiritual maximalism, his severe and sarcastic self-criticism, the high level of his speech and thought, and his end, worthy of a tragic hero — the difference between these heroes, these human types, is drawn as clearly as the difference between "petty Hamlets" and people spiritually akin to Hamlet.

What is it then — a Russian Hamlet without reservations? No, obviously not; the reservations are dictated by the age.

Ivanov, who is involved by the force of circumstances and the cast of his intellectual and conscience-ridden personality in a Hamlet situation, is, in contrast to the Danish prince, an ordinary man, according to Chekhov "not distinguished in any way," a typical person (although, compared with Laevsky, not shallow). In this there lies a characteristic not only of Chekhov's creative process, with his attraction towards "ordinary people," but also of the age itself, when Hamletism became the property not only of exceptional individuals, but of a wide circle of people.

The objectivity of Shakespeare and Chekhov lies in the fact that they show a man as being complex, contradictory, and capable of diversity. But with Shakespeare the complexity is created by the clash of good and evil on a large scale, while in Chekhov it is the clash of the significant and the ordinary, the tragic and absurd, the lofty and the commonplace. A prosaic and humdrum age has cheapened the material from which in former times tragic, romantic, demoniacal heroes used to be created; it has lumped it all up with the everyday humdrum things. In spite of all his relentless analysis, Ivanov does not think cosmically, like Hamlet, but within limits laid down by ordinary life. Neither does he indulge in "universal grief"—he grieves and is indignant basically because of his own fate.

With all his contradictions and dissatisfaction with himself, Hamlet remains a high-tragedy hero. But in Ivanov, Chekhov, as he himself admitted, "summed up" various features of "dull people," ranging from the tragic to the comic, and he did not immediately decide to give his hero the right to tragedy. . . .

Moreover, in principle, Chekhov did "not justify anyone." Although one may understand and explain his neurasthenia and confusion, there are moments when Ivanov's behavior really cannot be justified. There is his cruelty, which is not obviated either by his consciousness of it or by repentance. Hamlet's cruelty to his mother and Ophelia was just and was evoked by their treachery, what if the treachery was not intentional, but was carried out in the blindness of passion (Gertrude) or in filial obedience (Ophelia). Ivanov's cruelty to his sick wife, his dreadful words at the end of Act III ("Then know that you . . . soon will die . . .") stand between the hero and us and force us to hold him morally responsible. Nevertheless, cruelty is not in the nature of Ivanov, the formerly sincere man, as he lives in the memories of Sarah and Sasha. This is a symptom of the fatal and irreversible disintegration of personality, a disintegration which is stopped, put an end to, only by his final shot. It is as if Chekhov tests the measure of our, the reader's and the audience's, trust by the spectacle of Ivanov's neurasthenia or cruelty. At some moments he teeters on that dangerous line beyond which his hero will turn out to be a psychologically sick man or a Tartuffe, a sham, or a weak-willed hypochondriac who makes a cult of his mental indolence. But later the different approaches balance each other out, and, as a result, an objective characterization is achieved.

Other heroes in Chekhov's subsequent plays would also be complex and shown in two aspects — irony and understanding. But the irony is that of sorrowful sympathy, in contrast to the cold analysis of Ivanov: it is as if a young, experimenting doctor polemically demonstrates how relentless and correct is his method.

The point, however, is not only in the youthful fire and temperament of the experimenter. A deeper reason is Chekhov's complex attitude to Russian Hamletism and to the sort of people who are represented by Ivanov.

"I despise laziness, as I despise weakness and inertia in mental activity," Chekhov was to write towards the end of the nineties: he would have been fully justified in writing this earlier. But Ivanov, according to this criterion of Chekhov's, does not deserve contempt not only because he clearly despises himself, but because he is not lazy, weak or flabby. Having endowed him with straightforwardness, honesty and enthusiasm, wishing that the role should be played by a "versatile, energetic actor," who "can be tender at times, and enraged at others," Chekhov himself rules out satire or vaudeville, and turns the story of Ivanov into the tragedy of a man with a capacity for life but who cannot adapt himself to it.

It would be interesting to observe to what extent Hamletism was inherent in Chekhov himself. At first glance, in full measure, to judge by his correspondence in the eighties and nineties. The leitmotif is the already familiar yearning for a common cause, sometimes becoming extremely acute and sounding like the self-criticism of a generation: "God's earth is beautiful. The only thing that is no good is ourselves. And we? We! We paint life as it is, and beyond that — nothing. Beyond that, do to us what you will, flog us if you wish — nothing will help. We have neither immediate nor distant aims, and there is nothing in our souls."

But true Hamletism is to be found not in a way of thinking, but in the logic of living behavior and in the very nature of an introspective intellectual. Chekhov's nature was unusually effective and active, and he was endowed with an innate, life-long immunity against "loss of balance," while his Hamletism was enforced and prescribed by life. It is no accident that his contemporaries bear witness to Chekhov's merciless self-discipline: Ivan Bunin calls him the "personification of reserve, firmness and clarity." Ilya Repin writes that the young Chekhov "took pleasure in feeling that he was clad in 'the armor of courage,' " and so on. In a word, in Chekhov's life and work a very great deal stemmed from both artistic and moral duty, as he understood it.

And in selecting a hero to whom he was not too much attached, he saw his highest duty not in the expression of personal feelings, but in objectivity: "The main thing is to be fair, and the rest will fit into place." The story of Ivanov could have had different endings, and clear proof of this is in the two versions of the play, which were corrected by Chekhov himself. But in the great moment when he had to make a choice, there undoubtedly rose up before him the lofty image of Russian Hamletism, expressed not as the "Moscow Hamlets," but in a tragic intensity of spirit.

With regard to Chekhov's attitude to Hamletism, no "conclusive" answer can be given, because his attitude changed. Chekhov was mistaken in his prognosis of Ivanov: he could not put a limit to the theme he had chosen, since life did not lay down a limit. Noting that, in the figure of Ivanov, he had created "a type that has literary significance," Chekhov here saw the meaning in the summing up. He could not then know that this was also the meaning of the beginning, that in his own plays Ivanov would be followed by the creation of a whole row of heroes who are given to thought rather than to action, but whose thought ranges constantly more and more widely, tearing away from its own actual fate, and rising above it to problems of a truly Hamlet dimension.

The very inactivity of his heroes, which to the very end was to evoke his bitterness and irony, he was nevertheless to contrast with commonplace, base practices, and therefore his evaluation became more complex, even in regard to Ivanov—the strange man who did not want to be a Hamlet and yet became one—the Russian Hamlet of the eighties with all the amendments added by the age.

Microsubjects in *The Seagull*   Zinovii S. Paperny*

The study of Chekhov's text can be compared to the history of the investigation of matter, where researchers have come to employ smaller and smaller units of magnitude. What formerly seemed indivisible has proved a complicated structure consisting of interconnected microparticles.

Something similar is taking place in Chekhov studies. From general formulations investigators delving more deeply into the text have become increasingly convinced that the tissue of poetic narration displays a structure. Along with the main actors, there are also "microparticles" of a sort, and all these "macros" and "micros" are interconnected and subordinated one to the other.

In *The Seagull* the movement of the main subject—the history of the characters' development and their mutual relations—is complicated by microsubjects. The characters not only advance opinions, make confessions, argue, and act, they also offer each other various subjects for literary works, which express their understanding of life, their point of view, their basic "idea."

*From 'Vopreki vsem pravilam . . .': P'esy i vodevili Chekhova by Zinovii S. Paperny (Moscow: Iskusstvo, 1982), 154–67. Translated for this volume by David Woodruff. Reprinted by permission of the publisher.

This is an important feature of the play. Almost every character has not only his own personal drama or tragedy, but also a literary subject, a project that he intends to carry out himself or offers to someone else.

Let us recall the schoolteacher Medvedenko. He says to Trigorin, "Or how about writing and then staging a play that describes the life of teachers like me? Our life is hard, very hard!"

Fictive invention is totally foreign to this subject. Medvedenko proposes to "describe," that is, to tell everything as it really is, to reveal life in its reality. His subject betrays the single idea that runs through his every speech: material need, his difficulty in making ends meet.

Trigorin, the practiced literary master, has his subject:

NINA: What's that you're writing?
TRIGORIN: Just making a note. I had the glimmer of a subject. (*Putting away his notebook*) A subject for a little story: a young girl has lived on the shore of a lake since childhood, someone like you. She loves the lake the way gulls do, and she's happy and free like them. But a man happens by, sees her, and for lack of anything better to do, destroys her life — like this gull here.

This subject does not go to waste in Trigorin's literary economy. In the fourth act he will say to Treplev: "Tomorrow morning, if it's calm, I'm going fishing at the lake. By the way, I want to look over the garden and the place where your play was staged — remember? A motif has taken shape in my mind, and all I need now is to refresh my memory of the scene."

Everything that Trigorin sees and feels is skillfully and efficiently fashioned into subjects for novels, stories, and plays. His interest in life is above all professional. Even Nina interests him not only in herself but also as a kind of literary "raw material." "I don't often meet young girls — young and attractive," he tells her. "I've forgotten how it feels to be eighteen or nineteen and can't imagine it clearly, so young girls in my novels and stories generally don't ring true. I'd like to change places with you, even for an hour, to find out how your mind works and just what you're like."

There is a certain cruelty in Trigorin's "subject-creation," his tireless reworking of life into literature. He leaves Nina calmly and easily; nothing is left of his affair with the beginning actress but a literary project that, we may be quite certain, he will successfully carry out.

At the end of the play, Nina confesses to Treplev that she still loves Trigorin. But she does not want to be merely the occasion for one of Trigorin's subjects and argues with him, as if trying to free herself from painful chains: "I'm a seagull. No, that's not it. . . . You once shot a gull, remember? A man happened by, saw it, and for lack of anything better to do, killed it. A subject for a little story. . . . That's not it. . . ."

Here it is particularly clear how active the microsubjects are in *The Seagull* and how tellingly they touch, move, and disturb the characters. What for Trigorin is merely a theme that has taken shape, a subject for a little story, is for Nina her fate, her vocation.

The microsubjects in *The Seagull* are like little periscopes that connect what is happening on the surface with the very depths. Only here the direction is reversed, running not from the surface to the depths, but the other way around.

Treplev has his subject, and not just one, but two. The first is the one that formed the basis of his unfortunate play, whose performance was such a disaster. The second is the subject, vaguely and incompletely sketched, of the story he is working on in the fourth act, before Nina's arrival.

At the end of the play Nina takes issue with Trigorin's "subject for a little story," which assigns her the role of a defenseless victim and, as it were, returns to Treplev's play.

We see that Trigorin's and Treplev's subjects are profoundly connected to the general development of the action and the fortunes of the characters. They appear and reappear like leitmotivs throughout the entire narration, and this intermittent but insistent repetition of motifs and details is one of the most characteristic features of the play.

Both these subjects are present in the ending. But while Nina rejects Trigorin's, Treplev's subject becomes accessible to her once more. And when she runs off at the end, it is as if she takes it with her.

Old Sorin has a literary idea to propose: "I want to give Kostya Treplev a subject for a story," he says. "It is to be called 'The Man Who Wished,' 'L'Homme qui a voulu.' When I was young at one point I wanted to become a writer, but never did; I wanted to be a good speaker, but I spoke terribly . . . I wanted to marry, but I didn't; I always wanted to live in the city, but here I am ending my days in a village, and everything."

His life is drawing to a close, and he still has not started to live. Fortune has passed him by; it has not provided him what he sought or what he hoped to achieve.

The subject that he offers Treplev is not merely autobiographical. Do we not sense Masha's fate in it as well? Or that of her mother, the manager Shamraev's wife? It can be said that Sorin's microsubject helps a great deal in understanding Chekhov's larger subject.

At the beginning of the third act Masha says to Trigorin: "I'm telling you all this so that you can use it in your writing." And then: "In all honesty, if he had wounded himself seriously, I wouldn't have lived another minute."

What Masha tells Trigorin he can use is the story of her love for Treplev, the love she tries so assiduously and so vainly to tear out of her heart during the course of the whole play, the hopeless and ineradicable love that swallows up all her feelings and desires.

Thus in *The Seagull* the main subject unfolds before our eyes, performed by Chekhov's characters; and simultaneously this represented reality appears twisted, foreshortened, and brokenly reflected, as it is seen by different characters. The microsubjects of Medvedenko, Trigorin, Treplev, Sorin, and Masha are, as it were, micromodels of life that contend among themselves and contradict each other. In this peculiarity of the play's construction is crystallized an important aspect of its content: that attention to secondary characters that so struck sensitive early readers.

At the same time the microsubjects of the five characters reflect various relationships between art and life, from Medvedenko's despondency in the face of prosaic everyday demands, to Treplev's aspirations beyond the bounds of reality.

It is most significant that not only the writers propose subjects, but also the schoolteacher Medvedenko, Masha, and Sorin. Chekhov seems to imply that the boundary between art and life is elusive. Not everyone in *The Seagull* writes, but they are all as it were surrounded by waves of art, and nearly every character tries to make sense of life in his own way. Even if a character does not write himself, he takes his literary "commission" to a professional.

One can speak of a large and a small subject in Chekhov. This aspect of his plays, which has escaped scholarly attention, appears not only in the form of literary subjects proposed by the characters.

The principle of large and small subjects makes itself felt in the overall construction of *The Seagull* as well. We have a rather rare example of theater within theater, a play within a play, and even (if we recall the fate of the original Aleksandrinski Theater production) a failure within a failure: Treplev's play is ridiculed as was Chekhov's own.

The reader is confronted with two theaters. One is firmly established, the one that the actress Arkadina and the playwright Trigorin serve, and in which Treplev feels stifled (". . . the contemporary theater is convention, prejudice"). The second is Treplev's own, set up at the beginning of the first act. It does not look like a stone box, and nature itself and the real moon form the scenery. This theater will be misunderstood. At the conclusion it "stands naked, ugly as a skeleton, the curtain flapping in the wind." But after many wanderings, afflictions, and quests Nina will return here and weep as she remembers everything youthful, innocent, and pure connected with this stage.

In *The Seagull* the very word "theater" seems to split up. The play's microsubjects create a distinctive system of poetic mirrors that register various clashing "reflections."

Thus the constant, unitary symbolic image of the seagull seems to shatter and take the form of various "fragments," one of which reflects Treplev's fate, another Trigorin's, and a third Nina's.

During Chekhov's lifetime critics more than once resorted to such a simile: his works reflect reality not like a large, intact poetic mirror but rather like the broken pieces of a mirror that was once intact. Only taken as a whole do Chekhov's stories create a total impression. In reading *The Seagull* we see that the principle of "multimirrored" construction makes itself felt in the structure of the play as well, where microsubjects enter into complicated and tension-filled relations with each other.

A special type of microsubject consists of references to the classics, quotations that far from seeing mere anthological snippets, start to take on new life in their new context.

Three writers are mentioned in *The Seagull* — Shakespeare, Maupassant, and Turgenev — each of them not once but two or three times.

Just before the performance of Treplev's play begins, Arkadina suddenly and apparently without the slightest motivation, recites from *Hamlet*:

> O Hamlet, speak no more:
> Thou turn'st mine eyes into my very soul,
> And there I see such black and grained spots
> As will not leave their tinct.

Treplev answers with a quotation from the same source:

> Nay, but to live
> In the rank sweat of an enseamed bed,
> Stew'd in corruption, honeying and making love
> Over the nasty sty, —

Then a horn sounds and Treplev's play begins. The quotation from Shakespeare is like an overture.

From the very beginning of the first act one senses the tension in the relationship between Arkadina and her son, his dissatisfaction with her, his sense of injury, his jealous, unfriendly feelings toward her lover, Trigorin. The exchanges of speeches from *Hamlet*, in itself half-joking and playful, at the same time lends an unexpectedly tragic coloration to all that follows. Associations develop between Treplev and Hamlet, Arkadina and the Queen, and Trigorin and the King who has no right to his throne.

Of course in so putting it we coarsen Chekhov's meaning to some extent; in the play everything is put less definitely and is less "spelled out."

Shakespeare is mentioned next in Nina's monologue from Treplev's play ("I am the universal world soul, I! The soul of Alexander the Great is in me, and of Caesar, and of Shakespeare . . ."). And finally Shakespeare is mentioned for the third time (again it is *Hamlet*) in Treplev's conversation with Nina after the collapse of his play. Catching sight of Trigorin who is approaching, he says sarcastically, "Here comes real talent; he strides along like Hamlet and is even reading, too. (*Mockingly*) 'Words, words, words. . . .' "

It is not simply a matter of references and quotations, but of deeper correspondences between *The Seagull* and *Hamlet*.

A. I. Roskin accurately observed that "the lines from *Hamlet* in *The*

Seagull sound not like quotation but like a leitmotiv, one of the play's leitmotivs."[1]

Much in Chekhov's plays goes back to Shakespeare's *Hamlet*, in subject and in the development of the action where the main event is postponed.

The source of tension in Shakespeare's subject is not that the Prince of Denmark kills the false King, but rather the opposite, that for so long he does not.

The "Shakespearean" enters into the very nature and most essential character of Chekhov's subject.

Another link between *The Seagull* and *Hamlet* is the theater within a theater. The Prince arranges a performance that ends in an uproar and is broken off. The fate of Treplev's production seems in a way similar. Particularly interesting are the parallels between the conversations of the Prince with the Queen and Treplev with Arkadina in the third acts of both plays. It is lines from precisely this act that are quoted in *The Seagull*.

In *Hamlet* while the Prince is castigating his mother who has fallen into vice, the Ghost appears; and Hamlet's tone of voice alters and he begins to sound more sympathetic toward his mother, whom the Ghost of his father the King seems to defend.

A similarly abrupt transition takes place in *The Seagull* when after mutual insults mother and son cry, are reconciled, and embrace.[2]

Chekhov studies Shakespeare's art of abrupt reversals, discontinuities in the characters' states of mind, and sharp transitions from anger to remorse or from apparently irreconcilable quarreling to unexpected tranquillity.

In *The Seagull* Shakespeare is not merely a quoted classic. Like the ghost of Hamlet's father he appears in the play and exercises an unseen influence on the course of the action and on its character. Associations with *Hamlet* enrich our perception of *The Seagull* and enter into the very structure of Chekhov's play.

Guy de Maupassant is mentioned twice. Treplev speaks of him at the beginning of the play (". . . when I am served up the same stuff again and again and again, I run and run, as Maupassant ran from the Eiffel Tower which was crushing his brain with its vulgarity"). At the beginning of the second act Arkadina, Dorn, and Masha are reading aloud from Maupassant's *Sur l'eau*. Arkadina opens the book at a passage about a society woman who is trying to attract a writer: "She lays siege to him by means of every variety of compliments, attractions, and indulgence."[3] Arguing against Maupassant, Arkadina points to the example of herself and Trigorin.

Maupassant's *Sur l'eau* appeared in 1888. It consists of the description of a week's cruise on the yacht "Bel-Ami." It is a bitter book, full of skepticism and mockery of deceitful human society, particularly fashionable society.

Treplev in *The Seagull* attacks convention, banality, and vulgarity. For Maupassant, however, vulgarity is a synonym for life: "Happy are those whom life satisfies, who are amused and content."[4]

Upset by his mother's ironic remarks, Treplev, at the performance of his play, cries "Enough! Curtain!"

In *Sur l'eau* Maupassant directs this cry against life as a whole, for him a cheap and deceitful spectacle. "How is it that the worldly audience has not yet called out, 'Curtain,' has not yet demanded the next act, with other beings than mankind."[5]

A comparison of *Sur l'eau* with *The Seagull* helps us to feel more sharply the differences in world outlook of the two writers and lets us grasp the distinction between the total pessimism of the one and, as it were, the imperfect skepticism of the other.

Echoes of Maupassant's novel are to be heard in other parts of Chekhov's play as well. In one of the chapters of *Sur l'eau* Maupassant expresses disagreement with those who envy writers and says that writers are to be pitied, not envied. Reading these lines, it is hard not to be reminded of Trigorin's monologue:

> For (the writer) no simple feeling any longer exists. All he sees, his joys, his pleasures, his suffering, his despair, all instantaneously become subjects of observation. . . . If he suffers, he notes down his suffering, and classes it in his memory. . . . He has seen all, noticed all, remembered all, in spite of himself, because he is above all a literary man, and his intellect is constructed in such a manner that the reverberation in him is much more vivid, more natural, so to speak, than the first shock — the echo more sonorous than the original sound.[6]

And a little further on he compares the writer to "a terribly vibrating and complicated piece of machinery, fatiguing even to himself."[7]

Thus Treplev, Arkadina, and Trigorin unexpectedly intersect with Maupassant. And each of them approaches him from his own angle. It is true that in Trigorin's monologue there is no mention of Maupassant, but traces of *Sur l'eau* are none the less discernible.

Turgenev's presence in the play is equally varied. Trigorin feels mocked by Turgenev's unattainable eminence as a writer, of which people constantly remind him: " 'A marvelous piece, but Turgenev's *Fathers and Sons* is better.' . . . and when I die my friends will say as they go past my grave, 'Here lies Trigorin. He was a good writer, but not as good as Turgenev.' "

And at the end of the play it is as if Turgenev extends a hand to Nina: "Listen — do you hear the wind? Turgenev says somewhere, 'A man's all right if he has a roof over his head on nights like these, some place where it's warm.' I'm a seagull. No, that's not it. (*She rubs her forehead*) What was I saying? Yes, Turgenev. 'And God help all homeless wanderers.' It's nothing. (*She sobs*)"

Turgenev's words in the context of Nina's monologue lose their "quotedness" and become Chekhov's. The actor V. A. Podgorny, who performed with Kommissarzhevskaya and knew her well, tells this story about her last days, when she was rehearsing *The Seagull* with her company in Tashkent: " 'And God help all homeless wanderers,' said Kommissarzhevskaya in the sad words of Nina Zarechnaya, and looked at the actors with a smile. "We really are those homeless wanderers! Here in the middle of nowhere we are rehearsing and acting and living, and in a few days it will be time to go on and rehearse and act and live some more. . . ."[8]

Whom is she quoting? Formally, Turgenev; but actually it is Chekhov.

This example makes it particularly clear how a literary source changes on entering into Chekhov's text, and becomes no longer someone else's, but Chekhov's own.

Microsubjects in *The Seagull* are of various sorts. There are the literary subjects of the characters, both professional writers and people who have nothing to do with literature, and there are associations with classical works such as the quotations from Shakespeare, Maupassant, and Turgenev. There is still another variety: the anecdotes and funny stories that Shamraev and Sorin tell.

A few minutes after the end of Treplev's play, Nina steps down from the stage, Arkadina praises her and introduces her to Trigorin. They begin their first conversation.

On making the acquaintance of her idol Trigorin, Nina immediately starts talking about what pains her most: those who live for art, the chosen ones of fame who taste the higher pleasures. Arkadina, laughing, intervenes (she does not leave Trigorin alone for a minute). And at this dramatic moment, when conversation is starting up among the three characters who are to cause each other so much suffering — becoming close, separating, coming back together — at this point Shamraev begins telling his old story about a synodal cantor:

SHAMRAEV: I remember one time at the Opera House in Moscow, the famous Silva hit a low C. As luck would have it one of our synodal cantors happened to be in the gallery and — you can imagine our astonishment — we heard booming out of the gallery, "Bravo, Silva!," a whole octave lower. Like this: (*in a low approximation of a bass voice*) Bravo, Silva! The whole theater just died. (*pause*)

DORN: A quiet angel flew by — we are sitting here in silence.

NINA: It's time for me to go. Good-by.

This anecdote, perhaps amusing in itself, is totally out of place here, at this moment. No one is listening to Shamraev, and when he finishes, they do not know what to say.

Shamraev's anecdote is funny less because of its intrinsic humor than because it is totally unexpected and unmotivated.

Shamraev's second anecdote is even more at odds with its context ("We're twapped!" instead of "We're trapped!"). Shamraev enters as the scene between Trigorin and Arkadina has just concluded, where she tries to take him away from Nina. At this moment he enters and "with regret" announces that the horses are ready and tells his story about "twapped."

At first glance all these little anecdotes are pointless and only interrupt the course of the narration. However the stories told by Shamraev and Sorin ("Your voice, your Excellency, is powerful . . . but unpleasant"), are at once inappropriate and essential. Their very lack of harmony with the context makes them deeply organic elements of a play where everything is built on conflicts, contrasts, and discontinuities. One may say that these half-humorous microsubjects let us perceive life's lack of harmony, refracted by the play as if by a magnifying glass, and not only in the twists and turns of the larger subject, but on a smaller scale as well.

Shamraev's and Sorin's anecdotes play an important role in intensifying the play's polyphonic sound quality, in which tragedy and comedy merge into one.

Some readers, viewers, and interpreters of *The Seagull* have unintentionally tried to reduce the amplitude of oscillation from large to small, from tragic to comic. A curious example is provided by N. M. Ezhov's letter to Chekhov of 29 January 1899: ". . . there are things in *The Seagull* which I find most unattractive. The first is Sorin's singing and what he says about some gentleman's witticism, that the general's voice is powerful but repulsive [for "unpleasant"]. This is so jarring to the viewer that it is a shame! The second thing is the manager's story about 'trapped' and 'twapped.' I can't explain exactly why, but these two passages seem to me for some reason impossible in *The Seagull*."[9]

What seemed to Ezhov an unjustified and impermissible violation of the style and tonality of the play is actually the bold introduction of counterpoint, creating a sort of disharmonic structure with constant interruptions in the development of the subject, a lack of mutuality in the sympathies of the characters, and clashes between the tragic "Hamletic" impulse and the anecdotal.

As we have seen, Chekhov's microsubjects are least of all illustrations. They have various sources, ranging from the literary "claim checks" of the characters themselves, to quotations from the classics, to anecdotes. In their many-colored mosaic there is a whole range of transitional tints and shades.

"Thou turnst mine eyes into my very soul" and "We're twapped!" are equally microsubjects.

Chekhov did not immediately achieve so rich and complicated a palette of colors, of transitions from high to low, from tragic to laughable.

In his first play *Platonov* we do not find microsubjects at all.

In *Ivanov* the main character tells about the workman Semyon who heaved two sacks of rye up on his back and strained something: "I think

I've strained something, too." Here the microsubject simply illustrates what is going on with the main character. The unexpectedness that characterizes the microsubject in *The Seagull* is lacking and there is no contradiction between the large and small subjects.

In Chekhov's third play *The Wood Demon* the situation is just about the same as in *Ivanov*. With *The Seagull* he first attains multimirrored reflections of reality. They form a complicated system that at first glance seems a mosaic of disparate bits, but which in reality is profoundly consistent in affirming through images on various levels the disharmony of life, its conflicts and contradictions, and the agonizing discrepancy between dream and reality.

Notes

1. A. Roskin, *A. P. Chekhov; stat'i i ocherki* (Moscow: GIKhL, 1959), 131.

2. Chekhov was particularly fond of the scene between the Queen and her son in *Hamlet*. There is much evidence of this. One example is the review "*Hamlet* on the Stage of the Pushkin Theater," where, in discussing the performance of M. Ivanov-Kozlovsky, the twenty-two-year-old Chekhov notes that "the scene with the mother was done beautifully" (A. P. Chekhov, *PSSP*, 16:21).

3. *A Selection from the Writings of Guy de Maupassant*, vol. 4: *Sur l'eau and Other Tales* (New York: Review of Reviews Co., 1903), 20.

4. Maupassant, *Writings*, 26.

5. Ibid., 28.

6. Ibid., 56.

7. Ibid., 58.

8. V. A. Podgorny, *Pamiati* [Memories], in *Sbornik pamiati V. F. Komissarzhevskoi* (Moscow: GIKhL, 1931), 99.

9. In the archive of the Lenin State Library, Moscow, 331.43.11.

Craftsmanship in *Uncle Vanya*   Eric Bentley*

The Anglo-American theater finds it possible to get along without the services of most of the best playwrights. Aeschylus, Lope de Vega, Racine, Molière, Schiller, Strindberg — one could prolong indefinitely the list of great dramatists who are practically unknown in England and America except to scholars. Two cases of popularity in spite of greatness are, of course, Shakespeare and Shaw, who have this in common: that they can be enjoyed without being taken seriously. And then there is Chekhov.

It is easy to make over a play by Shaw or by Shakespeare into a Broadway show. But why is Chekhov preserved from the general oblivion?

*From *Chekhov, New Perspectives*, ed. René Wellek and Nonna D. Wellek (Englewood Cliffs, N.J.: Prentice-Hall, 1984), 118–39. Reprinted by permission of the publisher.

Why is it that scarcely a year passes without a major Broadway or West end production of a Chekhov play? Chekhov's plays — at least by reputation, which in commercial theater is the important thing — are plotless, monotonous, drab, and intellectual: find the opposite of these four adjectives and you have a recipe for a smash hit.

Those who are responsible for productions of Chekhov in London and New York know the commodity theater. Some of them are conscious rebels against the whole system. Others are simply genuine artists who, if not altogether consciously, are afflicted with guilt; to do Chekhov is for them a gesture of rebellion or atonement, as to do Shakespeare or Shaw is not. It is as if the theater remembers Chekhov when it remembers its conscience.

The rebels of the theater know their Chekhov and love him; it is another question whether they understand him. Very few people seem to have given his work the careful examination it requires. Handsome tributes have been paid Chekhov by Stanislavsky, Nemirovich-Danchenko, and Gorky, among his countrymen; and since being taken up by Middleton Murry's circle [in the 1920s], he has enjoyed a high literary reputation in England and America. The little book by William Gerhardi and the notes and obiter dicta of such critics as Stark Young and Francis Fergusson are, however, too fragmentary and impressionistic to constitute a critical appraisal. They have helped to establish more accurate general ideas about Chekhov's art. They have not inquired too rigorously in what that art consists.

I am prompted to start such an enquiry by the Old Vic's engrossing presentation of *Uncle Vanya* in New York. Although *Vanya* is the least well known of Chekhov's four dramatic masterpieces, it is — I find — a good play to start a critical exploration with because it exists in two versions — one mature Chekhov, the other an immature draft. To read both is to discover the direction and intention of Chekhov's development. It is also to learn something about the art of rewriting when not practiced by mere play-doctors. There is a lesson here for playwrights. For we are losing the conception of the writer as an artist who by quiet discipline steadily develops. In the twentieth century a writer becomes an event with his first best-seller, or smash hit, and then spends the rest of his life repeating the performance — or vainly trying to.

Chekhov's earlier version — *The Wood Demon* — is what Hollywood would call a comedy drama: that is, a farce spiced with melodrama. It tells the story of three couples: a vain Professor[1] and his young second wife, Yelena; Astrov, the local doctor, who is nicknamed the Wood Demon because of his passion for forestry, and Sonya, the Professor's daughter by his first marriage; finally, a young man and woman named Fyodor and Julia. The action consists to a great extent in banal comedic crisscrossing of erotic interests. Julia's brother seems for a time to be after Sonya. Yelena is coveted rather casually by Fyodor and more persistently by Uncle Vanya, the brother of the Professor's first wife. Rival suitors, eternal triangles, theatric adultery! It is not a play to take too seriously. Although in the third act there is a climax when Uncle Vanya shoots himself, Chekhov tries in the last and fourth act to reestablish the mode of light comedy by pairing off all three couples before bringing down the curtain on his happy ending.

Yet even in *The Wood Demon* there is much that is "pure Chekhov." The happy ending does not convince, because Chekhov has created a situation that cannot find so easy an outcome. He has created people who cannot possibly be happy ever after. He has struck so deep a note that the play cannot quite, in its last act, become funny again.

The death of Vanya is melodrama, yet it has poignancy too, and one might feel that, if it should be altered, the changes should be in the direction of realism. The plot centers on property. The estate was the dowry of Vanya's sister, the Professor's first wife. Vanya put ten years' work into paying off the mortgage. The present owner is the daughter of the first marriage, Sonya. The Professor, however, thinks he can safely speak of "our estate" and propose to sell it, so he can live in a Finnish villa on the proceeds. It is the shock of this proposal, coming on top of his discovery that the Professor, in whom he has so long believed, is an intellectual fraud—coming on top of his infatuation with Yelena—that drives Vanya to suicide. And if this situation seems already to be asking for realistic treatment, what are we to say to the aftermath? Yelena leaves her husband, but is unable to sustain this "melodramatic" effort. She comes back to him, defeated yet not contrite: "Well, take me, statue of the commander, and go to hell with me in your twenty-six dismal rooms!"[2]

The Wood Demon is a conventional play trying, so to speak, to be something else. In *Uncle Vanya*, rewritten, it succeeds. Perhaps Chekhov began by retouching his ending and was led back and back into his play until he had revised everything but the initial situation. He keeps the starting-point of his fable, but alters the whole outcome. Vanya does not shoot himself; he fires his pistol at the Professor, and misses. Consequently the last act has quite a different point of departure. Yelena does not run away from her husband. He decides to leave, and she goes with him. Astrov, in the later version, does not love Sonya; he and she end in isolation. Vanya is not dead or in the condemned cell: but he is not happy.

To the Broadway script-writer, also concerned with the rewriting of plays (especially if in an early version a likable character shoots himself), these alterations of Chekhov's would presumably seem unaccountable. They would look like a deliberate elimination of the dramatic element. Has not Prince Mirsky told us that Chekhov is an undramatic dramatist? The odd thing is only that he could be so dramatic *before* he rewrote. The matter is worth looking into.

Chekhov's theater, like Ibsen's, is psychological. If Chekhov changed his story, it must be either because he later felt that his old characters would act differently or because he wanted to create more interesting characters. The four people who emerge in the later version as the protagonists are different from their prototypes in *The Wood Demon*, and are differently situated. Although Sonya still loves Astrov, her love is not returned. This fact is one among many that make the later ending Chekhovian: Sonya and Astrov resign themselves to lives of labor without romance. Vanya is not resolute enough for suicide. His discontent takes form as resentment against the author of his misery. And yet, if missing his aim at such close quarters be an accident, it is surely one of those unconsciously willed accidents that Freud wrote of. Vanya is no murderer. His outburst is rightly dismissed as a tantrum by his fellows, none of whom dreams of calling the police. Just as Vanya is the kind of man who does not kill, Yelena is the kind of woman who does not run away from her husband, even temporarily.

In the earlier version the fates of the characters are settled; in the later they are unsettled. In the earlier version they are settled, moreover, not by their own nature or by force of circumstance, but by theatrical convention. In the later, their fate is unsettled because that is Chekhov's view of the truth. Nobody dies. Nobody is paired off. And the general point is clear: life knows no endings, happy or tragic. (Shaw once congratulated Chekhov on the discovery that the tragedy of the Hedda Gablers is, in real life, precisely that they do *not* shoot themselves.) The special satiric point is also familiar: Chekhov's Russians are chronically indecisive people. What is perhaps not so easy to grasp is the effect of a more mature psychology upon dramaturgy. Chekhov has destroyed the climax in his third act and the happy consummation in his fourth. These two alterations alone presuppose a radically different dramatic form.

II

The framework of the new play is the attractive pattern of arrival and departure: the action is what happens in the short space of time between the arrival of the Professor and his wife on their country estate and their departure from it. The unity of the play is discovered by asking the question: what effect has the visit upon the visited — that is, upon Vanya, Sonya, and Astrov? This question as it stands could not be asked of *The Wood Demon*, for in that play the Professor and Yelena do not depart, and Vanya is dead before the end. As to the effect of the Professor's arrival, it is to change and spoil everything. His big moment — the moment when he announces his intention to sell the estate — leads to reversal in Aristotle's sense, the decisive point at which the whole direction of the narrative turns about. This is Uncle Vanya's suicide. Vanya's futile shots, in the later version, are a kind of mock reversal. It cannot even be said that they make the Professor change his mind, for he had begun to change it already — as soon as Vanya protested. Mechanical, classroom analysis would no doubt locate the climax of the play in the shooting. But the climax is an anticlimax. If one of our script-writers went to work on it, his "rewrite" would be *The Wood Demon* all over again, his principle of revision being exactly the opposite of Chekhov's. What Chekhov is after, I think, is not reversal but recognition — also in Aristotle's sense, "the change from ignorance to knowledge." In Aristotle's sense, but with a Chekhovian application.

In the Greeks, in much French drama, and in Ibsen, recognition means the discovery of a secret which reveals that things are not what all these years they have seemed to be. In *Uncle Vanya*, recognition means that what all these years seemed to be so, though one hesitated to believe it, really is so and will remain so. This is Vanya's discovery and gradually (in the course of the ensuing last act) that of the others. Thus Chekhov has created a kind of recognition which is all his own. In Ibsen the terrible thing is that the surface of everyday life is a smooth deception. In Chekhov the terrible thing is that the surface of everyday life is itself a kind of tragedy. In Ibsen the whole surface of life is suddenly burst by volcanic eruption. In Chekhov the crust is all too firm; the volcanic energies of men have no chance of emerging. *Uncle Vanya* opens with a rather rhetorical suggestion that this *might* be so. It ends with the knowledge that it certainly is so, a knowledge shared by all the characters who are capable of knowledge — Astrov, Vanya, Sonya, and Yelena. This growth from ignorance to knowledge is, perhaps, our cardinal experience of the play (the moment of recognition, or experimental proof, being Vanya's outburst *before* the shooting).

Aristotle says that the change from ignorance to knowledge produces "love or hate between the persons destined by the poet for good or bad fortune." But only in *The Wood Demon*, where there is no real change from ignorance to knowledge, could the outcome be stated in such round terms. Nobody's fortune at the end of *Uncle Vanya* is as good or bad as it might be; nobody is very conclusively loving or hating. Here again Chekhov is avoiding the black and the white, the tragic and the comic, and is attempting the halftone, the tragicomic.

If, as has been suggested, the action consists in the effect of the presence of the Professor and Yelena upon Sonya, Vanya, and Astrov, we naturally ask: what *was* that effect? To answer this question for the subtlest of the characters — Astrov — is to see far into Chekhov's art. In *The Wood Demon* the effect is nil. The action has not yet been unified. It lies buried in the chaos of Chekhov's materials. In *Uncle Vanya*, however, there is a thread of continuity. We are first told that Astrov is a man with no time for women. We then learn (and there is no trace of this in *The Wood Demon*) that he is infatuated with Yelena. In *The Wood Demon*, Sonya gets Astrov in the end. In *Uncle Vanya*, when Astrov gives up Yelena, he resigns himself to his old role of living without love. The old routine — in this as in other respects — resumes its sway.

The later version of this part of the story includes two splendid scenes that were not in *The Wood Demon*, even embryonically. One is the first of the two climaxes in Act III — when Yelena sounds out Astrov on Sonya's behalf. Astrov reveals that it is Yelena he loves, and he is kissing her when Vanya enters. The second is Astrov's parting from Yelena in the last act, a scene so subtle that Stanislavsky himself misinterpreted it: he held that Astrov was still madly in love with Yelena and was clutching at her as a dying man clutches at a straw. Chekhov had to point out in a letter that this is not so. What really happens is less histrionic and more Chekhovian. The parting kiss is passionless on Astrov's side. This time it is Yelena who feels a little passion. Not very much, though. For both, the kiss is a tribute to the Might-Have-Been.

Astrov's failure to return Sonya's love is not a result of the Professor's visit; he had failed to return it even before the Professor's arrival. The effect of the visit is to confirm (as part of the general Chekhovian pattern) the fact that what seems to be so *is* so; that what has been will be; that nothing has changed. How much difference has the visit made? It has made the case much sadder. Beforehand Astrov had maintained, and presumably believed, that he was indifferent to women. Afterward we know that it is Sonya in particular to whom he is indifferent. The "wood demon," devoted to the creative and the natural, can love only Yelena the artificial, the sterile, the useless. To Sonya, the good, the competent, the constructive, he is indifferent.

The Professor's visit clarifies Astrov's situation — indeed, his whole nature. True, he had already confessed himself a failure in some of the opening speeches of the play. The uninitiated must certainly find it strange (despite the august precedent of *Antony and Cleopatra*) that the play starts with a summary of the whole disaster. Yet the rest of the play, anything but a gratuitous appendix, is the proof that Astrov, who perhaps could not quite believe himself at the beginning, is right after all. The action of the play is his chance to disprove his own thesis — a chance that he misses, that he was bound to miss, being what he was. What was he, then? In the earlier version he had been known as the Wood Demon or Spirit of the Forest, and in *Uncle Vanya* the long speeches are retained in which he advances his idea of the natural, the growing, the beautiful. Because he also speaks of great ennobling changes in the future of the race (not unlike those mentioned in the peroration of Trotsky's *Literature and Revolution*), he has been taken to be a prophet of a great political future for Russia in the twentieth century. But this would be wrenching his remarks from their context. Astrov is not to be congratulated on his beautiful dreams; he is to be pitied. His hope that mankind will some day do something good operates as an excuse for doing nothing now. It is an expression of his own futility, and Astrov knows it. Even in the early version he was not really a Wood Demon. That was only the ironical nickname of a crank. In the later version even the nickname has gone,[3] and Astrov is even more of a crank. When Yelena arrives, he leaves his forests to rot. Clearly they were no real fulfillment of his nature, but an old-maidish hobby, like Persian cats. They were ersatz; and as soon as something else seemed to offer itself, Astrov made his futile attempt at seduction. Freud would have enjoyed the revealing quality of his last pathetic proposal that Yelena should give herself to him in the depth of the forest.

The actor, of course, should not make Astrov too negative. If one school of opinion romanticizes all Chekhov characters who dream of the future, another, even more vulgar, sees them as weaklings and nothing else. Chekhov followed Ibsen in portraying the average mediocre man — *l'homme moyen sensuel* — without ever following the extreme naturalists in their concern with the utterly downtrodden, the inarticulate, the semi-human. His people are no weaker than ninety-nine out of every hundred members of his audience. That is to say, they are very weak, but there are also elements of protest and revolt in them, traces of will-power, some dim sense of responsibility. If his characters never reach fulfillment, it is not because they were always without potentialities. In fact, Chekhov's sustained point is precisely that these weeping, squirming, suffering creatures might have been men. And because Chekhov feels this, there is emotion, movement, tension, interplay, dialectic, in his plays. He never could have written a play like Galsworthy's *Justice*, in which the suffering creature is as much an insect as a man.

The Might-Have-Been is Chekhov's idée fixe. His people do not dream only of what could never be, or what could come only after thousands of years; they dream of what their lives actually could have been. They spring from a conviction of human potentiality — which is what separates Chekhov from the real misanthropes of modern literature. Astrov moves us because we can readily feel how fully human he might have been, how he has dwindled, under the influence of "country life," from a thinker to a crank, from a man of feeling to a philanderer. "It is strange somehow," he says to Yelena in the last scene, "we have got to know each other, and all at once for some reason — we shall never meet again. So it is with everything in this world." Such lines might be found in any piece of sentimental theater. Buy why is it that Chekhov's famous "elegiac note" is, in the full context, deeply moving? Is it not because the sense of death is accompanied with so rich a sense of life and the possible worth of living?

III

Chekhov had a feeling for the unity of the drama, yet his sense of the richness of life kept him clear of formalism. He enriched his dramas in ways that belong to no school and that, at least in their effect, are peculiar to himself. While others tried to revive poetic drama by putting symbolist verse in the mouths of their characters, or simply by imitating the verse drama of the past, Chekhov found poetry within the world of realism. By this is meant not only that he used symbols. Symbolism of a stagy kind was familiar on the boulevards and still is. The Broadway title *Skylark* is symbolic in exactly the same way as *The Wild Duck* and *The Seagull*. It is rather the use to which Chekhov puts the symbol that is remarkable. We have seen, for instance, what he makes of his "wood demon." This is not merely a matter of Astrov's character. Chekhov's symbols spread themselves, like Ibsen's, over a large territory. They are a path to the imagination and to those deeper passions which in our latter-day drama are seldom worn on the sleeve. Thus if a symbol in Chekhov is explained—in the manner of the *raisonneur*—the explanation blazes like a denunciation. Yelena says:

> As Astrov was just saying, you are all recklessly destroying the forests and soon there will be nothing left on the earth. In the same way you recklessly destroy human beings, and soon, thanks to you, there will be no fidelity, no purity, no capacity for sacrifice left on the earth either! Why is it you can never look at a woman with indifference unless she is yours? That doctor is right: it's because there is a devil of destruction in all of you. You have no mercy on woods or birds or women or one another.

What a paradox: our playwrights who plump for the passions (like O'Neill) are superficial, and Chekhov, who pretends to show us only the surface (who, as I have said, writes the tragedy of the surface), is passionate and deep! No modern playwright has presented elemental passions more truly. Both versions of *Uncle Vanya* are the battleground of two conflicting impulses—the impulse to destroy and the impulse to create. In *The Wood Demon* the conflict is simple: Vanya's destructive passion reaches a logical end in suicide. Astrov's creative passion a logical end in happiness ever after. In *Uncle Vanya* the pattern is complex: Vanya's destructive passion reaches a pseudo-climax in his pistol-shots, and a pseudo-culmination in bitter resignation. Astrov's creative passion has found no outlet. Unsatisfied by his forests, he is fascinated by Yelena. His ending is the same as Vanya's—isolation. The destructive passions do not destroy; the creative passions do not create. Or, rather, both impulses are crushed in the daily routine, crushed by boredom and triviality. Both Vanya and Astrov have been suffering a gradual erosion and will continue to do so. They cry out. "I have not lived, not lived . . . I have ruined and wasted the best years of my life." "I have grown old, I have worked too hard, I have grown vulgar, all my feelings are blunted, and I believe I am not capable of being fond of anyone." Chekhov's people never quite become wounded animals like the Greek tragic heroes. But through what modern playwright does suffering speak more poignantly?

At a time when Chekhov is valued for his finer shades, it is worth stressing his simplicity and strength, his depth and intensity—provided we remember that these qualities require just as prodigious a technique for their expression, that they depend just as much on details. Look at the first two acts of *Uncle Vanya*. While the later acts differ from *The Wood Demon* in their whole narrative, the first two differ chiefly in their disposition of the material. Act I of *The Wood Demon* is a rather conventional bit of exposition: we get to know the eleven principals and we learn that Vanya is in love with Yelena. In *Uncle Vanya* Chekhov gives himself more elbow-room by cutting down the number of characters: Julia and her brother, Fyodor and his father are eliminated. The act is no longer mere exposition in the naturalistic manner (people meeting and asking questions like "Whom did you write to?" so that the reply can be given: "I wrote to Sonya"). The principle of organization is what one often hears called "musical." (The word *poetic* is surely more accurate, but music is the accepted metaphor.) The evening opens, we might say, with a little overture in which themes from the body of the play are heard. "I may well look old!" It is Astrov speaking. "And life is tedious, stupid, dirty. Life just drags on." The theme of human deterioration is followed by the theme of aspiration: "Those who will live a hundred or two hundred years after us, for whom we are struggling now to beat out a road, will they remember and say a good word for us?" The overture ends; the play begins.

Analyses of the structure of plays seldom fail to tell us where the climax lies, where the exposition is completed, and how the play ends, but they often omit a more obtrusive factor—the principle of motion, the way in which a play copes with its medium, with time-sequence. In general, the nineteenth-century drama proceeded upon the principles of boulevard drama (as triumphantly practiced by Scribe). To deal with such a play, terms like exposition, complication, and denouement are perfectly adequate because the play is, like most fiction, primarily a pattern of suspense. The "musical" principle of motion, however, does not reflect a preoccupation with suspense. That is why many devotees of popular drama are bored by Chekhov.

Consider even smaller things than the use of overture. Consider the dynamics of the first three lines in *Uncle Vanya*. The scene is one of Chekhov's gardens. Astrov is sitting with the Nurse. She offers him tea. She offers him vodka, but he is not a regular vodka-drinker. "Besides, it's stifling," he says; and there is a lull in the conversation. To the Broadway producer this is a good opening because it gives latecomers a chance to take their seats without missing anything. To Chekhov these little exchanges, these sultry pauses, are the bricks out of which a drama is built.

What makes Chekhov seem most formless is precisely the means by which he achieves strict form—namely, the series of tea-drinkings, arrivals, departures, meals, dances, family gatherings, casual conversations, of which his plays are made. As we have seen, Chekhov works with a highly unified action. He presents it, however, not in the centralized, simplified manner of Sophocles or Ibsen, but obliquely, indirectly, quasi-naturally.

The rhythm of the play is leisurely yet broken and, to suspense-lovers, baffling. It would be an exaggeration to say that there is no story and that the succession of scenes marks simply an advance in our knowledge of a situation that does not change. Yet people who cannot interest themselves in this kind of development as well as in straightforward story-telling will not be interested in Chekhov's plays any more than they would be in Henry James's novels. Chekhov does tell a story—the gifts of one of the greatest raconteurs are not in abeyance in his plays—but his method is to let both his narrative and his situation leak out, so to speak, through domestic gatherings, formal and casual. This is his principle of motion.

The method requires two extraordinary gifts: the mastery of "petty" realistic material and the ability to go beyond sheer Sachlichkeit— materiality, factuality—to imagination and thought. (Galsworthy, for example, seems to have possessed neither of these gifts—certainly not the second.) Now, the whole Stanislavsky school of acting and directing is testimony that Chekhov was successfully sachlich—that is, not only accurate, but significantly precise, concrete, ironic (like Jane Austen). The art by which a special importance is imparted to everyday objects is familiar enough in fiction; on the stage, Chekhov is one of its few masters. On the stage, moreover, the Sachlichkeit may more often consist in a piece of business—I shall never forget Astrov, as played by Olivier, buttoning his coat—than in a piece of furniture. Chekhov was so far from being the average novelist-turned-dramatist that he used the peculiarly theatrical Sachlichkeit with the skill of a veteran of the footlights. The first entrance of Vanya, for instance, is achieved this way (compare it with the entrance of the matinee idol in a boulevard comedy): *"Vanya (comes out of the house; he has had a nap after lunch and looks rumpled; he sits down on the garden-seat and straightens his fashionable tie). Yes . . . (Pause.) Yes. . . ."* (Those who are used to the long novelistic stage-directions of Shaw and O'Neill should remember that Chekhov, like Ibsen, added stage-directions only here and there. But the few that do exist show an absolute mastery.)

How did Chekhov transcend mere Sachlichkeit and achieve a drama of imagination and thought? Chiefly, I think, by combining the most minute attention to realistic detail with a rigorous sense of form. He diverges widely from all the Western realists—though not so widely from his Russian predecessors such as Turgenev, whose *Month in the Country* could be palmed off as a Chekhov play on more discerning people than most drama critics—and his divergences are often in the preservation of elements of style and stylization, which naturalism prided itself it had discarded. Most obvious among these is the soliloquy. Chekhov does not let his people confide in the audience, but he does use the kind of soliloquy in which the character thinks out loud; and where there is no traditional device for achieving a certain kind of beginning or ending, he constructs for himself a set piece that will do his job. In *Uncle Vanya*, if there may be said to be an overture, played by Astrov, there may also be said to be a finale, played by Sonya. For evidence of Chekhov's theatrical talents one should notice the visual and auditory components of this final minute of the play. We have just heard the bells jingling as the Professor and his wife drive off, leaving the others to their desolation. "Waffles"—one of the neighbors—is softly tuning his guitar. Vanya's mother is reading. Vanya "passes his hand over" Sonya's hair:

> SONYA: We must go on living! (*Pause*). We shall go on living, Uncle Vanya! We shall live through a long, long chain of days and weary evenings; we shall patiently bear the trials that fate sends us; we shall work for others, both now and in our old age, and have no rest; and when our time comes we shall die without a murmur, and there beyond the grave we shall say that we have suffered, that we have wept, that our life has been bitter to us, and God will have pity on us, and you and I, uncle, dear uncle, shall see a life that is bright, lovely, beautiful. We shall rejoice and look back at these troubles of ours with tenderness, with a smile—and we shall have rest. I have faith, uncle, fervent, passionate faith. (*Slips on her knees before him and lays her head on his hands; in a weary voice*) We shall rest! (*"Waffles" softly plays on the guitar.*) We shall rest! We shall hear the angels; we shall see all heaven lit with radiance, we shall see all earthly evil, all our sufferings, drowned in mercy, which will fill the whole world, and our life will be peaceful, gentle, sweet like a caress. I have faith, I have faith. (*Wipes away his tears with her handkerchief.*) Poor, poor Uncle Vanya, you are crying. (*Through her tears*) You have had no joy in your life, but wait, Uncle Vanya, wait. We shall rest (*Puts her arms around him.*) We shall rest! (*The watchman taps; Waffles plays softly; Vanya's mother makes notes on the margin of her pamphlet; the Nurse knits her stocking.*) We shall rest! (*Curtain drops slowly.*)

The silence, the music, the watchman's tapping, the postures, the gestures, the prose with its rhythmic repetitions and melancholy import— these compose an image, if a stage picture with its words and music may be called an image, such as the drama has seldom known since Shakespeare. True, in our time the background music of movies and the noises-off in radio drama have made us see the dangers in this sort of theatricality. But Chekhov knew without these awful examples where to draw the line.

A weakness of much realistic literature is that it deals with inarticulate people. The novelist can of course supply in narrative and description what his milieu lacks in conversation, but the dramatist has no recourse— except to the extent that drama is expressed not in words but in action. Chekhov's realistic milieu, however, is, like Ibsen's, bourgeois and "intellectual"; a wide range of conversational styles and topics is therefore plausible enough. But Chekhov is not too pedantic about plausibility. He not only exploits the real explicitness and complication and abstractness of bourgeois talk; he introduces, or re-introduces, a couple of special conventions.

The first is the tirade or long, oratically composed speech. Chekhov's realistic plays—unlike Ibsen's—have their purple patches. On the assumption that a stage character may be much more self-conscious and aware than his counterpart in real life, Chekhov lets his people talk much more freely than any other modern realist except Shaw. They talk on all subjects from bookkeeping to metaphysics. Not always listening to what the other man is saying, they talk about themselves and address the whole world. They make what might be called self-explaining soliloquies in the manner of Richard III—except for the fact that other people are present and waiting, very likely, to make soliloquies of their own.

This is the origin of the second Chekhovian convention: each character speaks his mind without reference to the others. This device is perhaps Chekhov's most notorious idea. It has been used more crudely by Odets and Saroyan; and it has usually been interpreted in what is indeed its primary function: to express the isolation of people from one another. However, the dramaturgic utility of the idea is equally evident: it brings the fates of individuals before the audience with a minimum of fuss.

In Chekhov, as in every successful artist, each device functions both technically and humanly, serves a purpose both as form and as content. The form of the tirade, which Chekhov reintroduces, is one of the chief means to an extension of content; and the extension of content is one of the chief means by which Chekhov escapes from stolid naturalism into the broader realities that only imagination can uncover. Chekhov's people are immersed in facts, buried in circumstances, not to say in trivialities, yet— and this is what differentiates them from most dramatic characters— aware of the realm of ideas and imagination. His drama bred a school of acting which gives more attention to exact detail than any other school in history; it might also have bred a school of dramaturgy which could handle the largest and most general problems. Chekhov was a master of the particular and the general—which is another sign of the richness and balance of his mind.

IV

Obviously Chekhov is not a problem playwright in the vulgar sense. (Neither is Ibsen; neither is Shaw. Who is?) Nor is his drama about ideas. He would undoubtedly have agreed with Henry Becque: "The serious thing about drama is not the ideas. It is the absorption of the ideas by the characters, the dramatic or comic force that the characters give to the ideas." It is not so much the force Chekhov gives to any particular ideas as the picture he gives of the role of ideas in the lives of men of ideas—a point particularly relevant to *Uncle Vanya*. If Vanya might be called the active center of the play (in that he precipitates the crisis), there is also a passive center, a character whose mere existence gives direction to the action as a whole.

This is Professor Serebryakov. Although this character is not so satisfactory a creation as the professor in Chekhov's tale *A Tiresome Story*, and though Chekhov does too little to escape the cliché stage professor, the very crudeness of the characterization has dramatic point. Serebryakov is a simple case placed as such in contrast to Vanya and Astrov. His devotion to ideas is no more than a gesture of unearned superiority, and so he has become a valetudinarian whose wife truly says: "You talk of your age as though we were all responsible for it." Around this familiar and, after all, common phenomenon are grouped the others, each of whom has a different relation to the world of culture and learning. The Professor is the middle of the design; characters of developed awareness are, so to say, above him; those of undeveloped awareness below him. Above him are Vanya and Astrov, Yelena and Sonya—the men aware to a great extent through their superior intellect, the women through their finer feeling. Below him are three minor characters—Waffles, Vanya's mother, and the Nurse.

The Nurse, who is not to be found in *The Wood Demon*, stands for life without intellectuality or education. She sits knitting, and the fine talk passes her by. She stands for the monotony of country life, a monotony that she interprets as beneficent order. One of the many significant cross-references in the play is Vanya's remark at the beginning that the Professor's arrival has upset the household routine and the Nurse's remark at the end that now the meals will be on time again and all will be well.

Vanya's mother stands on the first rung of the intellectual ladder. She is an enthusiast for certain ideas, and especially for reading about them, but she understands very little. Less intelligent, less sensitive than Vanya, she has never seen through the Professor. Her whole character is in this exchange with her son:

MOTHER. . . . he has sent his new pamphlet.
VANYA. Interesting?
MOTHER. Interesting but rather queer. He is attacking what he himself
        maintained seven years ago. It's awful.
VANYA. There's nothing awful in that. Drink your tea, maman.
MOTHER. I want to talk.
VANYA. We have been talking and talking for fifty years and reading
        pamphlets. It's about time to leave off.
MOTHER. You don't like listening when I speak; I don't know why.
        Forgive my saying so, Jean, but you have so changed in the
        course of the last year that I hardly know you. You used to be a
        man of definite convictions, brilliant personality. . . .

On a slightly higher plane than the tract-ridden Mother is the friend of the family, Waffles. If Vanya is the ruin of a man of principle, Waffles is the parody of one. Listen to his account of himself (it is one of Chekhov's characteristic thumbnail autobiographies):

> My wife ran away from me with the man she loved the day after our wedding on the ground of my unprepossessing appearance. But I have never been false to my vows. I love her to this day and am faithful to her. I help her as far as I can, and I gave her all I had for the education of her children by the man she loved. I have lost my happiness, but I still have my pride left. And she? Her youth is over, her beauty, in accordance with the laws of nature, has faded, the man she loved is dead. . . . What has she left?

Just how Waffles is able to keep his equilibrium and avoid the agony that the four principals endure is clear enough. His "pride" is a form of stupidity. For him, as for the Professor, books and ideas are not a window through which he sees the world so much as obstacles that prevent him seeing anything but themselves. The Professor's response to the crisis is a magnanimity that rings as false as Waffles's pride: "Let bygones be bygones. After what has happened. I have gone through such a lot and thought over so many things in these few hours, I believe I could write a whole treatise on the art of living. . . ." Waffles also finds reflections of life more interesting than life itself. In *The Wood Demon* (where his character is more crudely drawn), having helped Yelena to run away, he shouts: "If I lived in an intellectual center, they could draw a caricature of me for a magazine, with a very funny satirical inscription." And a little later: "Your Excellency, it is I who carried off your wife, as once upon a time a certain Paris carried off the fair Helen. I! Although there are no pockmarked Parises, yet there are more things in heaven and earth, Horatio, than are dreamt of in your philosophy!" In the more finely controlled *Uncle Vanya* this side of Waffles is slyly indicated in his attitude to the shooting:

NURSE.   Look at the quarreling and shooting this morning—shameful!
WAFFLES.   Yes, a subject worthy of the brush of Aivazovsky.

Aside from this special treatment of the modern intellectual and semi-intellectual, aside from explicit mention of various ideas and philosophies, Chekhov is writing "drama of ideas" only in the sense that Sophocles and Shakespeare and Ibsen were—that is to say, his plays are developed thematically. As one can analyze certain Shakespeare plays in terms of the chief concepts employed in them—such as Nature and Time—so one might analyze a Chekhov play in terms of certain large antitheses, such as (the list is compiled from *Uncle Vanya*) love and hate, feeling and apathy, heroism and lethargy, innocence and sophistication, reality and illusion, freedom and captivity, use and waste, culture and nature, youth and age, life and death. If one were to take up a couple of Chekhov's key concepts and trace his use of them through a whole play, one would find that he is a more substantial artist than even his admirers think.

Happiness and work, for instance. They are not exactly antitheses, but in *Uncle Vanya* they are found in by no means harmonious association. The outsider's view of Chekhov is of course that he is "negative" because he portrayed a life without happiness. The amateur's view is that he is "positive" because he preached work as a remedy for boredom. Both views need serious qualification. The word *work* shifts its tone and implication a good deal within the one play *Uncle Vanya*. True, it sometimes looks like the antidote to all the idleness and futility. On the other hand, the play opens with Astrov's just complaint that he is worked to death. Work has been an obsession, and is still one, for the Professor, whose parting word is: "Permit an old man to add one observation to his farewell message: you must work, my friends! you must work!"[4] Vanya and Sonya obey him — but only to stave off desperation. "My heart is too heavy," says Vanya. "I must make haste and occupy myself with something. . . . Work! Work!" To Sonya, work is the noblest mode of self-destruction, a fact that was rather more than clear in *The Wood Demon*:

ASTROV. Are you happy?

SONYA. This is not the time, Mikhail Lvovich, to think of happiness.

ASTROV. What else is there to think of?

SONYA. Our sorrow came only because we thought too much of happiness. . . .

ASTROV. So! (*Pause.*)

SONYA. There's no evil without some good in it. Sorrow has taught me this — that one must forget one's own happiness and think only of the happiness of others. One's whole life should consist of sacrifices. . . .

ASTROV. Yes . . . (*after a pause*). Uncle Vanya shot himself, and his mother goes on searching for contradictions in her pamphlets. A great misfortune befell you and you're pampering your self-love, you are trying to distort your life and you think this is a sacrifice. . . . No one has a heart. . . .

In the less explicit *Uncle Vanya* this passage does not appear. What we do have is Sonya's beautiful lyric speech that ends the play. In the thrill of the words perhaps both reader and playgoer overlook just what she says — namely, that the afterlife will so fully make up for this one that we should learn not to take our earthly troubles too seriously. This is not Chekhov speaking. It is an overwrought girl comforting herself with an idea. In *The Wood Demon* Astrov was the author's mouthpiece when he replied to Sonya: "You are trying to distort your life and you think this is a sacrifice." The mature Chekhov has no direct mouthpieces. But the whole passage, the whole play, enforces the meaning: work for these people is not a means to happiness, but a drug that will help them to forget. Happiness they will never know. Astrov's yearnings are not a radical's vision of the future any more than the Professor's doctrine of work is a demand for a workers' state. They are both the daydreams of men who Might Have Been.

V

So much for *The Wood Demon* and *Uncle Vanya*. Chekhov wrote five other full-length plays. Three — *Ivanov, That Worthless Fellow Platonov*, and *The Wood Demon* — were written in his late twenties, and are experimental in the sense that he was still groping toward his own peculiar style. Two plays — *The Seagull* and *Uncle Vanya* — were written in his middle thirties; the last two plays — *The Three Sisters* and *The Cherry Orchard* — when he was about forty.

Chekhov's development as a playwright is quite different from that of Ibsen, Strindberg, or any of the other first-rate moderns. While they pushed tempestuously forward, transforming old modes and inventing new ones, perpetually changing their approach, endlessly inventing new forms, Chekhov moved quietly, slowly, and along one straight road. He used only one full-length structure: the four-act drama; and one set of materials: the rural middle class. For all that, the line that stretches from *Ivanov* (1887–9) to *The Cherry Orchard* (1903) is of great interest.

The development is from farce and melodrama to the mature Chekhovian *drame*. The three early plays are violent and a little pretentious. Each presents a protagonist (there is no protagonist in the four subsequent plays) who is a modern variant upon a great type or symbol. Ivanov is referred to as a Hamlet, Platonov as a Don Juan, Astrov as a Wood Demon. In each case it is a "Russian" variant that Chekhov shows — Chekhov's "Russians" like Ibsen's "Norwegian" Peer Gynt and Shaw's "Englishman" representing modern men in general. Those who find Chekhov's plays static should read the three early pieces: they are the proof that, if the later Chekhov eschewed certain kinds of action, it was not for lack of dramatic sense in the most popular meaning of the term. Chekhov was born a melodramatist and farceur; only by discipline and development did he become the kind of playwright the world thinks it knows him to be. Not that the later plays are without farcical and melodramatic elements; only a great mimic and caricaturist could have created Waffles and Gaev. As for melodrama, the pistol continues to go off (all but the last of the seven plays have a murder or suicide as climax or pseudo-climax), but the noise is taken further off-stage, literally and figuratively, until in *The Three Sisters* it is "the dim sound of a far-away shot." And *The Cherry Orchard*, the farthest refinement of Chekhov's method, culminates not with the sharp report of a pistol, but with the dull, precise thud of an ax.

These are a few isolated facts, and one might find a hundred others to demonstrate that Chekhov's plays retain a relationship to the cruder forms. If, as Jacques Barzun has argued, there is a Balzac in Henry James, there is a Sardou in Chekhov. Farce and melodrama are not eliminated, but subordinated to a higher art, and have their part in the dialectic of the whole. As melodrama, *The Seagull*, with its tale of the ruined heroine, the glamorous popular novelist, the despairing artist hero, might have appealed to Verdi or Puccini. Even the story of *The Cherry Orchard* (the elegant lady running off to Paris and being abandoned by the object of her grand passion) hardly suggests singularity, highbrowism, or rarefaction.

In the later plays life is seen in softer colors; Chekhov is no longer eager to be the author of a Russian *Hamlet* or *Don Juan*. The homely Uncle Vanya succeeds on the title page the oversuggestive Wood Demon, and Chekhov forgoes the melodrama of a forest fire. Even more revealing: overexplicit themes are deleted. Only in *The Wood Demon* is the career of the Professor filled in with excessive detail (Heidelberg and all) or Astrov denounced as a socialist. Only in the early version does Vanya's mother add to her remark that a certain writer now makes his living by attacking his own former views: "It is very, very typical of our time. Never have people betrayed their convictions with such levity as they do now." Chekhov deletes Vanya's open allusion to the "cursed poisonous irony" of the sophisticated mind. He keeps the substance of Yelena's declaration that "the world perishes not because of murderers and thieves, but from hidden hatred, from hostility among good people, from all those petty squabbles," and deletes the end of the sentence: ". . . unseen by those who call our house a haven of intellectuals." He does not have Yelena explain herself with the remark: "I am an episodic character, mine is a canary's happiness, a woman's happiness." (In both versions Yelena has earlier described herself as an "episodic character." Only in *The Wood Demon* does she repeat the description. In *The Wood Demon* the canary image also receives histrionic reiteration. In *Uncle Vanya* it is not used at all.)

Chekhov does not tone things down because he is afraid of giving himself away. He is not prim or precious. Restraint is for him as positive an idea as temperance was for the Greeks. In Chekhov the toned-down picture—as I hope the example of *Uncle Vanya* indicates—surpasses the hectic color scheme of melodrama, not only in documentary truth, but also in the deeper truth of poetic vision. And the truth of Chekhov's colors has much to do with the delicacy of his forms. Chekhov once wrote in a letter: "When a man spends the least possible number of movements over some definite action, that is grace"; and one of his critics speaks of a " 'trigger' process, the release of enormous forces by some tiny movement." The Chekhovian form as we find it in the final version of *Uncle Vanya* grew from a profound sense of what might be called the *economy* of art.

We have seen how, while this form does not by any means eliminate narrative and suspense, it reintroduces another equally respectable principle of motion—the progress from ignorance to knowledge. Each scene is another stage in our discovery of Chekhov's people and Chekhov's situation; also in their discovering of themselves and their situation (in so far as they are capable of doing so). The apparent casualness of the encounters and discussions on the stage is Chekhov linking himself to "the least possible number of movements." But as there is a "definite action," as "large forces have been brought into play," we are not cheated of drama.

The "trigger effect" is as dramatic in its way as the "buried secret" pattern of Sophocles and Ibsen. Of course, there will be people who see the tininess of the movements and do not notice the enormousness of the forces released — who see the trigger-finger move and do not hear the shot. To them, Chekhov remains a mere manufacturer of atmosphere, a mere contriver of nuance. To others he seems a master of dramatic form unsurpassed in modern times.

Notes

1. In cases where Chekhov changed the name of a character for his later version, I have used the later name only, to avoid confusion. And I have called each person by the designation that non-Russians most easily remember: "the Professor," "Waffles," "Astrov," "Sonya."

2. In general I quote from published translations of Chekhov: the English of *The Wood Demon* is S. S. Koteliansky's; of *Uncle Vanya*, Constance Garnett's. But I have altered these versions, consulting the Russian original wherever alteration seemed desirable.

3. From the title as well as from the dialogue. For not only does the center of interest shift from Astrov to Vanya, but Chekhov deliberately drops from his masthead the evocative demon in favor of the utterly banal uncle. If the name Vanya sounds exotic to non-Russian ears, one has to know that it is the equivalent of Jack.

4. So Constance Garnett. Actually Chekhov does not here use the Russian word for "to work" (rabotat), which is his leitmotiv; he uses an idiom meaning "you must do something!" ("Nado delo delat!")

The Three Sisters   Maurice Valency*

The theme of *The Three Sisters* is so elusive as to be almost indefinable. The play involves considerable discussion of current problems; there is talk of work and happiness, of the necessity for preparing the future through education, of hope for an earthly paradise to come, and of the present need for self-sacrifice and social service. The action illustrates a familiar aspect of the social process, and this process appears to be evolutionary in its workings, but it is not at all certain what its goal may be, or of how it is to be reached. On the far shore of these troubled lives, Moscow flashes like a beacon. But it is a useless mark, a source of aspiration, but even more a source of frustration and unhappiness; and it is eventually relinquished in favor of other landmarks, less bright and less alluring, but more certain.

The situation in *The Three Sisters* is treated with austere realism. Life has its little satisfactions, but on the whole it is not a pleasant experience. The recurrent question is: why? Vershinin ventures one sort of answer;

*From *The Breaking String: The Plays of Anton Chekhov* by Maurice Valency (New York: Oxford University Press, 1966), 241–50. Reprinted by permission of the author.

Tusenbach another; Chebutykin wastes no words. Apart from Vershinin and, in the end, Olga, none of these characters has any special awareness of the current which propels their lives. Individuals think of themselves as discrete entities, each with his own destiny. It is implied that they might better think of themselves in the aggregate as a wave, sharing a common impetus, and that their insistence on maintaining their individuality at any cost is a chief source of their discontent. Vershinin alone touches upon this point, but quite superficially, in the way of small talk in a drawing-room. His words are sufficiently impressive to induce Masha to stay to lunch, and Irina remarks that what he says should really be written down: this is their total effect. The implication is humorous.[1]

Olga echoes Vershinin's thought quite solemnly at the very last, it is true, but what she says is rather musical than meaningful. Her speech is less elegiacal and more energetic than Sonya's speech at the end of *Uncle Vanya*, and is therefore supported, not by a polka played on a guitar, but by drums and trumpets. Yet the net effect is not altogether different. The music, in fact, tells us as much as the speech:

OLGA (*puts her arms around both her sisters*): The music sounds so gay, so brave, that I want to live! Oh my God! The years will pass, and we shall die and be gone forever, we shall be forgotten, forgotten — our faces, our voices, they will even forget how many of us there were; but our sufferings will bring happiness to those who come after us; peace and joy will reign on earth, and there will be kind words and blessings for us and for our times. Oh my dear sisters, our lives are not yet over. We shall live! The music is playing so joyously, so happily, and it seems to me that, very soon now, we shall know why we are living, and why we are suffering . . . If only we knew! If only we knew!

(*The music grows fainter. Kulygin, smiling cheerfully, comes in with Masha's cloak and her hat. Andrey pushes in the baby carriage with Bobik in it.*)

CHEBUTYKIN (*sings quietly*):
Ta-ra-ra-boom de ay!
I'm getting tight today!
(*He looks into his newspaper*)
It's all one. All one.
OLGA: If only we knew! If only we knew![2]

It is on this antiphony that *The Three Sisters* ends, not on a positive note, but on two levels of uncertainty. There is a distinct expression of faith in the future; but, obviously, it puts a severe strain on the imagination to discount present sorrow in the expectation of better times to come in some hundreds of years. To substitute the dream of the earthly paradise for the dream of Moscow is perhaps sensible in the circumstances, and even useful, but chiefly as a device for sustaining the flagging spirits of those whom life has cheated. *Uncle Vanya* is, on the whole, pessimistic. The strain of idealism is strong in *The Three Sisters*, but whether the note of irony on which it ends is as sharp as its counterpart in *Uncle Vanya* is a matter of opinion. In any case, it hardly matters. From an artistic viewpoint the result is the same.

In *The Three Sisters*, Vershinin evidently speaks for Chekhov, and his views are clear. But Chebutykin also speaks for Chekhov, and his views are equally clear. The old skeptic believes in nothing, and expects nothing. He is cynical, spent, a little wicked, yet in his way quite as sympathetic as Vershinin, and for him it is all nonsense, the past, the future, and the present — it all adds up to nothing, and the play virtually closes with his words: *Vse ravno! Vse ravno!* — "It's all one! It's all one!"

The indeterminate area between faith and skepticism measures the extent of Chekhov's spiritual discomfort. Vershinin speaks for his faith; Chebutykin, for his doubt. Chekhov's soul was capacious. There was room in it for the one and for the other, and he saw no way to reconcile the two. We cannot doubt that this continual inner altercation was of major importance in his life as a dramatist. Possibly it represented in conscious terms the dynamic principle of his art, the polarity which gave it movement. His mind was calm, but his soul was not placid and, more clearly than any other of his plays, *The Three Sisters* reflects his spiritual tension.

The Three Sisters marks an important stage in the evolution of the type of drama which depends for its magnitude on the association of its characters with a cosmic process external to themselves. This is the tradition, essentially Hegelian, which we associate with Hebbel and Ibsen. The difference between *The Three Sisters* and a play like *Rosmersholm*, however, is that while Ibsen is often ironic at the expense of his characters, he is completely serious with respect to the order of change in which they are involved, while Chekhov takes nothing for granted. Chekhov concedes the possibility of the social process which Vershinin expounds, but he cannot accept the idea wholeheartedly, and the suggestion is inescapable that perhaps all these hopes, these dreams, and these efforts are in the end equally meaningless and equally absurd.

By the time of *Uncle Vanya*, Maeterlinck, Ibsen, and Hauptmann had amply demonstrated the uses of symbolism in the theater, and their works were being played in Russia. Chekhov came very readily under the spell of Maeterlinck. In *The Three Sisters* as much is conveyed symbolically as is expressed in words, and in the interplay of expression and suggestion Chekhov developed a more complex counterpoint than anyone had so far attempted in the theater. Apart from such solid stuff as the silver samovar, the baby carriage, Natasha's candle, and the lamps she is constantly extinguishing, there is the tissue of memories, and all the wealth of literary reminiscence against which the action is played — the image of the green oak and the golden chain from Pushkin's *Ruslan and Lyudmila*, the couplet from Krylov's fable, the scraps of verse, popular tunes, and odds and ends of rhyme and proverb that form the warp through which the narrative weaves its texture. But beyond this, the play itself is symbolic of a greater drama, the cosmic drama which it suggests, and with which it corresponds. The nature of this correspondence is broadly hinted at by Vershinin in several passages, but very subtly and delicately by Tusenbach in the scene at the end of the play:

> TUSENBACH: Strange how trifles, stupidities, sometimes become so important in our lives, suddenly, without rhyme or reason! You laugh at them, the same as always, you see that they're nonsense, yet all at once you find that you are being swept away by them, and have no power to stop. Oh, let's not talk about that! I am full of joy. It's as if I am seeing these pines and maples and birches for the first time, and they all seem to be looking at me, waiting. What beautiful trees! And, now I think of it, how beautiful life must be when there are trees like these! (*Shouts offstage*: "Hey! Hurry up!") I must go now . . . Look at that tree; it's dead, but it still sways in the wind with the others. Yes, when I am dead, I think, I too shall continue to have a share in life in one way or another. Good bye, my darling . . .[3]

The lyrical quality of a play conceived along these lines is achieved, necessarily, at the expense of more usual dramatic values. A fine play in the Scribean manner is a marvel of ingenuity, in which every line serves either to advance the action, or to characterize the speaker, or both. In such plays, no words are wasted; whatever does not serve to propel the plot is judged to be extraneous and dispensable; and the characters work their way forward with all their might, each intent on his desire. This kind of drama conveys, accordingly, a sense of urgency which in real life we feel only in our more hysterical moments, and also an enhanced awareness of the play of motives, the interchange of pressures, and the clash of wills. The design is primarily mechanical in principle, and the result is a piece of dramatic engineering, a machine.

Chekhov's plays are of another stamp. In general, his characters feel no urgency and transmit none; they create no suspense. In comparison with the characters of well-made plays, they seem languid and bored. Aside from the comic characters of such vaudevilles as *The Bear* and *The Proposal*, the personages who convey a sense of energy in Chekhov's plays are exceptional, and seem to belong to another world than the rest of the cast. The usual Chekhovian character is a half-hearted participant in an action that barely excites his interest. His desires, when they are manifested, seem to run against the grain of the action. The bustle which characterizes Scribean drama is nowhere evident in Chekhov's theater. There is a certain tension; but nobody is in a hurry, and even when, like Elena in *The Wood Demon*, a character desperately wishes to escape, there is nowhere to go. This very lack of direction is a source of uneasiness.

It is possible that in these incongruities Chekhov saw something comic. All of his later plays may be considered examples of *comédie rosse*.

They are not, of course, written in the style of Jean Jullien or Henri Becque; between the Russian spirit and the French there is half of a world of difference. But it is not altogether unlikely that Chekhov had something in mind when he wrote *The Three Sisters* and *The Cherry Orchard* which is analogous to the bitter comedy of Becque.

The type of vaudeville which Chekhov was accustomed to write would develop readily into hard comedy. Probably, plays like *La Sérénade* or *La Parisienne* came quite close to Chekhov's idea of *comédie-vaude-ville*; indeed, it is by no means certain that it was not through the vaudeville that Becque arrived at the comic genre which he evolved. From the comic point of view, at any rate, the inappropriate efforts of Chekhov's characters to compensate for their shortcomings are perhaps laughable. In *The Three Sisters*, Chebutykin makes up for his ignorance by a compulsive addiction to the fillers in his newspaper. Vershinin compensates for an unhappy life by fixing his mind on the future happiness of the race. Solyony tries in vain to sweeten his sourness by sprinkling his chest and hands with scent. There is certainly something funny about Irina's periodic Tolstoyan impulse toward a life of social service, just as there is something both touching and ridiculous in Vershinin's love-making, and something both tragic and clownish in Chebutykin's nihilism. In the days of Molière, it would probably have been easy to laugh at these characters, to smile at Masha, or to chuckle over the infinitely pathetic Kulygin. In our day, however, after some centuries of sensibility, it is hardly possible to play these roles comically, and it was perhaps unreasonable of Chekhov to insist that they should be given a comic interpretation.

Even if we concede that all its characters lend themselves to irony, it is impossible to give a comic bias to *The Three Sisters*. In order to treat characters comedically it is necessary, at the very least, to view their behavior with the detachment proper to a predominantly intellectual experience. Sympathy is not conducive to merriment, and the more intense our emotion, the further we move from comedy. The principal characters in Chekhov's later plays are all conceived in such a way as to invite a very high degree of identification on the part of the spectator; one can laugh at them only by laughing at oneself.

It may be, of course, that Chekhov was capable of maintaining his artistic objectivity to a degree beyond the ordinary. Kind and generous as he was as a man, he was sometimes accused by those closest to him of something like inhumanity in his lack of emotional identification. If this is true, he certainly went to extraordinary lengths in his plays to compensate for his lack of warmth. Almost every scene in *The Three Sisters* makes a demand on the emotions. It is true, on the other hand, that Chekhov's characters have an amusing tendency to dramatize themselves and that, in their efforts to give tragic magnificence to their lives, they occasionally invite a smile. Certainly the final tableau of *The Three Sisters* — the girls grouped in the center, as if sitting for their portrait, Chebutykin on one side buried in his newspaper, and Andrey on the other with his baby carriage—makes an effect, at least visually, that is much closer to comedy than to tragedy. But *The Three Sisters* strikes far too deep for laughter. It would be inhuman to chuckle through Olga's final speech; and it is unlikely that anyone ever will.

After *Ivanov*, Chekhov's mistrust of melodrama, and his fear of overstatement, were such that he rarely permitted his climaxes to rise much above the level of the preparatory action. In *Uncle Vanya* the climax is deflated by Vanya's ineptitude; in *The Seagull*, it is sabotaged by Nina's determination to play a tragic scene; in *The Three Sisters*, the climaxes are so unobtrusive that one is hardly aware of them. Evidently Chekhov did not see life in terms of climaxes and *scènes à faire*, that is to say, in terms of theater. None of his later plays is theatrical; and the indefinable sense of paradox that his works evoke is very likely the result of the application of a dramatic system designed to arouse passion to a subject-matter which stubbornly resists any such treatment.

This curious incongruity was the consequence of Chekhov's naturalistic bias. In his opinion, a dramatist who desires to depict life honestly must put on the stage the experiences of ordinary people, and deal with the laughter and tears inherent in ordinary happenings. In real life what is visible is generally trivial and commonplace. But for centuries playwrights had been in the habit of associating drama with moments of high excitement, great gestures, and impressive utterances, precisely those things which are lacking in our ordinary experience. The result was the impassable gulf which has always divided reality from the fantasies of the theater.

It was Chekhov's ambition to bridge this gulf. As he said:

> After all, in real life, people don't spend every moment in shooting one another, hanging themselves, or making declarations of love. They do not spend all their time saying clever things. They are more occupied with eating, drinking, flirting, and saying stupidities, and these are the things which ought to be shown on the stage. . . . People eat their dinner, just eat their dinner, and all the time their happiness is taking form, or their lives are being destroyed.[4]

There was nothing especially new in this idea. But while both Zola and Maeterlinck had quite recently described the drama of everyday life, nobody had so far attempted actually to write such a play. It was very difficult in the theater to relinquish the extraordinary. The novelty of Chekhov's technique lay not in his theory, but in his practice. He was the first dramatist to write realistically for the stage.

Because he was primarily a realist, one looks in vain to Chekhov for that quality of neatness which was so highly prized by the dramatists of the Second Empire. Chekhov's plots are not neat. "Plays should be written badly, insolently," he told his brother Alexander. In his later plays, when the action ends, the narrative is not concluded; it is merely suspended. *The Three Sisters* ends with a tableau. The audience is invited to contemplate for a moment those who have departed, and those who remain. For a moment the play is at rest. But in fact, nothing is at rest—the tableau holds together only for that moment. Like the final tableau in *Revizor*, the scene is charged with energy and ready to fly apart the moment the author relinquishes his control.

Here, as elsewhere, Chekhov succeeds in giving his characters an extension of vitality that goes beyond their dramatic utility. They have a dimension that is peculiarly theirs, in which they are free to live. As characters, they are enlisted to serve the plot; but they have an autonomy of their own. Certain characters—Chebutykin, for example—appear at a certain point to secede from the ensemble, as if they refused to take any further part in the action. In general, Chekhov's personages preserve the imprecise outlines and the enigmatic quality of people. They exhibit a normal reluctance to engage themselves, and the author makes no effort to penetrate their reserve. The consequence is not only the strange relation of character to narrative that is peculiar to Chekhov's plays, but also a derogation of plot which presages a different order of drama from anything that properly belongs to the nineteenth century.

Notes

1. *The Oxford Chekhov*, trans. Ronald Hingley (London: Oxford University Press, 1964), III, 84.

2. Ibid., 139.

3. Ibid., 132.

4. V. Feider, *A. P. Chekhov, Literaturny byt i tvorchestvo po memoarnym materialam* (Leningrad, 1928), 160.

The Cherry Orchard   John L. Styan*

The Cherry Orchard, the supreme achievement of the naturalistic movement in the modern theatre, was Chekhov's last play. It was written and revised when its author was a dying man, his tuberculous condition forcing him to live in the milder air of Yalta on the Black Sea, six or seven hundred miles from rehearsals at the Moscow Art Theatre. Luckily, he had married Olga Knipper, one of the M.A.T.'s leading actresses, on 25 May

*From *Chekhov in Performance: A Commentary on the Major Plays* by John L. Styan (Cambridge: Cambridge University Press, 1971), 239–48. Reprinted by permission of the publisher.

1901, and he and his wife corresponded freely about the details of the play, so that our first-hand knowledge of its author's intentions is very full.[1]

Chekhov told Nemirovich-Danchenko that he had spent three years preparing the play,[2] and it seems that he was already planning it during rehearsals for *Three Sisters* in 1901. Two years later he had only just begun to write, and the first draft was not finished until October 1903. This teasing and weighing of his material is characteristic of Chekhov at the end: he used this long period of gestation as Ibsen might have done, until, as he said, the play was completed in his head.[3] It is clear, for example, that at the beginning he intended to make his play more of a light comedy, and he described it as a "vaudeville," a term synonymous with "farce," although he may have been speaking idiosyncratically in order to emphasize his comic intentions to those who thought of him as a writer of tragedy.[4] At all events, the detail of the working compelled him to modify his first ideas, and he finally called the play "A Comedy in Four Acts."

As with *Three Sisters*, Chekhov was again able to plan his play with the actors in mind, but this time the facility was more of a headache. Olga Knipper, then aged thirty-four, was first imagined in the part of Varya, then of Mme Ranevsky and then of Charlotta, since he wanted an actress with a sense of humor for the part; she finally played Mme Ranevsky.[5] The part of Charlotta, first conceived for Lilina or Olga Knipper, was finally played by Muratova. Lilina herself was thought of for Varya, who as a character accordingly became a more attractive young woman, then as Charlotta, but she finally played the young girl Anya. Stanislavsky was at first to play Lopahin, but he cast himself as Gaev, and Lopahin was in fact played by Leonidov. This juggling suggests that, far from gaining any easy verisimilitude for his characters by a close acquaintance with the players, in his last years Chekhov had grown as fussy about his characters as a mother about her babies.

The play was first performed in Moscow by the M.A.T. on 17 January 1904, on its author's forty-fourth birthday. It was published in June of that year, a few days before he died (1 July 1904).

In spite of the play's slow gestation, Chekhov's advances in craftsmanship in *The Cherry Orchard* suggest a complete confidence in what he was doing at the last. One might point to the progress of the setting of the play from act to act, moving from the house out to the estate itself (almost, indeed, to the town beyond) and back to the house again; and, within the house, from the most intimately evocative room, the nursery, to more public rooms, and back again to the nursery. Parallel with these visual changes, Chekhov makes a more thematic use of the weather and the seasons, passing from the chill of spring with its promise of warmth to the chill of autumn with its threat of winter. In this, the lyricism of *The Seagull* returns to Chekhov's dramatic writing. The growth of the year from May to October is precisely indicated, and the cycle of the cherry trees, from their blossoming to their fruiting and their destruction, matches the cycle of joy and grief, hope and despair, within the family. As in *Three Sisters*, time and change, and their effects wrought on a representative group of people, are the subject of the play. But in feeling for this, Chekhov knows that the realism of the chosen convention can dangerously narrow his meaning until it seems too particular and finally irrelevant. He thus works hard to ensure that his play projects a universal image, giving his audience some sense that this microcosm of the cherry orchard family stands, by breadth of allusion and a seemingly inexhaustible patterning of characters, for a wider orchard beyond.

The cherry orchard is a particular place and yet it is more. It represents an inextricable tangle of sentiments, which together comprise a way of life and an attitude to life. By the persistent feelings shown towards it, at one extreme by old Firs, the house-serf for whom the family is his whole existence, and at another by Trofimov, the intellectual for whom it is the image of repression and slavery; by Lopahin, the businessman and spokesman for hard economic facts, the one who thinks of it primarily as a means to wiser investment, and by Mme Ranevsky, who sees in it her childhood happiness and her former innocence, who sees it as the embodiment of her best values — by these and many other contradictions, an audience finds that the orchard grows from a painted backcloth to an ambiguous, living, poetic symbol of human life, *any* human life, in a state of change.

Inseparable from these patterns are those into which the cherry orchard characters are woven by their brilliant selection. Chekhov claimed that his cast for the play was small, but in performance they seem curiously to proliferate. Offstage characters increase the complexity, like the lover in Paris, the Countess in Yaroslavl, Pishchik's daughter Dashenka, Lyubov's drowned son Grisha. But the true reason for this sense of proliferation is because the same dozen players, each supplied with a character of three-dimensional individuality in Chekhov's impressive way, are encouraged to group and re-group themselves in our minds. He had always been meticulous in delineating the social background to his situation. Now he plans the play's context as a living environment. What is "a cross-section of society"? It may be a division by birth and class, by wealth, by age, by sex, by aspirations and moral values. Chekhov divides the people of the cherry orchard in a variety of ways, so that the orchard and its sale take on a different meaning for each group.

By birth and class, we see the members of the land-owning upper middle class, Mme Ranevsky, Gaev, Anya and, accordingly, the foster-daughter Varya, slipping from their security: we are made to feel what it is like to be uprooted. Lopahin, Epihodov, Yasha and Dunyasha, the servants and former peasants, are straining, comically it may be, to achieve a new social status. For some, Charlotta, Trofimov and Pishchik for much of the play, their future security is in doubt. Forty years after the Emancipation,[6] each character is still making a personal adjustment to the social upheaval according to age, sex or rank, and according to his lights. As a group, the cherry orchard people demonstrate the transition between the old and the new, bringing life to Chekhov's idea of an evolving social structure. The passing of time is thus represented *socially*. The three classes on the stage, owners, dependents and the new independents like Lopahin, are a social microcosm at a given point in time, so that any shift in the pattern of dependence forces an audience to acknowledge the reality of social time.

From economic considerations, the one-time wealthy landowners, Mme Ranevsky, Gaev and Pishchik, are in great distress. The responsible ones, Lopahin, Charlotta and Varya, are intimately concerned: to those who must battle the real world, money matters. However, the new generation, Trofimov and Anya, are largely indifferent, and the servants are unaffected. But money is the least of it.

By age, those of middle years who live in and for the past, like Mme Ranevsky and Gaev, the sale of the orchard is a blow striking at their very souls. For Anya, Trofimov, Dunyasha and Yasha, the young who, naturally, live for the future, the event is an opportunity for enterprise of one kind or another, self-interested or altruistic as the case may be. For those who are neither young nor old, for Varya, Lopahin and Charlotta, those concerned with the pressing problems of the present, the auction is an urgent call for decisions and practical measures. Firs, aged eighty-seven, is beyond time. *The Cherry Orchard* is thus, in part, a "generations" play, marking the conflict between the old and the young, the substance of a thousand dramatic themes. To watch the interactions of the four age-groups is to watch the cycle of life itself. Time will be alive on the stage, and the characters will seem human milestones.

By sex, the departure from the orchard means an assessment of marital needs and opportunities, and the spinsters, Charlotta, Varya and Dunyasha, are troubled in varying degrees. But Pishchik, Lopahin and Yasha, because of other pressures, fail to respond. While Anya and Trofimov claim idealistically to be "above love," at least for the time being, Mme Ranevsky is thrown back on her other resource, her Paris lover; as instinct or impulse brought her back to the orchard, so one or [the] other drives her back to Paris. Only Firs has arrived at that time of life when nothing, neither status, money, past nor future, can affect him any more. With exquisite irony, it is he whose neglect by the family in the last act passes the final comment on them all.

This is not the best place to indicate the echoes and parallels and parodies built into this restless group of people: these are better observed as the action of the play proceeds. Mme Ranevsky finds her counterpart in the feckless optimist Pishchik, the neighboring landowner. Epihodov the clerk counters Pishchik's trust in fate with an equally pessimistic fatalism. While Epihodov declares that he has resigned himself to his position, Yasha, who aspires to higher things than the life of a servant, is treading on necks as he climbs. When Gaev finds Yasha, a servant, playing his own aristocratic game of billiards, the valet's impertinence measures his master's own precarious status. Gaev, sucking his caramels, will, in spite of his disclaimers, never do a day's useful work, and Chekhov sets this weakness against the practical energies of Lopahin. And Lopahin against Trofimov. And Trofimov against Mme Ranevsky. *La ronde* continues ceaselessly.

Patterns of characters, then, make patterns of dramatic emphasis, and this "plotless" play is one with *too many* plots, however fragmentary, to permit analysis finally to untangle all its threads. In *Three Sisters*, Chekhov traced the passing of the months and years from scene to scene, and we watched the visible transformation of the people of the play. In *The Cherry Orchard*, time past, present and future are at the last all one, the play's last act as integrated moment of revelation. We know the orchard must go, just as surely as the curtain must fall, and in Act IV Chekhov counts out the minutes, as in the first three acts he counted out the days to the sale. As the minutes pass, we scrutinize the whole family. Every exchange, between Lopahin and Trofimov on their futures, between Mme Ranevsky and Pishchik on the vagaries of fate, between Varya and Lopahin in their abortive proposal scene, refocuses the image of the play. When Varya seems to strike Lopahin with a stick, the notions both of differences in class and of sexual need are by one gesture violently yoked together, simultaneously reintroduced to contradict one another. When Trofimov refuses Lopahin's generous offer of a loan, the student's youth and idealism are in pathetic contrast with Lopahin's maturity and common sense. When Mme Ranevsky gives away her purse to the peasants at her door (her name "Lyuba" means "love"), we see in the gesture her failure to be realistic about her financial circumstances as well as her paternalistic affection for all the orchard stood for in the past. One incident comprehends and generates the next, endlessly, and the last act is a masterpiece of compact concentration.

"The entire play is so simple, so wholly real, but to such a point purified of everything superfluous and enveloped in such a lyrical quality, that it seems to me to be a symbolic poem."[7] So wrote Nemirovich-Danchenko, early recognizing the gratifying contradiction that a play can be naturalistic and poetic at the same time. *The Cherry Orchard* has the poetic strength of simplicity. The interweaving in the play, the relationships between one generation and another, between master and servant, between the love-lorn and the less concerned, with the ebb and flow of such relationships, are the source of *poetic* energy in the play. But the subtle shifts across the social fabric are also the source of the play's *comic* energy, compelling its audience to remain both alert and amused as it watches. In *The Cherry Orchard*, Chekhov consummated his life's work with a *poetic comedy* of exquisite balance.

The Cherry Orchard was conceived as a comedy, but its author had difficulty in persuading Stanislavsky and his company that it was not full of tearful people. "Where are they? Varya's the only one, and that's because Varya is a cry-baby by nature, and her tears shouldn't distress the audience."[8] He wanted his Moscow audience to laugh at tears. "There isn't a cemetery in Act Two," he expostulated. It is evident from his letters to Olga after the first production that he felt Stanislavsky and Nemirovich-Danchenko had created a *drame*, as indeed they advertised it: "Why is it that on the posters and in the newspaper advertisements my play is so persistently called a drama? Nemirovich and Stanislavsky see in my play something absolutely different from what I have written, and I am ready to bet anything that neither of them has once read my play through attentively. Forgive me, but I assure you it is so."[9] In spite of Stanislavsky's ecstatic praise of the play, he had misunderstood it. E. P. Karpov reported the same reactions from Chekhov after a provincial performance of the play at Yalta: "Is this really my *Cherry Orchard*? Are these my types? With the exception of two or three roles, none of this is mine. I describe life. It is a dull, philistine life. But it is not a tedious, whimpering life. First they turn me into a weeper and then into a simply boring writer. However, I've written several volumes of merry tales."[10] In the role of Gaev, Stanislavsky had "dragged things out most painfully" in Act IV.[11] The whole thing was played flamboyantly. What is the truth behind this difference between conception and realization? Farce, which prohibits compassion for human weakness, and tragedy, which demands it, are close kin. The truth is that *The Cherry Orchard* is a play which treads the tightrope between them, and results in the ultimate form of that special dramatic balance we know as Chekhovian comedy.

An audience, of course, will find there what it will, depending upon how it approaches the theater experience. If, like recent Soviet audiences, it wants rousing polemics from Trofimov, it can hear them. If, like many Western audiences, it wishes to weep for Mme Ranevsky and her fate, it can be partly accommodated. It is possible to see Lyubov and Gaev as shallow people who deserve to lose their orchard, or as victims of social and economic forces beyond their control. It is possible to find Anya and Trofimov far-sighted enough to want to leave the dying orchard, or ignorant of what they are forsaking. But if production allows either the heroics of prophecy or the melodrama of dispossession, then all of Chekhov's care for balance is set at nought and the fabric of his play torn apart. Chekhov himself must have known that he was taking this risk, and it is for us to ask why.

In *The Cherry Orchard*, Chekhov struck his final blow at nineteenth-

century theatrics. There is no shot fired, either on or off the stage. In Act
II, Charlotta has a rifle and Epihodov a pistol, but these weapons are now
handled by comedians purely for the joke, and they are not mentioned
again. Even the amorous pairing of characters common to the earlier plays
has been turned entirely into comedy: the "love scenes" between Varya and
Lopahin are illuminatingly still-born; between Anya and Trofimov they
remain pathetically ludicrous; and between Yasha and Dunyasha they
border on farce. The play is "about" the purchase of a great imperial estate
by a former peasant who at one time worked on it, but Chekhov makes
nothing political of this; rather, it is emphasized that the man who buys it
had no intention of doing so, and Chekhov takes immense pains to subvert
any easy alignment of the spectator either with the old or the new owner.
If the "action" concerns the sale of the orchard, its fate is sealed from the
start, and Chekhov denies his audience the satisfaction of a sensational
crisis. In its place the play that Chekhov wrote allows only an intelligent,
objective curiosity about how the sale of the estate will affect the
individual lives of those who live there. Chekhov takes no stand on the
issues themselves; there is no triumph, no villainy, no message, no lesson,
no argument. But "there is not five minutes space, anywhere in the
dialogue, which would not, like a drop beneath a microscope, be found
swarming with life,"[12] and, in the theater, to this life we are forced to
attend.

Chekhov's anti-theatricalism was more obvious in *Uncle Vanya*,
where it appeared as an almost sensational anti-sensationalism. The
technique in *The Cherry Orchard* is more subtle, more submerged and
pervasive, and a stage examination of this pervasiveness may go some way
towards resolving the controversy about the genre of the play. In *The
Cherry Orchard*, every detail fits, not just by a progressive illumination of
a character's roots or the ramifications of a social situation as in any good
naturalistic play, but by its contribution to an embracing structure of
comi-tragic ambivalence. "Undercutting" as a method of objective communication in the theater has become a style and a mode on *The Cherry
Orchard* stage. Chekhov knows that by reversing a current of feeling,
muting a climax, toppling a character's dignity, contradicting one statement by another, juxtaposing one impression with its opposite, he is
training his audience to see the truth of the total situation. To be
compassionate and yet cool at the same time is to take a big step nearer
this truth, and Chekhov's final, hard discipline is to prove that the truth is
relative by trying it dialectically on his audience's feelings. In this
Chekhov is again the scientist and the doctor, and the result is perfect
comedy—Chekhovian comedy.

At the same time his unrelenting methods of undercutting lend the
play a vitality which penetrates and activates its audience's perceptions.
This nourishment is at the source of all good theatre, and has nothing to
do with the final direction his story takes. His procedures on the stage

result in a lively extension of our involvement with the play. In the last act, when with outrageous baby noises Charlotta mimics the bitter-sweet dreams of Anya and her mother on the sofa in the chilling nursery, Chekhov is both setting the play back on its course of comic objectivity and demanding of his audience a newly creative frame of mind. In the control of an audience's response, this is pruning for stronger growth.

Ambivalence is the source of all that is truly participatory in comedy. By promoting in his thousand and one details at once our sympathy with his characters and our alienation from them, Chekhov has refashioned for a proscenium arch drama the time-honored ironies of the traditional aside. For ambivalence as it flourishes in *The Cherry Orchard* reveals its author's sense of the playhouse as well as his sense of the play. Compensating us for the loss of an earlier participatory theater, he must draw us into the world of the characters at one moment, into the illusory world through the arch, and at the next push us back into our seats, more critical than before. The tone of his play therefore constantly edges on satire, without being distinctively satirical. He divides us against ourselves and splits our attention in order to arouse us.

A split theater is a dialectical theater. The director Michel Saint-Denis has tried for many years to sound the true note of Chekhovian comedy, and he thinks of it as one which strikes the perfect dialectical balance. For him, it is Mme Ranevsky herself who exemplifies this balance, a balance between her fear of the ill-fated situation she is in and the irresponsible, if charming, behavior with which she tries to avoid it. We must neither condemn nor condone. He argued that the English tradition of Chekhovian production militated against the complete success of his work on the play when he presented it at the Aldwych, London, in 1961.

> The "connoisseurs" have fallen in love with the scenery, with the dear creatures, representing the threatened past; they mock Trofimov and have little sympathy for Lopahin; they were bound to resent the degradation of romantic values purposely displayed in my recent production. The contradictions of the Press contributed to the liveliness of the public's reactions; some complained they were not moved enough while others regretted not being given more opportunities to laugh. It is my belief and my hope that our interpretation has brought many people, particularly among the young, to a new understanding of this many-sided masterpiece.[13]

It is this balance on the stage, producing an exactly irritating result in the auditorium, which can be tested only in performance.

Chekhov's achievement in naturalism, therefore, was to do more than create the conditions for our belief in the happiness and misery on the stage. They had to be conditions which he could also control by calling up sympathy at one moment, and dispelling it at the next. The human personality is many-faced, just as Mme Ranevsky may be sad and yet smile, be stupid yet generous, or as Lopahin may be a tough businessman and yet a clumsy lover, a peasant's son always calling himself a pig and yet a man with a gentle nature who loves the poppies he must destroy. Social and human "doubleness" touches every line of dialogue in the play, and "Chekhovian" is the endearment that describes as much our response as Chekhov's characteristically quizzical way of looking at life. Just as the best tragedy engages the intelligence, so the best comedy, in spite of Henri Bergson, engages the emotions.

Notes

1. Chekhov saw some rehearsals in December 1903, and was present on the opening night.

2. Letter of 2 November 1903: Chekhov's *Complete Works and Letters* (PSSP), Moscow, 1951, vol. 20, p. 173.

3. Letter to Stanislavsky of 5 February 1903 (ibid., p. 37). Nemirovich-Danchenko asserted, "Not a single play, not a single story, did he write so slowly as *The Cherry Orchard*" (V. I. Nemirovich-Danchenko, *My Life in the Russian Theatre*, reprint: New York: Theatre Arts Books, 1968, p. 214).

4. See Nemirovich-Danchenko, ibid., pp. 214–215: "If I write anything that resembles a play it will be a vaudeville piece." Cf. his letter to Lilina (Stanislavsky's wife): "Not a drama but a comedy emerged from me, in places even a farce" (Ernest J. Simmons, *Chekhov, a Biography*, Boston-Toronto: Little and Brown, 1962, p. 604). The point is reiterated in a letter to Olga Knipper: "The last act will be merry, and indeed the whole play will be merry and frivolous" (21 September 1903, vol. 20 [see footnote 2], p. 135).

5. She was still playing this role for the three hundredth anniversary performance of the play in 1943, when she was seventy-three.

6. The Act of Emancipation of 1861, indirectly one of the better results of the Crimean War, freed some fifteen million serfs, although for many years they continued paying for the land they were allotted.

7. Nemirovich-Danchenko, p. 218.

8. Letter to Nemirovich-Danchenko of 23 October 1903 (vol. 20, p. 162).

9. Letter to Olga Knipper of 10 April 1904 (vol. 20, p. 265).

10. Simmons, p. 624.

11. Letter to Olga Knipper of 29 March 1904 (vol. 20, p. 258).

12. Desmond MacCarthy, *Drama* (London, 1940), p. 87.

13. Introduction to *Anton Chekhov: The Cherry Orchard*, a version by John Gielgud (London, 1963), p. xi.

SELECTED
BIBLIOGRAPHY

Primary Works

Complete Works

Anton Chekhov, *Complete Works and Letters (Polnoe Sobranie Sochinenii i Pisem)*. 20 volumes. Moscow, 1944–51.

Anton Chekhov, *Complete Works and Letters (Polnoe Sobranie Sochinenii i Pisem)*. 30 volumes. Moscow, 1974–83.

The Oxford Chekhov. Edited and translated by Ronald Hingley. 9 volumes. London: Oxford University Press, 1964–80. This is the most complete edition of Chekhov's works translated into English; it contains the plays and all the later stories.

Letters

Anton Chekhov's Life and Thought: Selected Letters and Commentary. Edited and translated by Simon Karlinsky and Michael Heim. Berkeley and Los Angeles: University of California Press, 1976.

Letters of Anton Chekhov. Selected and edited by Avrahm Yarmorlinsky, New York: The Viking Press, 1947, 1968, 1973.

The Life and Letters of Anton Tchekhov. Translated by Samuel S. Koteliansky and Philip Tomlinson. New York: Doran, 1925; reprint, New York: Blom, 1965.

Secondary Works

Bibliographies

Lantz, Kenneth A. *Anton Chekhov: A Reference Guide to Literature*. Boston: G. K. Hall, 1985. This is the only annotated bibliography, containing mostly Russian and English titles (but also some in German and French) from 1886 to 1983; included is an introductory essay, "Images of Chekhov."

Sendich, Munir. "Anton Chekhov in English: A Comprehensive Bibliography of Works about and by Him" (1889–1984). *Russian Language Journal* 39, nos. 132–34 (Chekhov volume) (1985): 227–379. Reprinted in *Anton Chekhov Rediscovered* (see below).

Books in English

Anton Cechov, 1860–1960: Some Essays. Edited by Thomas Eekman. Leiden, (The Netherlands): E. J. Brill, 1960.

Anton Chekhov as a Master of Story Writing. Edited by Leo Hulanicki and David Savignac. The Hague: Mouton, 1976.

Anton Chekhov Rediscovered. A Collection of New Studies with a Comprehensive Bibliography. Edited by Savely Senderovich and Munir Sendich, East Lansing, Mich.: Russian Language Journal, 1987.

Anton Tchekhov: Literary and Theatrical Reminiscences. Edited and translated by Samuel S. Koteliansky. New York, 1927; reprint, New York: Blom, 1965.

A. P. Chekhov, 1860–1960. Edited by Julius Katzer. Moscow: Foreign Language Publishing House, 1960.

Avilova, Lydia A. *Chekhov in My Life, a Love Story*, translated by David Magarshack. London: John Lehmann, 1950.

Bitsilli, Peter. *Chekhov's Art: A Stylistic Analysis*, translated by Toby W. Clyman and Edwina J. Cruise. Ann Arbor, Mich.: Ardis Publishers, 1983.

Brahms, Carol. *Reflections in the Lake: A Study of Chekhov's Four Greatest Plays*. London: Weidenfeld & Nicolson, 1976.

Bruford, Walter H. *Anton Chekhov*. New Haven, Conn.: Yale University Press, 1957.

———. *Chekhov and His Russia: A Sociological Study*. London: Kegan Paul, Trench, Trubner, 1948; reprint, Hamden, Conn.: Archon Books, 1971.

Chekhov. A Collection of Critical Essays. Edited by Robert L. Jackson. Englewood Cliffs, N.J.: Prentice Hall, 1967.

A Chekhov Companion. Edited by Toby W. Clyman. Newport: Greenwood Press, 1985.

Chekhov: New Perspectives. Edited by René Wellek and Nonna D. Wellek. Englewood Cliffs, N.J.: Prentice-Hall, 1984.

Chekhov's Art of Writing: A Collection of Critical Essays. Edited by Paul Debreczeny and Thomas Eekman. Columbus, Ohio: Slavica, 1977.

Chekhov's Great Plays, A Critical Anthology. Edited by Jean-Pierre Barricelli. New York: New York University Press, 1981.

Chekhov: The Critical Heritage. Edited by Victor Emelyanow. London: Routledge & Kegan Paul, 1981.

Chudakov, Aleksandr P. *Chekhov's Poetics*, translated by Edwina J. Cruise and Donald Dragt. Ann Arbor, Mich.: Ardis Publishers, 1983.

Chukovsky, Kornei I. *Chekhov the Man*, translated by Pauline Rose. London: Hutchinson & Co., 1945; reprint, New York: Haskell House, 1974.

Elton, Oliver. *Chekhov: The Taylorian Lecture*. Oxford: Clarendon Press, 1929.

Ermilov, Vladimir V. *Anton Pavlovich Chekhov, 1860–1904*. Moscow: Foreign Languages Publishing House, 1954.

Gerhardie, William A. *Anton Chekhov: A Critical Study*. New York: Duffield & Co., 1923; revised edition, London: Macdonald & Co., 1974, and New York: St. Martin's, 1974.

Gilles, Daniel. *Chekhov: Observer without Illusion*, translated by Charles Lam Markmann. New York: Funk & Wagnalls, 1968.

Gorky, Maxim, Alexander Kuprin, and Ivan A. Bunin. *Reminiscences of Anton Chekhov*, translated and edited by Samuel S. Koteliansky and Leonard Woolf. New York: Huebsch, 1921.

Gottlieb, Vera. *Chekhov and the Vaudeville: A Study of Chekhov's One-Act Plays*. Cambridge: Cambridge University Press, 1982.

————. *Chekhov in Performance in Russia and Soviet Russia*. Alexandria, Va.: Chadwyck Healey, 1984.

Hahn, Beverly. *Chekhov: A Study of the Major Stories and Plays*. Cambridge: Cambridge University Press, 1977.

Hingley, Ronald. *Chekhov: A Biographical and Critical Study*. New York: Barnes & Noble, 1950.

————. *A New Life of Anton Chekhov*. New York: Knopf, 1976.

Kirk, Irina. *Anton Chekhov*. Boston: Twayne Publishers, 1981.

Kramer, Karl D. *The Chameleon and the Dream: The Image of Reality in Cexov's Stories*. The Hague: Mouton, 1970.

Kutscheroff, Alexander. *Chekhov and His Place in World Literature*. Middletown, Conn.: Wesleyan University, 1946.

Laffitte, Sophie. *Chekhov, 1860–1904*, translated by Moura Budbert and Gordon Lata. New York: Scribners, 1973; reprint, Cremore, Australia, and London: Angus & Robertson, 1974.

Magarshack, David. *Chekhov: A Life*. London: Faber & Faber, 1952; reprint, Toronto: Nelson-Fodor-Scott, 1955, and Westport, Conn.: Greenwood Press, 1970.

————. *Chekhov the Dramatist*. London: John Lehmann, 1952; reprint, London: Eyre Methuen, 1980.

————. *The Real Chekhov: An Introduction to Chekhov's Last Plays*. London: Allen & Unwin, 1972; reprint, New York: Harper & Row, 1974.

Melchinger, Siegfried. *Anton Chekhov*, translated by Edith Tarcov. New York: Frederick Ungar, 1972.

Moss, Howard. *Chekhov*. New York: Albondocani Press, 1972.

Némirovsky, Irène. *A Life of Chekhov*, translated by Erik de Mauny. London: Grey Walls Press, 1950; reprint, New York: Haskell House, 1974.

Peace Richard. *Chekhov: A Study of the Four Major Plays*. New Haven, Conn.: Yale University Press, 1983.

Pitcher, Harvey. *The Chekhov Play: A New Interpretation*. New York: Barnes & Noble, 1973; reprint, Berkeley and Los Angeles: University of California Press, 1985.

————. *Chekhov's Leading Lady: A Portrait of the Actress Olga Knipper*. London: Murray, 1979; reprint, New York: Franklin Watts, 1980.

Priestley, John B. *Anton Chekhov*. London: International Textbook, 1970.

Rayfield, Donald. *Chekhov: The Evolution of His Art*. New York: Barnes & Noble, 1975.

Saunders, Beatrice. *Tchehov, the Man*. Arundel, England: Centaur Press, 1960.

Shestov, Leo. *Chekhov and Other Essays*. Ann Arbor: University of Michigan Press, 1966.

Simmons, E. J. *Chekhov: A Biography*. Boston: Little Brown & Co., 1962; reprint, Chicago: University of Chicago Press, 1970.

Smith, Virginia L. *Anton Chekhov and "The Lady with the Dog."* Foreword by Ronald Hingley. London: Oxford University Press, 1973.

Speirs, Logan. *Tolstoy and Chekhov*. Cambridge: Cambridge University Press, 1971.

Stowell, Peter H. *Literary Impressionism: James and Chekhov*. Athens: University of Georgia Press, 1981.

Styan, John L. *Chekhov in Performance: A Commentary on the Major Plays.* Cambridge: Cambridge University Press, 1971.

Toumanova, Nina A. *Anton Chekhov, the Voice of Twilight Russia.* New York: Columbia University Press, 1937.

Tulloch, John. *Chekhov: A Structuralist Study.* London: Macmillan Press, 1981.

Valency, Maurice. *The Breaking String: The Plays of Anton Chekhov.* New York: Oxford University Press, 1966; reprint, New York: Schocken Books, 1983.

van der Eng, Jan, Jan M. Meijer, and Herta Schmid. *On the Theory of Descriptive Poetics: Anton P. Chekhov as Story-Teller and Playwright.* Lisse: Peter de Ridder Press, 1978.

Winner, Thomas. *Chekhov and His Prose.* New York: Holt, Rinehart & Winston, 1966.

INDEX

Aeschylus, 169
Aiken, Conrad, 1, 4
Aivazovsky, Ivan K., 182
Alexander the Great, 164
Alexander II, Tsar, 131, 135
Aristides, 11
Aristotle, 172–73
Ashmore, Basil, 153n2
Austen, Jane, 178
Avilova, Lidia, 119, 147
Aykhenval'd, Yuri, 137n6

Balzac, Honoré de, 184
Barzun, Jacques, 184
Becque, Henri, 180, 190
Bellow, Saul, 47
Bentley, Eric, 6
Bergson, Henri, 200
Bernard, Claude: *Introduction to the Study of Experimental Medicine*, 71, 73
Berthoff, Ann E., 116n7
Bettelheim, Bruno, 56–57
Bicilli, Petr, 90n10
Boborykin, Petr D., 71
Borges, Jorge, 54
Bulgakov, S. N., 2
Bulgakov, S. V., 101, 102n7
Bunin, Ivan A., 151, 159
Byron, George G., 2; *Don Juan*, 184–85; *Manfred*, 155

Caesar, Julius, 164
Chaucer, Geoffrey, 46
Cheever, John: "The Country Husband," 53
Chekhov, Alexander P., 141, 192
Chekhov, Anton P., action in the plays, 189; antithesis in the plays, 182; boredom and guilt, 55–57; dramas, general, 1–2, 126–36; humor, 29, 61–68; romantic elements, 78–91; short stories, general, 1–2; short story technique, 21–25; symbolism, 175–76; the tirade, 180

STORIES (only the longer stories listed):
About Love, 5, 103–4, 109–16
Ariadna, 35, 38
An Attack of Nerves, 5, 74–77
The Betrothed, 42, 44, 145
The Bishop, 60
The Black Monk, 65, 78, 84–89
A Case from a Doctor's Practice, 41, 43
The Darling, 41, 64
The Duel, 29, 42, 47, 65, 121, 145, 157
Gooseberries, 5, 103–4, 107–10, 112, 115, 116n7
The House with a Mezzanine, 27, 42
In the Cart, 27
In the Ravine [*Hollow*], 24, 27, 54
Ionych, 36–38, 65, 72
Kashtanka, 62
The Kiss, 78, 81–84
The Lady with the [*Little Pet*] *Dog*, 31, 41–42, 116n8, 118–23
Lights, 61
The Man in a Shell, 5, 103–7, 109, 112, 115
A Murder, 59
My Life, 23, 27, 36, 42, 65
Neighbors, 64, 148
The New Villa [*Dacha*], 26–27, 43
On Official Business [*Duty*], 27, 44
The Peasants, 2
Rothschild's Violin, 43
The Steppe, 12, 23
The Student, 43, 60
A Tedious [*Dreary, Tiresome*] *Story*, 18, 23, 40, 60, 70, 72, 76, 146, 156, 181
Terror, 64
Three Years, 29, 65, 121
An Unknown Man's [*Anonymous*] *Story*,

42, 58, 64
Verochka, 78–81, 84, 88
A Visit to Friends, 2
Ward No. Six, 49–52, 144
A Woman's Kingdom [*World*], 5, 43,
    91–102

PLAYS:
The Bear, 146, 189
The Cherry Orchard, 2, 7, 41, 127–29,
    134–35, 145, 149–50, 152, 184–85,
    190, 192–200
Ivanov, 6, 12–14, 38, 40, 52, 56–58,
    128, 131–34, 138n23, n26, n35,
    141–44, 146–48, 151–52, 154–60,
    168–69, 184, 191
Platonov, 128, 131–32, 138n26, 139–53,
    168, 184
The Proposal, 146, 189
The Seagull, 6, 14, 56, 127, 130, 132,
    136, 147–49, 160–69, 176, 184, 191,
    193
[*The*] *Three Sisters*, 2, 6, 64, 127–28,
    130, 144–46, 148–49, 152, 184,
    186–92, 193–94, 196
Uncle Vanya, 2, 6, 49, 56, 127–28, 130,
    134, 145–47, 149, 152, 170–85,
    187–88, 191, 198
The Wood Demon, 127, 134, 136,
    146–49, 152, 169, 170–73, 176–77,
    181–85, 189

Chekhov, Evgenia Ya., 151
Chekhov, Mikhail P., 3, 90n18, 140, 153n5
Chekhov, Nikolai, 141
Chekhov, Pavel E., 151
Chudakov, Alexander P., 3, 75–76, 78
Chukovsky, Kornei, 3
Conrad, Joseph L., 5

Derman, Avram B., 4, 140
Des Pres, Terrence: *The Survivor*, 56
Dickens, Charles, 29: *Bleak House*, 51
Dobrolyubov, N. A., 133–34, 138n35
Dostoevsky, Fedor M., 11, 18, 19, 31, 46,
    58, 93, 131; *The Brothers Karamazov*,
    19; *Notes from Underground*, 46; *The
    Village of Stepanchikovo and its Inhab-
    itants*, 130
Duncan, Phillip A., 5

Eichendorff, Joseph von, 78
Elliott, George P., 4
Ermilov, V. V., 3
Ermolova, Maria N., 1, 140

Eugénie, Empress, 82
Ezhov, N. M., 168

Fergusson, Francis, 170
Flaubert, Gustave, 28, 29
Fonvizin, Denis I.: *The Brigadier*, 130,
    137n17
Freedman, John, 5
Freud, Sigmund, 45, 59, 172, 175; *The
    Interpretation of Dreams*, 52

Galsworthy, John, 3, 178; *Justice*, 175
García Márquez: *One Hundred Years of
    Solitude*, 53
Garnet, Constance, 186n2
Garnett, Edward, 3
Gass, William: "The Order of Insects," 54
Gerhardi(e), William, 3, 170
Goethe, Johann W., 11
Gogol, Nikolai V., 22, 29, 72, 126,
    137n16; *The Government Inspector
    (Revizor)*, 130, 192
Goncharov, Ivan A., 131, 134; *Oblomov*,
    132–35
Goncourt, Brothers de, 22
Gorky, Maxim, 26, 31, 33, 43, 138n34,
    170
Gornfeld, A. G., 43
Gradov-Sokolov, Leonid A., 143
Griboedov, Alexander S., 126; *Woe from
    Wit*, 128–32, 138n26, 141
Gromov, M. P., 3
Grossman, Leonid, 70, 72–73

Hauptmann, Gerhard, 188
Hebbel, Christian, F., 188
Hingley, Ronald, 60n1, 116n5, n9, 138n31
Hoffmann, E. T. A., 78

Ibsen, Henrik, 48, 60, 171, 173, 175–80,
    182, 184, 186, 188, 193; *Hedda Gabler*,
    172; *Peer Gynt*, 184; *Rosmersholm*, 188;
    The Wild Duck, 176
Isaiah, 57
Ivanov-Kozlovsky, M., 169n2

Jackson, Robert L., 3, 5
James, Henry, 4, 24, 29, 48, 178, 184
Joyce, James, 48
Jullien, Jean, 190

Kafka, Franz, 59
Kapnist, V. V.: *Malicious Litigation*, 130
Karlinsky, Simon, 3

Karpov, E. P., 197
Kataev, Vladimir B., 3, 5, 116n7
Kavelin, Konstantin D., 17
Knipper, Olga L., 2, 119–20, 192–93, 197, 200n4, n5, n9
Kommissarzhevskaya, Vera F., 167
Korolenko, Valdimir G., 138n23
Krylov, Ivan A., 188

Lavrin, Janko, 103
Lawrence, David H., 48
Lenin, Vladimir I., 47, 157
Leonidov, L. M., 193
Lermontov, Mikhail Yu., 126, 131, 141
Lessing, Doris: The Golden Notebook, 53
Liatsky, Evgeni, 106
Lilina, M. P., 193, 200n4
Linkov, V. Ia., 3
Lope de Vega, 169

Maeterlinck, Maurice, 136, 188, 191
Magarshack, David, 139, 149–50, 153n20
Maikov, Valerian, 71
Mann, Thomas, 33
Matthewson, Rufus, 90n13
Maugham, William Somerset, 114
Maupassant, Guy de, 4, 12, 22–23, 28, 32–33, 164–65, 167; Bel ami, 28; Sur l'eau, 165–66; Une vie, 28
Maxwell, David E., 109
Mayakovsky, Vladimir V., 103
Mays, Milton A., 108, 116n7
Meilakh, B. S., 123nl
Merezhkovsky, Dmitri S., 2
Mikhailovsky, Nikolai K., 2, 10, 19, 156
Miller, Arthur, 53
Mirsky, Dmitri, S., 116n5
Mizinova, Lika, 119
Molière, Jean B., 169, 190
Monroe, Marilyn, 53
Moravcevich, Nicholas, 71
Murasaki, Lady, 57
Muratova, E. P., 193
Murry, John Middleton, 3, 170

Nabokov, Vladimir V., 4, 59
Nadson, Semyon Ya., 155
Nekrasov, Nikolai A., 17
Nemirovich-Danchenko, Vladimir I., 128, 170, 193, 196–97, 200n3, n4
Nicholas I, Tsar, 132
Nietzsche, Friedrich, 13
Nivat, Georges, 103, 116n3
Novalis, Friedrich, 78

Odets, Clifford, 180
Olivier, Sir Laurence K., 178
O'Neill, Eugene G., 176, 178
Ostrovsky, Alexander N.: The Forest, 137n14; The Thunderstorm, 128
O'Toole, L. M., 90n14
Ovsianiko-Kulikovsky, Dmitri N., 71–72, 76

Pagès, Alain, 74, 76
Paperny, Zinovii S., 6
Pascal, Blaise, 13
Peace, Richard, 3, 6
Pirogov, Nikolai I., 17
Pisemsky, Alexei T.: A Bitter Fate, 141
Pitcher, Harvey, 127, 137n11
Pleshcheev, Alexei N., 40
Podgorny, V. A., 167
Poe, Edgar Allan, 4
Polonsky, Yakov P., 40
Polotskaia, Emma A., 3
Protopopov, Mikhail A., 71
Przewalski, Nikolai M., 151
Puccini, Giacomo, 185
Pushkin, Alexander S., 126, 141; Evgeni Onegin, 123n3, 129, 137n13; "Geroi," 109; Ruslan and Lyudmila, 130, 188

Racine, Jean, 169
Rayfield, Donald, 3, 131, 137n17
Repin, Ilya E., 159
Roskin, Alexander I., 73, 164
Roth, Philip, 47
Rousseau, Jean J., 48

Saint-Denis, Michel, 199
Saltykov-Shchedrin, Mikhail E., 106; "The Adventures of Kramolnikov," 135; The Golovlyov Family, 116n6
Sardou, Victorien, 184
Saroyan, William, 180
Schiller, Friedrich, 137n14
Schmid, H., 3
Schopenhauer, Arthur, 87, 91n22
Scribe, Eugène, 177
Segal, Lore: Lucinella, 54
Shakh-Azizova, Tatiana, 6
Shakespeare, William, 23, 59, 157–64, 167, 169–70, 179, 182; Antony and Cleopatra, 174; Hamlet, 6, 7n4, 132, 154–57, 164–65, 169n2, 184–85; Richard III, 180
Shaw, George Bernard, 48, 169–70, 172, 178, 180, 184

Shchukin, S., 35
Shestov, Leo(n), 1, 2, 3, 103
Smith, Virginia L., 6
Socrates, 13
Solzhenitsyn, Alexander I.: "As Breathing and Consciousness Return," 57
Sophocles, 57, 177, 182, 186
Spencer, Herbert, 48; *Principles of Psychology*, 52
Stanislavsky, Konstantin S., 128, 135–36, 170, 174, 178, 193, 197
Strindberg, August, 48, 169, 184
Styan, John L., 3, 7, 130, 137n10
Suvorin, Alexei S., 133–35

Tieck, Ludwig, 78
Timiriazev, Kliment A., 151
Tolstoy, Lev N., 13–14, 17, 28, 46–48, 55, 58, 72, 90n9, 126, 134, 151; *Anna Karenina*, 14, 123n1, n3; *The Death of Ivan Ilyich*, 13–14, 51; *The Power of Darkness*, 141; *War and Peace*, 14
Toumanova, Nina, 2
Trotsky, Leon: *Literature and Revolution*, 174
Tulloch, John, 131

Turbin, V. N., 65–66
Turgenev, Ivan S., 4, 25, 29, 33, 34, 89, 106, 126, 128, 131, 141, 164, 166–67; *Fathers and Sons*, 134; "The Hamlet of the Shchigrovsky Region," 132; "A [King] Lear of the Steppes," 24; *A Month in the Country*, 128–29, 178; *Rudin*, 132

Updike, John, 51, 53, 115; *Couples*, 54

Valency, Maurice, 6, 128, 136, 137n5
Verdi, Giuseppi, 185
Vinogradova, K. M., 123n2

Wertmüller, Lina, 56
Wilks, Ronald, 116n5, n9
Williams, Tennessee: *A Streetcar Named Desire*, 49
Winner, Thomas, 3, 71, 116n7
Woolf, Virginia, 3, 116

Yavorskaya, Lidia B., 119
Young, Stark, 170

Zola, Émile, 5, 70–74, 76–77, 191